ALASKA EDGE ISLAND

Yupiks of St Lawrence Island and Siberia

Jay Miller, PhD, Editor

© 2017

CONTENTS

#1 – 34 Footnotes

INTRODUCTION

St Lawrence Islanders, at the coastal edge of Alaska 36 visible miles from the Chuckchi Peninsula, are Yupiks with close kin in Siberia and its men traditionally wore monkish hair tonsures. With global warming, this island is again toehold for spreading Bering landscapes emerging from the sea.

A century ago, a young couple, Farrar and June Burn, came to the island as local superintendent of the reindeer herd and as teacher. After a year, they returned to their homestead on Waldron Island in the San Juan Islands of Washington State to welcome the birth of sons North and South ~ Robert Burn. In 1978, the latter contacted me to find a use for these reports, notes, and musings so I passed them to students working in Alaska, who have subsequently died, returning them. Making good on my own promise to see this information put to use and taking advantage of better equipment and electronic outlets, this volume has been assembled for posterity, along with my 30 backlogged titles providing future treasuries.

Miscommunications with University of Washington led to donating Burn family papers to Western Washington University in Bellingham, where the originals of these assembled materials will join them. Some carbons were left at Gambell school, but burned.

June Burn (1893-1969) was born Inez Chandler Harris on June 19, 1893 in Anniston, Alabama, to a Methodist circuit riding minister. After graduating from Oklahoma State University, she became a staff writer in 1917 for McCall's in New York City. In 1919 near Washington, DC, she married Farrar Burn (1888-1974), a World War I veteran and musician, whose brother Bob worked with Bing Crosby. For fifty years they traveled around the US, homesteading in the San Juan Islands, teaching Eskimos, and touring in a covered wagon, while writing for various periodicals and books. Burn's autobiography *Living High: An Unconventional Autobiography* (1941) treats early life on Waldron and St Lawrence islands. They both are buried in Van Buren, Arkansas.[1]

---

[1] Center For Pacific Northwest Studies ~ The June and Farrar Burn Papers: Biographical Note http://www.acadweb.wwu.edu/cpnws/burn/burnbio.htm

Placed within greater contexts,[2] relying on the Smithsonian's Arctic Handbook, Alexander and Dorothea Leighton's[3] Gambell interviews from summer 1940, ethnographies by their student Charles Hughes (1960), by Carol Jolles (2002) and by Ann Fienup-Riordan (1990, 1991, 1994), historical value has been assumed and editing has been minimal, with obvious spelling and grammar faults silently corrected. Footnotes amplify details. Idiomatic words and phrases remain, with distinctive terms like "Outside, Go Outside" referring to leaving Alaska itself. Punctuation is simplified.

Internal subheadings was suggested by the material itself, and related materials from the book, reports, and stories have remained adjacent. Typed pages are distinguished from handwritten {hw}, and added ^insertions^ are ^ marked. Original source [page numbers] from publications are between square brackets. Idiosyncratic use of "thot" for "thought" and "tho" for "though" have been kept. Though remarkably tolerant and understanding, the Burns, as unassuming agents of colonialism, are trapped in unflattering evaluations, judgmental phrases, and racial terms long out of favor. Yet they aptly convey a sense of their engagement with that place and this time. Hostilities, duels, and feuds with Siberians are considered by Roger Silook, a convert who refers to spirits as 'devils' but to shamans as magicians instead of 'sorcerer'.[4]

Eskaleut 'igloo' meaning 'house' is not limited to 'ice house' of Arctic Canada and popular image. Most distinctive are the place named *ramka* ~ gens ~ patriclan, such as *uyá•li•t*, founder ~"owner" of Gambell itself. Derived from Eskimo Siberia, including Chuckchee, they recruit and name vital boat crews selected from among father's brother's sons.

---

[2] Unavailable are three community collections for Bering Strait School District, Unalakleet, by Anders Apassingok, Willis Walunga, Edward Tennant, eds, Lore of St. Lawrence Island: Echoes of Our Eskimo Elders 1985 ~ Gambell, 1987 ~ Savoonga, 1989 ~ Southwest Cape.

[3] Alexander and Dorothea Leighton, Eskimo Recollections of their Life Experiences, Northwest Anthropological Research Notes 17 (1/2), Fall/Spring 1983. See contents list p241. Its stories are Grimmesque.

[4] *Seevookuk* ~ Stories the Old People Told on St Lawrence Island 1973. See p251. His father taught with the Burns (Leightons 1983: 112, 193, 338).

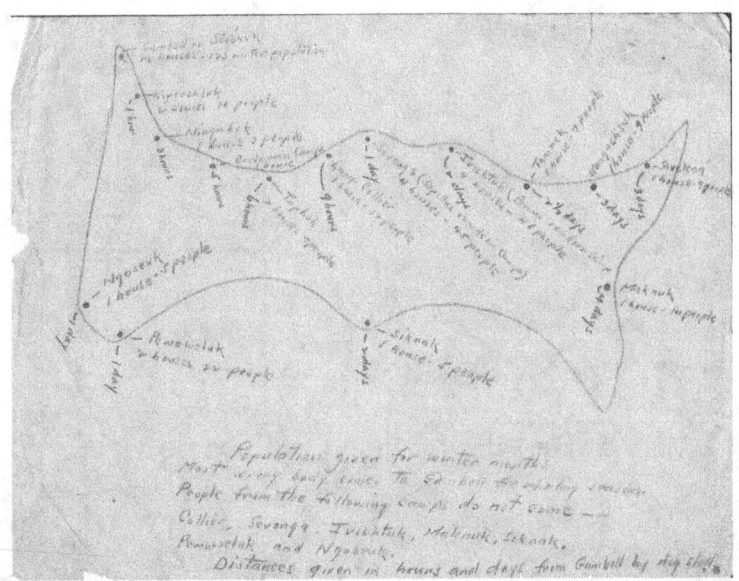

Burns' Map of St Lawrence Island

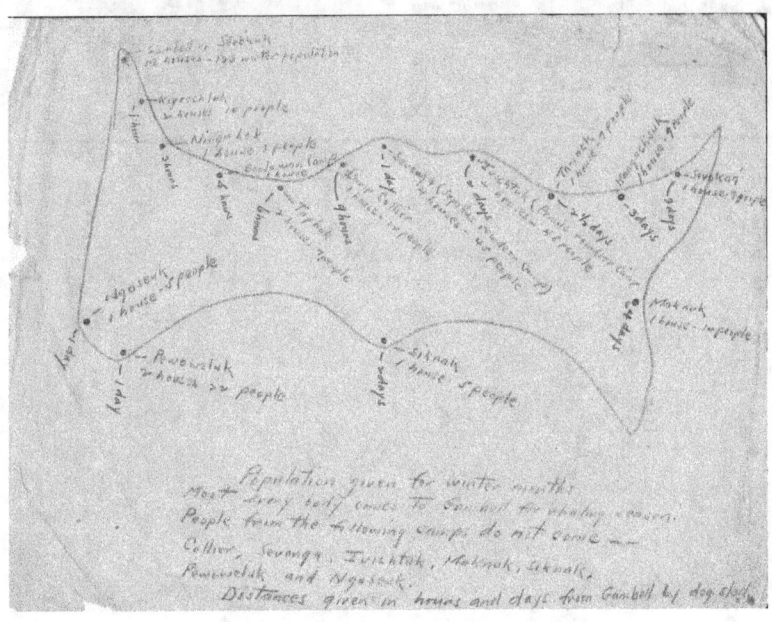

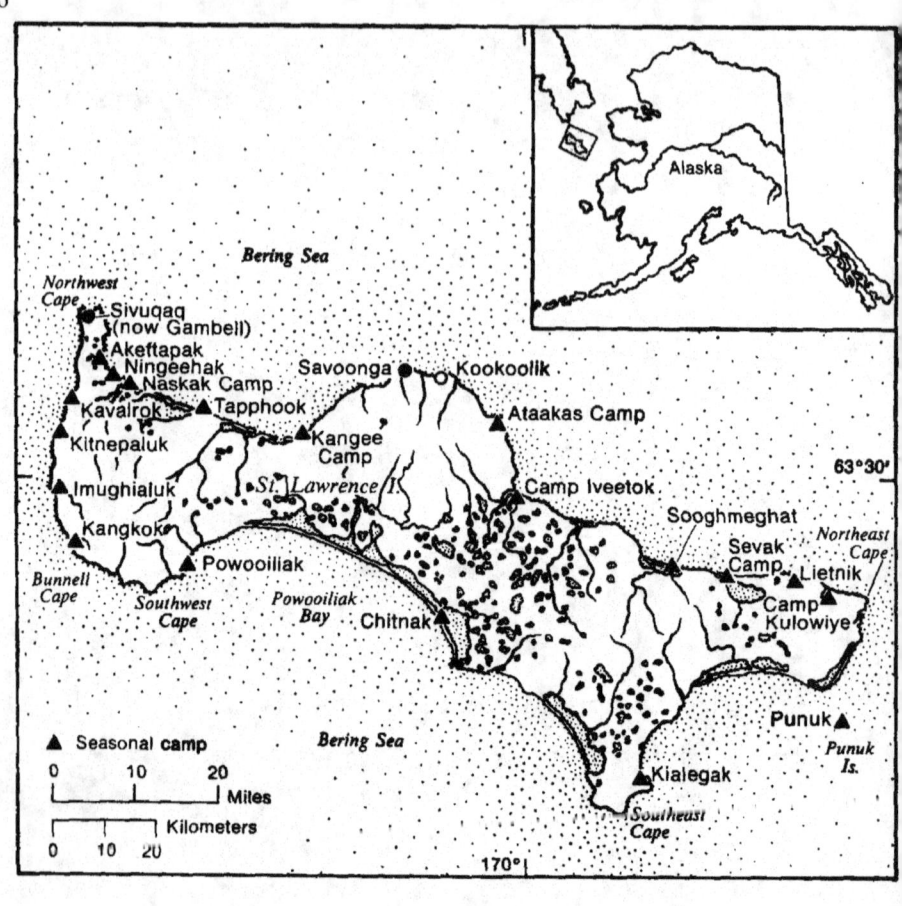

St. Lawrence Island settlements and seasonal camps
occupied before 1879-1880 famine;
some still used as summer camps in the 1980s.

Siberian Yupik Spelling

* Eskimo place-names and band ~ lineage names are normalized to the standard spelling of the Saint Lawrence Island practical orthography, with a phonemic transcription added in italics at the first occurrence. The words spelled *atrruk* and *chkwaek* were not available to the editors in phonemic transcription. [265]

IPA Writing System

p	t	k	k^w	q	q^w	voiceless stops
v	z	ɣ	γ^w	ẏ	$\dot{\gamma}^w$	voiced fricatives
f	s	x	x^w	x̲	$\underline{x}^w$	vl fricatives
m	n	ŋ	η^w			vl nasals
M	N	Ꞥ	η^w			vl nasals
ř	l					vd retroflex & lateral
Ř	L					vl retroflex & lateral
y	h					glides

i	a	u	ə	short vowels
i•	a•	u•		long vowels
i:	a:	u:		extralong vowels

St Lawrence Spelling System

p	t	k	kw	q	qw	vl stops
v	z	g	w	gh	ghw	vd fricatives
f	s	gg	wh	ggh	gghw	vl fricatives
m	n	ng	ngw			vl nasals
mm	nn	ngng	ngngw			vl nasals
r	l					vd retroflex & lateral
rr	ll					vl retroflex & lateral
y	h					glides

i	a	u	ə	short vowels
ii	aa	uu		long vowels
i:	a:	u:		extralong vowels

1984: 244 note *

St Lawrence Island Territory and Environment[5]

Saint Lawrence Island was given its European name by Vitus Bering in 1728, while on his first voyage of discovery into the North Pacific. Obviously it had been "discovered" many centuries earlier by ancestors of people now called Eskimos, for it is the largest island in the Bering Sea, about 100 miles long and averaging from 20 to 30 miles wide. Less than 200 miles south of Bering Strait and about 125 miles southwest of Nome, Alaska, its northwestern tip is only 40 miles from Siberia, which can be seen on a clear day.

Although technically located in the Subarctic rather than the Arctic (lying between 168°45' and 171°50' west longitude and between 63°00' and 63°38' north latitude), in a functional sense Saint Lawrence Island is fully an Arctic environment. It is a largely flat, treeless, tundra island, punctuated by several mountainous features of volcanic, igneous, and sedimentary origin. Surrounded by the ice pack for much of the year, it is beset by winds of high velocity alternating with heavy fog and cloud cover. There is no great accumulation of snowfall, but what does come down is piled into high drifts by the winds. The lowest recorded temperature is -30°F, but with the high winds, the wind chill factor seems considerably lower – especially to hunters out on the ocean ice. The ground cover is termed subarctic, containing the types of lichens, grasses, mosses, and flowering plants found elsewhere in such an inclement environment.

The island is one of the few remaining nonsubmerged parts of what had been a wide land bridge intermittently connecting the New World with the Old during the Pleistocene period and serving as a wide portal of entry for migrants from Asia, who were to become the indigenous peoples of North America, the first wave beginning possibly as long ago as 25,000BC. The key structural position of Saint Lawrence Island in such an episodic land bridge can be illustrated best by noting that a decline in present sea level of only 46 meters would create a land passage between Siberia and Alaska by way of Saint Lawrence, and sea level fell that much, and more, several times from about 30,000 years ago to possibly 10,000

---

[5] Charles C Hughes, Saint Lawrence Island Eskimo, Handbook of North American Indians ~ Arctic 5 1984: 262-277.

years ago. Also, during the several periods of submergence [262b] of the rest of the bridge over that time, the mountainous land mass that was eventually to be named Saint Lawrence Island might well have served as a refuge for populations that did not move elsewhere to escape the encroaching waters. This could be particularly likely for a human group that had developed subsistence techniques based upon exploitation of maritime and shoreline resources – groups such as the ancestors of present-day Eskimos and Aleuts.

Prehistory

In any case, an impressive artifactual record of sea-mammal hunters was left on the island, which began to be uncovered by archeological investigations in the 1920s. The island has provided highly significant sites in the development of Bering Sea prehistory. It was on the basis of work in the 1930s that the major outlines of the archeologically known cultures on the island – Old Bering Sea, Okvik, Punuk, Birnirk, and Thule – were laid out, although, as will no doubt continue with additional finds and reformulations, there are alternative views [263a] among scholars on certain questions, such as how Okvik relates to Old Bering Sea or whether Birnirk was indigenous or intrusive. However, there does appear to be concurrence on a dating of about 2,000 years ago for the appearance of Okvik and Old Bering Sea on Saint Lawrence Island, with Punuk appearing several hundred years later, followed by intrusive Thule influences. In all cases the artifactual evidence points to a people who were very efficient at hunting and extensively utilizing sea mammals: walruses, seals of various types, and several kinds of whales provided flesh for food, light, and heat; bones and tusks for tools; and skins for implements, clothing, boots, and house and boat covers. They had done so for centuries before Euro-American contact, when first the rifle and then the pressure lamp, canned foods, heating oil, mail-order clothing, imported lumber for houses, gasoline-run vehicles, and electricity greatly changed the subsistence patterns by which the Saint Lawrence Islanders adapt to their Arctic environment.

History

After the sighting and naming of Saint Lawrence Island by Bering in 1728, the island was seen by several other Russian and European explorers over the next century, including Otto von Kotzebue, Gleb Shishmaref, and Capt James Cook in 1778. Toward the middle of the nineteenth century the island became caught up in activities connected with the appearance of American and other commercial whaling ships in the North Pacific Ocean, and the Bering, Chukchi, and Beaufort seas. It became the regular pattern for such ships to stop at Eskimo villages to replenish water casks, to carouse, and to trade for ivory, baleen, and warm skin clothing. In return the Eskimos acquired firearms, whaling equipment (such as bomb guns, hemp rope, steel cutting-tools, and wooden whaleboats), liquor, disease, and sometimes long-term guests, for in a few places on the Alaskan shore stations were established for some members of the ships' crews to stay over the winter to hunt whales with the help of local Eskimos until the return of the ship the following spring. It is uncertain whether such stations were established on Saint Lawrence Island, but it is not unlikely, and at any rate it is quite apparent that people of the island had considerable commerce with visiting vessels. An account explicitly comments on Saint Lawrence Islanders' being taken on as crew members of whaling ships.

Saint Lawrence Island Eskimos suffered wholesale tragedy. Versions contradict, but one account has it that in the [263b] fall of 1878 some of the whaling vessels moving south with the oncoming winter freeze-up traded large amounts of liquor just at the time when normally intensive hunting of the walrus herds would have occurred. In the debauch that followed, little hunting was done and consequently meat supplies for the coming months – until the usual walrus harvest in the spring – were very low. Such bad weather followed that it was impossible to hunt the few remaining animals over the winter.[6] Starvation, then sickness, then slow death for much of the island's population ensued. Whatever the cause –

---

[6] A native reason was punishment for abuse of animals. "Kukulik ... don't whale, but they have ... mostly male walrus ... [during] a shortage of meat ... Somebody struck a young male walrus and pulled it on top of the ice and cut it up before it died – kind of a cruelty ... having a good time cutting that live walrus (Kogoyak Leightons 1983: 296).

alcoholic debauch or simply the periodic year of stormy weather and bad hunting – it is estimated that about 1,000 of the island's population of 1,500 or so had died by the next summer, a loss never recovered. The population in the late 1950s was still only about 600; in 1970 it was about 700; the 1980 census gives 936 for Gambell and Savoonga (which includes non-Natives). So devastated was the island that when the US revenue cutter *Corwin* investigated reports of mass starvation in the summer of 1880, one of its passengers, the noted naturalist John Muir, described entire settlements with nothing but bleached bones, with bodies lying in houses, about the village, or on the path to the burial ground.

The first recorded long-term residence by a White man began in 1894, when the Presbyterian missionary Vene C Gambell arrived with his wife and established a station in the major village of the island, then known as Sivuqaq (*sivú•qaq* ~ "squeezed"; Sivokakh in Gambell 1898). Located on the northwestern tip of the island, it had been a place of habitation for several thousand years, with signs of earliest settlement found on the slopes of the mountain that stands as a bold landmark for many miles out to sea. Gambell drowned with his family in 1898 when their ship was lost at sea. The village was renamed in his honor (in English usage), and others came to take up his post as missionary, teacher, and representative of the United States government. One of the most effective was Dr Edgar Omar Campbell, a medical missionary, who remained for over 10 years after the turn of the century and kept a detailed diary of many of important events. In it he recounts his battles with shamans for the conversion of the Eskimos to Presbyterianism, with Siberians over trading whiskey to local Eskimos, with domineering Eskimo boat captains who wanted no part of his interference with traditional hunting rites, and with his own isolation and disappointments at lack of success. One of the legacies he left was the building of the reindeer herd on the island. As part of a general scheme by the US government to restore stability to the native economy, in 1900 42 reindeer and several Lapp herders were placed on the island to help the Eskimos develop and manage a food resource. The [264a] herd was successful with respect to that aim for about 30 years or more (reaching a size of at least several thousand animals), but by the mid-1950s it had practically disappeared, most likely through range devegetation. In the early

island

1970s the herd had increased to 800-1,000.

Other missionaries and government-appointed teachers followed Dr Campbell. The notes of one of these record the first use of an outboard motor on the hunting boats in 1917, and those of another, [264b] some 10 years later, the formation of the first village council on an elective basis.

The 1920s were good years for the Saint Lawrence Islanders, based upon a mixed economy of indigenous pursuits and trapping the Arctic fox (*Alopex lagopus*), whose pelts brought up to $60 each. Indeed, some of the most successful trappers could earn several thousand dollars a year during those years from trapping alone. Such income even surpassed what had been possible some 30 and more years [265a] earlier, when the Eskimos had had a highly profitable trade in whale baleen with commercial vessels, a market that had begun to decline after the turn of the century, leaving the Eskimos with only the sale of Arctic fox furs as an important source of cash income, supplemented by the sale of carved ivory objects. But the Arctic fox market also began to fade in the late 1930s. With the onset of World War II it became highly uncertain and remained so after the war.

The Saint Lawrence Islanders were affected in other ways also by the war. Some of their young men served in the Alaska Territorial Guard, a few even seeing combat in the Alaskan theater of operations, and at one point the Islanders felt threatened with invasion by Japanese forces. Following the war what had been mostly year-round isolation from close contact with the outside world came to an end, when there was established near the village a small US military installation and a weather station. The effects of both of these firsthand illustrations of mainland life upon the evolving cultural system of the Saint Lawrence Islanders were profound (Hughes 1960). By the middle 1950s the pattern had been set: the teacher, missionary, and public health nurse were still the "traditional" representatives of the mainland world, but increasingly the island has become more interdependent with the Alaskan mainland. By the middle [265b] 1970s, the following changes had begun to influence the island: statehood and its implications for local government; implementation of the Alaska Native Claims Settlement Act (under which the island is owned by the Native people and managed by the native corporations in Gambell and

Savoonga); stricter controls on the hunting of maritime animals and sale of their products (under provisions of the 1972 Marine Mammals Protection Act); tourism as an industry, dependence on monetary income from jobs; enhanced communication capabilities (exemplified in satellite-beamed television reception); exploration for mineral resources; and emigration to the Alaskan mainland. Above all, Natives needed to deal with three separate but overlapping local governmental structures in each village – the council established by the Indian Reorganization Act, the city council, established under Alaska state authority, and the village corporation, established under the Alaska claims act. While the cultural pattern presented here derives from data gathered in the mid-1950s, its principal outlines, especially social structure, remained valid into the 1980s.

Culture

The Saint Lawrence Islanders belong culturally to the Asiatic Eskimo population, rather than to that of North America. This relationship is shown by a number of major cultural features but especially by their language, which is nearly identical to the variety of Eskimo spoken on the Siberian mainland called Chaplinski in the Soviet Union; the two together constitute the Central Siberian Yupik language. *[See Yupik Spelling page 7]

Besides the speakers of Central Siberian Yupik, who bridge the international boundary, other Asiatic Eskimos are found in Siberia. In addition to language, features differentiating Asiatic from North American Eskimos are the existence of patrilineal descent groups; the absence of the formal men's house found in Alaska villages; house, clothing, and cosmetic styles; and major features of the ceremonial system (which shows strong similarities to that of Maritime Chukchees on the Siberian shore). [266a]

Social Organization

In most respects, any treatment of Saint Lawrence Island Eskimos should be viewed as a particular discussion of the larger cultural grouping, the Siberian or Asiatic Eskimos; this is particularly true of any discussion of [266b] social organization. For

island

several hundred years at least (and probably a few millennia), there has been considerable interchange between the Saint Lawrence Islanders and Eskimos and Chukchees living on the Siberian shore, only 40 or so miles to the northwest. Such interactions involved extensive trade relations, intermarriage, warfare, and migration; in fact, at least one of the existing clan groups on Saint Lawrence Island is known historically to have originated in the village of Old Chaplino (*Ungaziq, uŋá•ziq*) on Indian Point (*Mys Chaplino*) on the Siberian shore, and one of the clans living there in 1962 bore the same name, Aymaramket (*aymáȓamkət*).[7]

One of the principal features of traditional Siberian Eskimo social structure is the existence of patrilineal clans or lineages. Soviet scholars broaden this issue, asserting that a clan structure was found everywhere in Eskimo societies, and that an evolutionary process had occurred whereby such groups had changed from a primitive communal form of social structure to a matrilineal organization and finally would reach a patrilineal mode of organization. One aspect of this argument is that vestiges of the presumed former matrilineal stage of development are everywhere to be seen as "survivals" in cultural [267a] features such as the presence of female deities in the religion, the participation of females in rituals, and the like.

The general issue of clans among the Eskimos notwithstanding, there is no question of the existence – and viability – of patrilineal descent groups among the Saint Lawrence Islanders in historic times. These groups may be called clans.

The development and stabilization of these patrilineal clans

---

[7] (What is the name of your tribe?) Aimarumkit. Poduk's and Gotulik's family, I think, and Laskok's and Kakoktok's family are all relatives. Some relatives are in a different tribe, Gotulik, Tuko, and Koneak. They are closely related to Aimarumkit but have a different tribal name. Tuko's and Koneak's fathers were Kukulumit, which means those people belonged to Kukulik. Gotulik and Ed of Savoonga are another tribe, also closely related, called Anawasat. That name comes from Gotulik's great-grandfather. Aimarumkit ....

Amarumkit has another name, too, for the same reason. Every time they would get a walrus or mukluk or anything, one or two of the older men would help themselves to what they liked to eat and not divide it all among the crew. So somebody called them Imbarumkit. That's the way the extra names are given. This one means "this is mine and nobody else can have it," Imbarumkit (Kogoyak Leightons 1983: 324-5)

island

may be conjectured as an outcome of particular historical, social, and ecological circumstances. In brief, the Saint Lawrence Islanders formerly were dispersed into a number of settlements scattered around the island, each settlement a patrilineally dominated extended family group similar to the social organizational and settlement pattern found in traditional North American Eskimo bands. In general the bands were [267b] designated, by themselves and others, by the place-name; they were, for example, the Meregtemiit (*məɾəxtəmi•t*) 'the people of Meregta (*məɾɔ́xta*)'. In a sense such groups may be thought of as "tribes," or at least incipient tribes (early reports called them this – for example); for each had an overall group identification that was meaningful to members of the group itself and also served to differentiate each group from all others. In addition, it is said that there were slight dialectal differences apparent among the bands, as well as some distinctive religious practices and social lore. [268a]

For reasons having to do with hunting opportunities as well as the catastrophic famine and decimation of the population in the winter of 1878-1879, all of these small outlying settlements were completely destroyed. The only survivors were about 30 at Powooiliak (*Pugu-ghileq, puyu•ẏiləq*) on Southwest Cape, about 300 at what became the principal village on the island, Gambell, and one at Kialegak (*Kiyalighaq, kiya•liẏaq*) on Southeast Cape, who went to Powooiliak. This catastrophe no doubt simply accelerated and consolidated a process of seasonal settlement from a central base that had already been going on, given the excellence of Gambell as a hunting site. The population of Powooiliak was absorbed by Gambell in the twentieth century. The other year-round settlement, Savoonga (*Sivunga, sivú•ŋa*), was started as a reindeer camp in 1914 as an offshoot of Gambell village; its social organizational format is similar to that of Gambell, which it surpassed in population in the 1970s.

In the context of that new social environment, Gambell village, the band or extended-family designations by which people were known became more pronounced. Whereas in the outlying settlements, the issue of what group a person belonged to was seldom raised in that local context (it being taken for granted), in Gambell village, with its heterogeneous population, such [268b] a group affiliation became a more important dimension of ongoing interpersonal relations, thus reinforcing a person's sense of kinship with a patriline. In addition, these groups continued to function in such a manner as to underscore the sense of identification and mutual need, for example, hunting together, conducting their own indigenous religious services, and serving as a person's reserve line of defense in quarrels with other villagers. In Gambell village since about the 1940s three such clans were dominant, the Meregtemiit, Aymaramket, and Pugughileghmiit (*puɣu•ɣiləmi•t*), with several others having fewer members and, largely because of that, being relatively powerless in intravillage politics.

It should also be noted that there are subclans within these larger descent groupings and that the specific terms by which the group and subgroup are known might well depend on the situation and the level of specificity required. For example, the broad group to which a person belongs might be the Meregtemiit when the issue is one of differentiating him from the Aymaramket; but if the focus is on the internal structure of the Meregtemiit, his "real" affiliation might be with the Nangupagagh-miit (*nanú•payáymi•t*).

• KINSHIP ~ Using Murdock's (1949) criteria, one may label the social organization of the Saint Lawrence Islanders as a variant of Iroquoian, that is, there are distinctive cousin terms for father's brother's children (*atálɣun*, sg.) and mother's sister's children (*aẏnálɣun*, sg.), with one term covering cousins linked to ego through father's sister and mother's brother. This single cross-cousin term, *ilú•ẏaq*, designates what is primarily a joking relationship, with none of the more serious and helpful interpersonal dimensions found with the other two types of cousin bonds. The two parallel cousin relationships are not the same, for the bond between a male (especially) and his father's brother's children is one of the strongest and most enduring of all relationships in the entire social organization. It is the base on which the boat crew is built and is the cornerstone of the patrilineal descent group. There is, in fact, social recognition of the importance – and closeness – of this relationship, expressed in a collective term for a group of patrilineal parallel cousins (*kəməkRakúlẏi•t*), which is translated 'those that have the same flesh'. So close behaviorally are individuals who stand in this relation that commonly, in fact, terms for one's own siblings rather than cousin terms are used in reference and in direct discourse.

The rest of the kinship terminology may be described as bifurcate collateral, with relatively more development of the patrilineal principle as expressed in number of terms and importance of social function accorded to persons standing in that relationship. Thus the patriline is firmly ensconced both in extended family and lineage activities, while matrilineal relatives function only [269a] periodically and irregularly in activities relating to ego's life-cycle events and small-scale domestic needs (for example, sharing of food or borrowing of tools).

Thus, for a given individual, there are concentric circles of social groupings, varying according to their bases and the scope of activities for which they are relevant to ego. The inmost grouping is the domestic family, which may be either nuclear or extended. Beyond the nuclear family the extended form may include either a grandparental generation, or else married or unmarried siblings at the parental level. The next kind of social grouping – and this is especially important for a male – is that of the patrilateral parallel cousin grouping. Then there is the kindred, ego's close relatives on both [269b] father's and mother's sides. Finally comes the most influential and dominant of the social bonds, this one expressed in a definite social group that has time and generational depth, the patrilineal clans (*ilá•k^{w}á•qulẏi•t*).

• MARRIAGE ~ Even though there was a clear lineage principle as the organizing structure of the social system, at least in historic times this was apparently not coupled with any consistent rule so far as exogamy was concerned, although clan exogamy was perhaps the dominant mode. The Siberian Eskimos are varyingly reported to have been exogamous between clans. In this respect Saint Lawrence Island cultural practice appears to resemble that of North American Eskimo groups, the only restriction upon marriage partner being that [270a] against marrying a "close" relative (in kindred terms). Thus on Saint Lawrence Island a person could and did marry someone belonging to the same descent group, and in the past, when the population lived in the small settlements before the gathering of the clans into the two dominant villages, this probably occurred frequently.

Traditionally, arrangements for marriage were made by the

parents and elders of the young people concerned. Sometimes, in fact, there was infant betrothal. In any case, at some point in adolescence deemed appropriate, the sequence of events that comprised the "marriage" began. The first step was that of the young man's moving into the home of the young woman's parents to render "groom-work" for a period of time, usually about a year in duration. The move was preceded by gifts of tools, weapons, and other economic goods from the boy's family to that of the girl. His duties were practically boundless: he was to hunt with his future father-in-law (and in his boat) and to do all other things appropriate to a male in the household {kinship diagram removed}. It is said that some men took advantage of this arrangement, exacting great labors from the prospective son-in-law, only then to refuse to carry through the rest of the bargain by giving the daughter up.

At the end of the work period, during which time the young people usually began sexual relations, the next formal step in social recognition occurred, and this one was the most decisive. The young couple moved back into the house of the boy's parents. The traditional rule of residence was thus matri-patrilocal or, more accurately, uxori-virilocal. The actual move was accompanied by a group of the girl's kinsmen (or close relatives if the marriage was lineage-endogamous) pulling a sled loaded with gifts of useful goods, such as walrus-hide rope, walrus skins, hunting tools, stores of food (meat, preserved plant food), ivory or baleen. With the receipt of the girl and the sledload of gifts, the marriage contract was sealed. No other formal ritualization occurred to mark the event.

The ensuing adjustment of the young bride to a new home environment was not always easy. Frictions either with the in-laws or with the new husband not uncommonly led to divorce. When it did occur, divorce, like the marriage itself, was not highly formalized. In fact, all that was required was for the woman either to leave or to be told to leave, returning to her original home and kinsmen. Although both marriage and divorce have changed with respect to Alaska state law, most features of the traditional pattern remained in the 1950s.

• PARTNERSHIP ~ One other type of institutionalized social bond – the trading and singing partner – is very important in Eskimo groups. On Saint Lawrence Island 270 this fictive kin relation was known as *naŋsá•yaq*. The [270b] principal form such a relationship took was that of an alliance between two nonclan mates, whereby they functioned as "brothers" in support of each other – sharing goods, giving support and hospitality, providing staged occasions of entertainment and singing matches, as well as sexual access to each other's wives. In the past, such "brother" relations were most often found between two men living on different parts of the island or with someone in Siberia; because of the distance, the other partner's residence would serve as a "home away from home." Once a relationship had been agreed upon by two men, they would formalize it in a ritual that included participation by their wives, exchange of gifts, and the public sanction provided by many guests participating in the affair.

Subsistence

Saint Lawrence Islanders have always relied chiefly upon the sea for food and for many of their tools to wrest a living from their severe environment. The island lies astraddle migration routes for the Pacific walrus (*Odobenus divergens*) and several species of whales, the bowhead (*Balaena mysticetus*), finback (*Balaenoptera physalus*), and the gray ~ summer whale (*Eschrichtius robustus*). The spotted seal (*Phoca vitulina*), ringed seal (*P. hispida*), and the bearded seal ~ *ugrug* (*makiak, mukluk*) (*Erignathus barbatus*) are found in considerable numbers at different times of the year, either along coasts or out among the ice floes. The flesh of these animals, with occasional polar bears, provided the great bulk of food. [271a]

Particularly important was the walrus. In the 1950s, (for example, in a good year hunters of Gambell village would often kill up to 300 of these large animals, the males each weighing about a ton; in 1982, 1,000 were killed. And it was not simply the flesh and internal organs that were used (practically everything except the spleen was eaten – flesh, heart, lung, kidney, stomach, intestines), but also the hide of the females, the ivory tusks, and the flippers (of baby walruses). If not eaten, the intestines were used to make waterproof parkas. Until the 1970s, when snowmobiles replaced dog teams for transportation, walrus meat was also vital dog food.

Other clothing was made of sealskins – parkas, boots, pants, mittens – and reindeer furs, obtained in trade from Siberia before the

Saint Lawrence Islanders had [271b] their own herd. Tough ropes for whaling were made from baby walrus hide; before the coming of the whaling vessels the harpoon heads were of walrus ivory tipped with stone; and the floats used on both the whaling line and the harpoon line for walrus or seals were made of inflated sealskins. Finally, seal and walrus blubber gave heat and light, and walrus hides were used as covers for the hunting boats and one of the types of houses built by the Saint Lawrence Islanders. That house was the *maŋtə́ẏaq*, a structure of driftwood roofed with skin, adopted from Siberia during the nineteenth century as an alternative to the traditional semisubterranean, sod-covered *nəŋlu ~ ningloo* winter house used into the late 1800s. Traditionally summer houses were skin tents. With the importation of [272a] lumber during the affluent 1920s, a single lumber structure became used year round. By the 1950s, this was the style of all homes.

Although maritime mammals were the basis of life, diet was supplemented by fishing in streams, through the winter ice, or from boats; by netting birds; and by the picking and preserving of many types of plants. The most commonly used plant was the *nuni•vak* (*Sedum rosea*, roseroot), the leaves of which were tightly packed and stored in a water-filled sealskin to preserve ~ ferment for the winter, when it was used as a succulent for ordinary meals and, in small portions, ceremonial offerings on ritual occasions.

Patterns of hunting took two basic forms. In one, an individual hunter would stalk seals and walruses at the ice edge where currents opened up breathing spaces in the ocean ice, or else would stand – sometimes for hours – at breathing holes on the stable ice. This type of hunting occurred only during the heart of the winter, when the ocean was so covered with ice that it was [272b] unfeasible to use boats. There were other times of the year also when boats were not used, such as early fall, when seals would come close to shore for feeding and could be netted or, after the introduction of the rifle, shot and their carcasses snared with a thrown hook.

But the chief mode of hunting, and the most productive, took the form of hunting walruses, seals, and especially whales with use of a boat. The most intensive hunting, in fact, occurred during the spring breakup of the ocean ice, at a time when walruses were beginning to work their way back north in huge herds, and whales were sporting about in the opening ocean. For the Saint Lawrence Islanders this was from March through May. After May, the walruses had mostly passed, the whales were rarely seen, and the seals could easily avoid being shot in the open sea.

The boats used were principally *umiaks* (*aŋyaq* 'boat', or *aŋya•pik* 'authentic boat'), constructed of driftwood and covered with split female walrus hides. In recent historic times, at least, this was the boat mostly used by the Saint Lawrence Islanders. Data are unclear on how much the kayak (*qayaq*) was used. Certain archeological artifacts from the Old Bering Sea and Punuk cultures are interpreted as belonging to kayak frames (Collins 1937; Bandi 1969); and a drawing in a late nineteenth-century US government publication depicts the Islanders using kayaks for harpooning walruses. But the data base for that drawing is not discussed and it is highly relevant that kayaks are not mentioned in other contemporary accounts of the Islanders. Otto von Kotzebue, who visited in 1816, also does not mention them and Nelson, in fact, denies their presence: "A smaller boat or canoe, called [*kayak*], is also used along the American coast and the adjacent islands; but I have never seen one among the people of the Siberian coast nor among the St Lawrence Islanders." Corroborating Nelson is the lack of reference to kayaks among the twentieth-century Eskimos on the Siberian coast by Rubfsova. Fieldwork in the 1950s also did not discover either their use or remembered use on Saint Lawrence Island. [273a] On the other hand, Doty noted that "kayaks are used in the summer and early fall by a few natives on lagoons."

In any case, the open umiak, powered by paddles – and for whaling, by sail – was the most efficient and productive hunting device for centuries (fig. 17), made even more effective when outboard gasoline motors were placed in it and high-powered rifles added to its weaponry after contact with the American mainland.

The makeup of the crew for each boat also served as a key example of the functioning of the principal structure in the social organization, the patrilineal clans, for crews were composed of some six to eight members drawn from the sons of a man (acting as captain), sometimes his brothers, and his brother's sons. This group was highly solidary, working together as a hunting unit and tied together with overriding bonds of kinship and clanship. Indeed, the core of the boat crew, companions on whom a person could rely through the many dangers of ice floe, freezing weather, and animal vengeance, was the group of patrilateral parallel cousins.

Religion

Saint Lawrence Island traditional religion was a variant of the beliefs and practices oriented to the supernatural world found elsewhere in Eskimo groups, although it showed strong similarities to that of the Chukchee on the Siberian shore. It was, as elsewhere, directed primarily at the mollification and beseechment of animals to ensure continued good hunting, and at the warding off or cure of sickness. Its social forms were individual and personal (as taboos and prescriptions placed upon the hunter) as well as collective and public (as rituals of thanksgiving upon the killing of a whale). Finally, into a number of these religious contexts, both private and public, there came the person of the shaman (*aŋáłkuq, alignalghiit*), the vital link between man and encompassing spiritual world.

The spiritual world is best described as highly animistic. Most features of observable nature were thought to have indwelling spiritual essences, in some cases capable of taking diverse forms. Rocks, mountains, and other features of landscape were included under such a spiritual umbrella. But more important in the affairs of men were the souls of animals – seals, walruses, whales, polar bears – that were the quarry in the life-and-death encounters out on the sea. The souls of these animals [274a] were conceived to be very much like those of human beings, subject to the same range of emotions and thoughts, of resentments and desires. Hence it was important to treat them with respect and dignity, such as offering a prayer to the soul of a seal before killing or lifting a cup of water to the animal's lips before the carcass was taken inside the house. Legend has it that such souls, if properly treated, would willingly release the body for use of man and harbor no grudge; indeed, they would return to villages at the bottom of the sea where they were thought to live, there to tell their fellows of the respectful manner in which they had been treated by men. A great many of the individual, private ritual prescriptions placed upon the hunter and upon his wife had to do with this goal of showing the animal that it was a valued co-being with man in the scheme of things.

At times, such respect took the form of public ceremonies.

Strangely (given its importance in the diet) there were no mass ceremonies in honor of the walrus, nor any to honor the seal comparable in magnitude and importance to those of the Alaskan mainland. The most dramatic ceremonies of this nature were performed for the polar bear and, especially, for the whale; they involved the ritual sacrifice of foodstuffs, singing and dancing in honor of the soul of the slain animal, and activities that functioned to unify the boat crew and its clan.

• ~ WHALE CEREMONIALISM Whaling was a focal concern, one that acted in the social realm as the principal arbiter of prestige and value, for the hunters considered to be the greatest and most powerful boat captains were those who had killed at least one whale. The supernatural ritualization of the whale's importance extended over several months, being marked by discrete events, either those of preparation for whaling or thankfulness [274b] after a successful hunt. The main ritual event of the winter occurred from February through April, when each of the hunting boats conducted a ceremony in preparation for whaling. This was called the *atrruk* or *chkwaek* (meaning 'the sacrifice'), and its details were traditional for each clan with its one or several hunting boats. The ceremony was held only at the time of the full moon, and it was customary that no two boats could conduct the ritual on the same day.

Preparations for the ceremony were begun long in advance. Throughout the previous spring and summer, greens from the mountain had been collected and sorted in a special place; reindeer fat (gotten from Siberia in the days before the Saint Lawrence herd) was similarly set aside; tobacco traded from the Russians made up part of the sacrificial foods; and a final item usually was fish of some kind. All these foods were considered extremely holy and were placed in sealskin pokes on a meat rack, out of the reach of children and dogs.

When later in the winter the day for the ceremony finally arrived, the boat captain, his wife, his harpooner, and sometimes the rest of the crew took all the foods down from the meat rack and, working on several wooden platters, molded them into long low mounds. These were placed in the center of the room in the boat captain's house and covered with a walrus skin. Over the foods were hung the captain's hunting gear – such as his special visor, worn only on the hunt and symbolic of his status as well as presumably possessing an inherent power. The captain's bag of special hunting charms was also hung over the foods, which was a small sealskin container in which were placed various bits of flesh or organs of animals the captain had killed – whale, polar bear, walrus, or sometimes even a sea gull if there had been something unusual about its killing. The captain and the rest of the group then sat around the foods singing and praying through the night.

Long before sunrise all the participants went down to the shore, carrying the trays of food with them. There they lowered the boat into the water, all the crew got into the craft, and they paddled out a short distance from shore, where once more they uttered prayers. Then they returned to the shore to await the coming of sunrise. At dawn, the sacrifice of food began. The captain took a small portion from each platter, broke this into small bits, and threw these into the air, into the sea, and onto the land. As he did so, he recited prayers asking for a successful hunt during the coming season. Following the sacrificing of ritual foods, the crew ate what was left on the platters, and anything remaining after that was distributed to other people in the village.

If a boat was successful in killing a whale, a different sort of ceremony occurred. First, out on the water before the animal was towed back to land, the captain, raising his special paddle (another mark of status and, like the visor, embodying supernatural power), shouted [275a] "Ho-ho-ho-ho." Then his boat circled the whale, stopping at the front and at the back once again while the captain shouted in the same way. The purpose of such shouting was to inform *kiyáy̓nəq*, the all-powerful. Supreme God (also known as *apa* 'grandfather'), that the whale had been captured and to thank him. Before towing the animal to the shore, the captain cut four small pieces of flesh from the tips of the tail and flukes and threw them back into the sea. This was again a mark of sacrifice to *kiyáy̓nəq* and to the animal spirits. During the towing to shore the captain twice shouted in his distinctive way.

With the animal finally tied up to the shore, the cutting began. While this was occurring, women of the captain's clan gathered to sing in front of his house, with the captain's wife wearing a special costume for the occasion, part of which was a band of white reindeer hair decorating her head.

island

From the cutting in of the whale, several pieces had been saved: bits of the flukes, eyes, and nose. Immediately after the cutting in was completed, the boat crew (along with the entire clan of the boat that had killed the whale) went to the captain's house, in front of which all these various parts of the animal were spread out on the ground in a diagrammatic form suggestive of the whale's body. A fire was built in front of the animal's nose, and then the captain's wife brought a pail of water containing small pieces of whale meat and *nuni•vak*. She offered a part of the water and *nuni•vak* to the whale, symbolically putting some into its mouth. Next she threw portions of the whale meat into the fire (in an act of feeding the ancestors). After this all the family walked around the parts of the whale and then on top of them.

Finally, all the pieces were taken into the captain's house and hung up over the fire for five days, while songs were chanted and stories told. No hunting was possible during this time, similar to the prohibition on hunting after the killing of a polar bear. At the end of the period, most of the parts of the animal were distributed among clan relatives and eaten. Parts not eaten were the mid-section of the tail, which was saved for a ceremony during the coming summer, and the eyeball of the whale, from which was made a black substance used for painting special ritual designs on the captain's paddle and on the bow of the boat.

• SPIRITS ~ While it was the souls of animals that, in their incarnate form, sustained the Saint Lawrence Islanders in the empirical world, other spirits made them fearful and apprehensive. Aside from the spirits of observable natural phenomena (rocks, hills) and beyond the souls of animals, there were thought to be at least two other types of spirits. One of these types was sometimes beneficial to man, responding to an appeal for aid or special power (as in regard to the shaman's alliance with a spiritual helper). These were the *taẏnə́ẏa•t* [275b] (*taẏnə́ẏaq* sg.), and they, like the second kind, could assume many forms, visible and invisible. The second aid or special power (as in regard to the shaman's always evil and maleficent toward man. They caused accidents, sickness, poor weather, loss of soul or of valuable objects, and all other manner of ill fortune. In the translation of the early missionaries these were known as 'devils', and however ethnocentric the term may be, in orientation it connotes the essential character of these spirits, who were said to be everywhere, but especially around the village, looking for the chance to create trouble and worry.

• SHAMANS ~ When sickness or some other perplexing problem arose that did not respond to home solutions, the Saint Lawrence Islanders turned to a shaman for help. Shamans, most of whom were men, acquired their presumed powers and their special alliance with the spiritual world through a quest out on the tundra or in some other lonely, isolated place. After striking a bargain with one or more spirits – by which the shaman was given power in return for what could be called a token or symbolic part of the valuable goods he would receive from clients – the shaman set himself up in the business of divination, prophecy, diagnosis, and therapy. His approach included dreams, ventriloquism, sleight-of-hand artistry, and, no doubt, acute observational and inference skills.

In the case of sickness of the Saint Lawrence Islanders, three causes were believed paramount – loss of soul, intrusion of some malignant object or spirit, and breach of taboo. The shaman's task was to discover which cause or causes were operating, and then to bring about the conditions for health. If loss of soul was indicated, the shaman would conduct a séance – with darkened lights in the room crowded with relatives, beating of the walrus-stomach drum, singing in an archaic language – in which his own soul would depart his body to wander in search of the soul of the patient. If it was theft of soul, then through his power he would overcome the evil spirit that had done the deed. The shaman's soul would "return" from wandering the spiritual world, reenter his own body, and tell those in the room and the patient what he had done and what the patient should now do to get better. Usually this would include some directives for the patient's behavior – to abstain from certain food, or to wear a particular amulet, and the like – and sometimes, too, restrictions of similar nature were placed on the patient's family.

In his curative procedures the shaman also was adept at use of empirical medicine – giving emetics, applying poultices, staunching wounds – but he was no doubt careful never to let such common-sense techniques overshadow the definition of the situation he had created in the minds of the viewers, namely, that this was a religious, and hence dangerous, procedure, one in which he was the expert and not they. [276a]

For such expert aid he was, of course, paid, and paid well. The patient's family gave him walrus-hide rope, food, reindeer fat, and many other kinds of valuable goods. After the patient-oriented ceremony was over, the shaman then had to satisfy his own spiritual obligation to those agents that had helped him, by throwing down into a fire small bits cut from each of the items he had been paid, uttering as he did so prayers of thanksgiving to his spirit-familiars, and, while tossing up other bits, prayers also to the supreme being *kiyáy̌nəq*, thought to have ultimate control (however loose it was at times) over all affairs of humans.

• CULTURAL PERSISTENCE ~ The preceding descriptions of ritual and belief belong to a past time in the culture history of the Saint Lawrence Islanders. Yet a number of the dominant beliefs that structured the Saint Lawrence Islanders' view of the supernatural world still operate to some degree in the current scene: in attitudes toward animals; in vague, inchoate fears of spirits or retributive events of nature; and in an apperception of an unseen power that influences man's fate, his health, and his well-being. It is probable that only to some extent have these beliefs been eradicated by Christianity, which began to influence their lives when Presbyterian missionaries arrived in 1894, followed during the 1940s by another Christian denomination, the Seventh-Day Adventists. Both groups had been so successful that by the late 1950s there was only one person still avowedly and openly practicing the indigenous religion. For the rest, the social influences of American culture on the Alaska mainland were as profound in the area of religious practice as they were in most other spheres of life – esthetic, recreational, material-cultural, and ideological. The one area where the press of a dominant environment retains its impact upon social, psychological, and economic reality is hunting, representing perhaps the most dramatic continuity of Saint [276b] Lawrence Island Eskimo present with its past.

Synonymy by Charles C Hughes and Ives Goddard

In the 1970s the Saint Lawrence Islanders applied the name *Sivuqaq* (*sivú•qaq*) to both the entire island and the town of

island

Gambell, and the derived form *sivú•qaxMi•t* could mean either 'Saint Lawrence Islanders' or 'Gambellites'.

The meaning of this name and its original application are uncertain, and the historical sources and islanders interviewed in 1955 appear to vary on the scope of the terms. From a man who had lived on the island before 1820 Khromchenko recorded its name as Chuakak. Kotzebue learned Tschibocki as the name of the island from the people he met in the southwest and found that those in the northwest likewise called themselves Tschi-bocko, but he later understood from people on the east that they applied the name Tschibocka to the western part and Kealegack (the same as the settlement name *kiyá•liẏaq*) to the east. These and other early spellings, like Chibukak and Chebukak, render *sivú•qaq* and reflect the nineteenth-century pronunciation [*čiBó•qaq*], before the shift of [*č*] (recorded as late as 1901) to s. Moore claims that in 1922 the group name (*Sivokakhmeit*) was used for the inhabitants of Gambell, but in 1955, although one informant used Sivuqaq for the entire island, others did not commonly use the group name to refer even to all the people just in Gambell, but rather only to some of them. This can be understood as reflecting the importance of clan groupings and clan identification in the traditional social structure.

Part of the difficulty in fixing a single term for the Saint Lawrence Islanders may be the assumption by outsiders that geographic space must be identical with social psychological reality. In view of Saint Lawrence Island cultural history, this clearly is not so. Shifting frames of social affiliation and identification have overlain the dispersion and consolidation of groups, such that at only one point in recent history might it have been possible to characterize the population of the island by the one term – when (in 1912) all the population was, in fact, centered in Gambell village as the basic point of residence.

The Chukchee name of Saint Lawrence Island has been recorded as Eiwugi-nu, 1792, also Eivugen, E-oo-vogen, Eivoogiena, and eiwhue'n, and the Chukchee name for the people has been given as *eiwhue'lit*; in the form Eiwhuelit this has been used as the English name for the islanders in [277a] some. There is evidence that this term traditionally designated only one of the groups living in Gambell, the (now small) *uyá•li•t* clan whose ancestors founded and therefore "own" the village.

island

The claim that the Saint Lawrence Islanders and the Chaplinski-speaking Siberian Eskimos called themselves Massinga 'good men' appears to be based on a misunderstanding of a polite term of address derived from Chukchee. Hodge BAE-B 1:419 gives a few other names.

Sources

An excellent review of the relevant literature up to the mid-1930s is in Collins (1937), which includes excerpts from early explorers such as Semen Dezhnev and Otto von Kotzebue. An extensive review, with illustrations, of the material culture of the nineteenth century is given by Nelson (1899), which is skimpy on social organization. Other observations from the late nineteenth century are those of Hooper (1881) and Muir (1917); and in the renowned study of the Chukchees by Bogoras (1904-1909), there are numerous comments about the Islanders. Materials also exist in government reports (for instance, Maynard 1898; Elliott 1898). An excellent source of information (sometimes erroneous, sometimes quite accurate) is the annual reports on the introduction of domestic reindeer into Alaska (US Bureau of Education 1896-1905). Of particular interest in that source are statements by Gambell (1898) and a lengthy "ethnographic" report by his successor, Doty (1900). Several photographs of interest are also found in these volumes.

The earliest formal "ethnological" account of the Saint Lawrence Islanders is that of Moore (1923), based on data gathered in 1912. Basic archeological monographs contain much valuable information on contemporary cultural patterns as well (Collins 1937; Geist and Rainey 1936). Hughes (1960) provides a comprehensive ethnography and study of sociocultural change through the middle 1950s; and J M Hughes (1960) analyzes mental health data from the same field study. Corroborative material on marriage is found in Shinen (1963). A brief overview of the archeology and contemporary culture of the island, focusing especially on Savoonga, is provided by Ackerman (1976), which speaks of economic and sociopolitical developments up to the middle 1970s. A collection of myths has been published by Silook (1976). Ethnobotany is described by Young and Hall (1969). Finally, a novelistic account of several [277b] nineteenth-century historical

island

events in the life of the Saint Lawrence Islanders based upon the field notes of Otto Geist is found in Murie (1977).

Burgess (1974) provides a report on resource utilization of the Islanders, including a detailed compilation of documentary and archival sources relating to the nineteenth century history of the island. Two other dissertations dealing with the people of the Island – both in biological anthropology – have been completed (Byard 1980; Heathcote 1982). A brief grammar of the language has been produced by Jacobson (1977).

Various reports since the 1960s relate to aspects of planning for the political, social, and economic changes that would be affecting Eskimo populations. The comprehensive review of the situation of Alaska natives (US Federal Field Committee for Development Planning in Alaska 1968) is one such example. Others are that by Ellana (1980), a background document relating to the sociocultural impacts of petroleum exploration in the Bering Sea-Norton Sound area, and the two reports produced by the US Bureau of Indian Affairs (1977, 1977a) intended as resource documents for the people of Gambell and Savoonga as they plan their economic futures. See Little and Robbins (1982).

Unpublished data exist in the diaries, letters, and reports written by missionaries and school teachers, for example, those of Dr Edgar Omar Campbell, missionary from 1901 to 1911. Reputedly his diary – as well as other such diaries and reports – were sent to the Bureau of Indian Affairs office in Juneau; including many other types of primary data in the form of reports and memoranda. The papers of Sheldon Jackson are available in the Presbyterian Historical Society, Philadelphia.

AH Leighton and DC Leighton conducted research on Saint Lawrence in 1940. Their field notes on life histories are deposited in the archives of the University of Alaska, Fairbanks. [Hughes did his MA and PhD with them.]

Popular or semipopular accounts date from Gambell's posthumously published article (Stephens 1900) and include articles appearing in *Alaskan Sportsman* through the years, occasionally in magazines such as Life, and in Alaska newspapers. In the 1960s documentary films were made that show aspects of Saint Lawrence Island life and people (*At The Time of Whaling* and *On the Spring Ice*, available from Documentary Educational Resources, Inc.,

Somerville, Massachusetts). A biography of one of the pioneers in Saint Lawrence Island archeological and cultural research, Otto Wilhelm Geist, contains some useful and previously unpublished cultural data, especially on ceremonies that were not being performed in the 1950s (Keim 1969). It also has excellent photographs showing people, housing and clothing styles, graves, hunting scenes, and other views from the 1920s and 1930s.

Before they divorced, Jane Murphy[8] and Charles Hughes spent a year of fieldwork following up on the 1940 Leightons interviews. She focused on health issues, including shamanism, an Arctic mainstay. In 1955, 250 islanders included 18 known shamans, with 8 currently active, 6 in familistic contexts and 2 professionals who also had become Christian converts.

A shaman ~ *aliginalre* ~ *aŋátkuq* is a cross-dressing gender-bender specializing in treating culture-bound Siberian arctic hysteria ~ copying mania ~ *amurakh* and *pibloktoq* with psychoterapetics, as well as 5 etiologies of 1) soul loss, 2) breach of taboo, 3) disease sorcery 4) object intrusion, & 5) spirit intrusion.

A shaman is likely to be an orphan, physically disabled, and gender bending as *anasik* ~ soft man or *uktasik* ~ womanly man. Their transvestism might also include homosexuality by convoluted logic since a shaman who looked and acted androgynous was nonetheless wife of a man. Islanders with telepathic abilities are called "thin", and all shamans are "thin", not all those "thin" are shamans. Malevolence was attributed to the sorcerer ~ *auvinak* ~ witch. Their success relied on group participation, awe, spirit possession, diagnosis, and patient involvement.

---

[8] Jane Murphy, Psychotherapeutic Aspects of Shamanism on St Lawrence Island, Alaska: 53-83. *Magic, Faith, and Healing* ~ Studies in Primitive Psychiatry Today. Ari Kiev, ed. NY: Glencoe Free Press.

YUP'IK of Southwestern Alaska

Better known and published are the Yup'iks of coastal Alaska, summarized here for comparison. As with self-names of other peoples, Central Yup'ik derives from _yuk_ "person" and _-pik_ "real, genuine" in their Eskaleut language. By far the largest, densest population of Eskimos, they view themselves as part of a web of relations which includes all "persons," both humans and animals, who have ever lived in their region. The souls of all these persons are immortal, provided their remains were treated with reverence after death. This allows for the rebirth of that soul within another body. Throughout this endless cycling, the same soul and name remain together.

Mainland Alaskan Yupik culture is based on the respectful maintenance of boundaries and of passages between human, animal, and spirit worlds. It is unlike Euro-American notions that rely on the diversity of individuals united only through self-interest and a concern with essences and core substances. Yup'ik believe in a primordial, undifferentiated universe whose shifting and permeable boundaries depend especially on human action. They keep everything in place, both in public and private, so as to circumscribe and usefully direct any flow of activity. Such human attention to rules, especially about sharing food and other gifts, involve active participation both to create differences and to maintain connections.[9]

Foremost in importance was "awareness" (_ella_), whose ubiquity included that of the universe itself (_ella yua_) and of each and every component (see below). Today, as in the past, Yup'ik out on the tundra "feed the land" by burying food and offerings to show their regard for this greater mindfulness. Everything had to be done with slow, careful deliberation to avoid offense. Berries were picked with individual regard, and a good person always turned driftwood to relieve its tedium and discomfort from lying in one position. This universal watchfulness was decorated on many artifacts as the circled dot motif ☉, sometimes with five rings

---

[9] Ann Fienup-Riordan, <u>Boundaries and Passages</u> ~ Rule and Ritual in Yup'ik Eskimo Oral Tradition 1994: 46, 48, 59.

indicating these levels above the earth.[10]

Each dot was, of course, a *tysic* {* = nexus of time, space, and affect centering}. In Yup'ik, such simultaneous fusion of time and space occurs in words such as *ciuliaq* = ancestor, leader. It is derived from *ciu-* meaning "the forepart of a body, front area, or time before"; in contrast to *kingu-* meaning "rear end, back area, or time after".[11]

They were missionized by Russian Orthodoxy in the 1830s, Moravians since 1885, Catholics after 1888, and devastated by epidemics of smallpox (1838) then influenza (1890, 1900, 1918). Yup'ik are now shareholders in their own regional Calista Corporation (meaning "worker," from *cali-* work) for the Yukon-Kuskokwim Delta. Their cosmology remains vitally integral to their lives as hunters and earth stewards.

The Moravian Alaska mission was particularly ironic because of the role of Rev. John Kilbuck, a Delaware Indian descended from famous men like Chief Netawatawas and his son Captain Killbuck, who were active in Ohio during the Revolution. John was raised and ordained by Moravians to appreciate another, more individualized, sense of community. Yet both Yup'ik and Moravians believe that waste is a result of being morally lax, not just of mindless carelessness.

Creatively, Yup'ik became Christians by restating European notions of responsibility and accountability in terms of their fundamental belief in awareness, and of salvation in terms of rebirth, not as separate individuals but within a community of believers. Only the doctrine of original sin had to be wedged into their prior beliefs.[12]

Yup'ik elders have been willing to discuss these tenets because they regard "their words as the conduit for immortal facts about the way the world is", firmly believing "people must not be stingy with their knowledge. They must give away [share] what they know or it will rot their minds."[13]

Two epics reflect Yup'ik views of their universe. The first is about a boy who lived with Seal immortals and came back to teach

---

[10] Ann Fienup-Riordan, Eskimo Essays 1990: 55.
[11] Ann Fienup-Riordan, Eskimo Essays 1990: 202, 212.
[12] Ann Fienup-Riordan, The Real People and the Children of Thunder 1991: 367.
[13] Ann Fienup-Riordan, Boundaries and Passages 1994: xii, xvii.

people how to show respect and regard for these prey. Boys who wanted to become successful hunters were told to keep busy, often shoveling snow away from doorways and entrances, keeping water buckets full, and acting with reserve and decency.

A good hunter focused on making a passage, a clear way, between himself and the animals he hunted. He was constantly thinking about and working hard to attract their attention. By clearing snow away from openings, these animals got a clear view of his face and agreed to benefit him by offering their own flesh. After proper treatment of their outer remains, the spirits of these animals were reborn again. Indeed, for Yup'ik, existence was an endless cycle of birth and rebirth, with the same "persons" (both human and nonhuman) interacting over eons.

The second tale was about the girl who returned from the dead to teach people how to feed and clothe their deceased kin by giving gifts to living namesakes and burning offerings in a fire.

Until 1900, Yup'ik men and woman lived separately, the men in a lodge (_qasgiq_) and the families in a sod covered house (_enet_). The men's lodge was "sweat house, hotel, workshop, medicine lodge, and dance hall."[14] Sea mammals in turn lived in their own underwater lodges with a skylight to watch human actions. These favored proper behavior, right thought, and good deeds by those who were decently restrained and circumspect.

Women and children provided food, clothes, and support. The family or woman's house was variously associated with womb, moon, and holy homes of _tuunraat_ {* = spirit bosses (keepers) of animals}. The purplish spot at the base of a newborn's spine was a mark left by the old woman who was believed to push each baby out of a womb. In general, the lodge represented spiritual reproduction, and the sod house the sexual reproduction of the community.

Everything in these worlds had a _yua_ {* = an in-dwelling human-like, fully-aware being}. Those of sea animals, at death, contracted into the air bladder to await rebirth. Each human had many components, such as breath, mind, vitality, shade, and name, inherited within its own immortal cycle of rebirths. These names were not gender-specific so rebirths as often as not changed sex.

Awareness allowed animals to know the thoughts and

[14.] Ann Fienup-Riordan, The Real People and the Children of Thunder 1991: 53.

mainland

intentions of hunters and others. Humans trained throughout life to increase awareness, building upon experiences, stories, instructions, taboos, and religious insights to improve their own minds. Children, in particular, had to be taught to use all their senses to synthesize information during each and every day. Upon awaking, they were sent outside to get a sense of any effects of wind, weather, and wayfarers on the day.

The aim of childhood was _ellange-_, to obtain awareness as a lasting memory of experiences. After they were five years old, boys moved into the men's lodge, where women brought food every day. When a girl waited for the empty bowl, she too was instructed in moral behavior toward the universe. At her first menstruation, these lessons intensified until she "stood up", reborn as a woman.

Marriage negotiations were not concerned with beauty, wealth, or mere status, but whether the potential partner handled food in a careful, honest, and respectful manner. The groom's family made new clothes for the bride, especially a parka decorated with designs from his mother or grandmother. The foremost rule of any marriage was not to "injure each other's mind."[15] Hardships were shared. A husband restricted his activities every time his wife was in menstrual or postpartum seclusion.

At the beginning, the primordial world was thin when all beings, from humans and animals to extraordinary creatures, interacted more easily. Now it is hardening and thickening. Humans have a greater moral duty to act responsibly to prevent illness because a body reacted physically "to the way a person chose to live life." If standard treatments failed, a patient received a new name to start over.

These extraordinary persons, going back to ancient times when the earth was very thin, include nine beings with more human forms, and eight or more with partial human characteristics.

Those more humanoid are often shape-shifting fantasticals. Their names and attributes follow.

(1)   _ircenrrat_ ~ look like humans most of the time, though sometimes only a yard tall, or take outer forms that are half human/half animal, or fully those of wolves, foxes, or whales (orca,

---

15. Ann Fienup-Riordan, <u>Boundaries and Passages</u> 1994: 62-87, 175, 189.

balukha). Living in hilly places and gathering into lodges, when humans might overhear their songs, they provide warning of death and disasters, while capture of their artifacts brings good luck;

(2) *egacuayiit* ~ are tiny people who mimic, echo, and mock humans in humorous ways, and take fish from traps to carry off inside their enormous sleeves;

(3) *cingssik* ~ derived from "point, tip," are tiny with pointed heads covered by conical hats, sometimes using a thimble for a hat and a shiny needle for a cane to visit human lodges when everyone was away;

(4) *tenguirayulit* ~ are very fast, move through the air, and like to take out livers from humans they adopt;

(5) *amikuk* ~ are huge, yet able to travel through everything, whether land or water, though only in straight lines. For variety, they sometimes take human form pulling a sled as a (6) *qamulek*;

(7) *qununiq* ~ live out on the ice as a man-like seal wearing five rain parkas, mittens, and boots;

(8) *agiirrnguat* ~ appear from a long distance, attracted by someone waiting too anxiously;

(9) *tengmiarpiit* ~ are giant bird-like people nesting at low hills and volcanic domes, protecting friendly humans, but destroying others.

The other semi-humanoid creatures follow.

(10) *itqiirpak* ~ a huge hand in the ocean with a mouth in its palm and on each finger to devourer any child who makes too much noise;

(11) *meriiq* (from *meq* 'water') ~ sucks blood from a big toe if a family carelessly lacks water in the home;

(12) *muruayuli* sinks into the ground while walking;

(13) *arularaq* (from *arula* 'be in motion, move back and forth') ~ has three toes per foot and six toes (not fingers) per hand;

(14) *quugaapiit* ~ live underground, swimming through solid land, where their buried bones suggest a connection with prehistoric mastodons;

mainland

(15) *amllit* ~ are abrasive, living in shallow, milky-colored lakes, where, only by stepping over them, never going around, can a human prevent a quick death;

(16) *ingluilnguq* (from half of a pair) ~ are one side of a normal person with only one eye, ear, arm, leg;

(17) *miluquyuli* ~ are teenager size, fond of maliciously throwing heavy rocks at humans;

(18) *ulurrugnaq* ~ is a sea monster that eats whales.

Movements between domains and dimensions, both extraordinary and ordinary, were carefully monitored. Passages were blocked by thoughtlessness. This included clumsy handling of a knife, sleeping late, eating and drinking carelessly, bumbling through a door, being noisy, or wasting personal talents. A proper person was ever concerned to restrict his or her breath, sight, thought, speech, and body movement. He or she carefully wears a belt and hood to bind their actions, deter unclean influences, and hold in their life force.[16] Weapons, tools, and containers were carefully made and decorated both to please that artifact itself and to attract game animals to such a pretty lure.

Before the annual seal hunt, men prepared beautiful gear, while women made them new, handsome clothing. Hunters prepared by fumigating their bodies and tools (sitting mat, pack basket, food supplies, and kayak) so as to smell like the land, which was attractive to seals. During a hunt, the hunter's wife had to remain motionless like the land. This encouraged seals to be listless. If she ate, slept, or groomed, her husband lost his concentration. Their spousal cooperation resulted in formal "ownership" of a slain seal by the husband while it was outside the house, then by the wife once it was inside.

At death, the constituents of a human body separated into mind, breath, feeling, life, warmth, shade, and name soul. The corpse was washed, bound in five places, and taken to a grave. Five stops were made along the way if a woman, four if a man. Similarly, the family remained quiet five days for a woman, four for a man. A surviving spouse was considered "sealed" (confined) for a

---

[16] Such restraint was like the moral force of Victorian women wearing a corset, whose stays, not incidentally, were often made from whale bone.

mainland

year to safeguard his or her survival. Over time, a spirit could reincarnate five times within the endless flow of rebirths.

Five major rituals of the traditional Yup'ik celebrated such renewals. Bladder Festival returned to the sea all the air sacks of animals slain by hunters during the previous year so they would be reborn. For five days, men evoked their spirit helpers in song and dance. Each year, with greater elaboration every ten years, a Feast for the Dead invited these shades into the *qasgiq* to receive fresh water, clothing, and sustenance. The _Kelek_ masked dance invited animal spirits into the lodge to be entertained by men and women reversing normal roles and cross-dressing. At the center of most masks was a tiny humanoid identified as the "thinking part" of that being. A Messenger Feast hosted a visit from another village. The Asking Festival honored cross-sex cousins within one community.

Most significant in all these relationships was the quality of one's mind, as revealed through the senses to enhance "awareness." Appeals to these senses opened passages between worlds as aptly illustrated by two examples. Human "ghosts" craved fresh water, provided by the living during rituals, because their own was too salty from all the tears shed by their kin. At death, mourners wailed loudly to make sure the spirit was awake for its journey to the beyond. Similarly, a seal had to be harpooned while it was awake so its spirit would retract into its air bladder. To kill a sleeping or inattentive seal was to murder it forever.[17]

Immediately after a seal was killed, it was anointed with fresh water in its mouth and on four flippers. Similar regard was shown to land animals, except the five-point anointing used seal oil, because these spirits yearned for the sea. Their separate habitats and desires decreed a firm boundary that kept land and sea foods apart at every meal. In Yup'ik the word for fish also meant food, so many restrictions applied to their handling and preparation, according to whether they were taken by trap or by net.

In everything, Yup'ik observed their duty to carefully perform "acts of differentiation – cutting, binding, covering, circling – to create the possibility of future relation."[18] When approaching boundaries between worlds, Yup'ik prevented any crossover by

---

[17] Ann Fienup-Riordan, The Real People and the Children of Thunder 1991: 113.
[18] Ann Fienup-Riordan, Boundaries and Passages 1994: 355, 360.

covering their bodies with gut parkas; by painting themselves with soot, clay, and urine; or by placing grass mats or skins between themselves and the thin earth lest they slip through.

Always, Yup'ik probity showed their active awareness of human duty toward this moral universe, connectinf as community members (not as isolated or alienated individuals) willing to fulfill obligations to other persons by supplying what these lacked, such as fresh water to seals, light and heat to belukha whales, and dry land to fish.[19]

Emphatically, to Yup'iks, "people were social beings first and individuals only if they forgot themselves, in which case their downfall was assured."

In the Bering Straits, Siberian Yupiks face challenges to US defense. On 23 June 1955, a US Navy P2V Neptune with a crew of 11, attacked by two Soviet fighters along the International Date Line between Siberia's Kamchatka Peninsula and Alaska, crashed near Gambell. Villagers rescued the crew, with 3 wounded by Soviet fire and 4 injured in the crash. Soviets offered to pay the US for 50% of damages, but the US was grudgingly satisfied with the Soviet expression of profound regret and the offer.

Operating 1952 to 1972, Northeast Cape Air Force Station consisted of an Aircraft Control and Warning (AC&W) radar site, Security Service listening post; and White Alice Communications System (WACS). Most of it was removed in a $10.5 million cleanup program in 2003, yet today people who grew up at Northeast Cape have high rates of cancer and other diseases, possibly due to PCB exposure.

All of the island was returned to native ownership 28 July 2016, five decades after the Alaska native Land Claims Settlement Act of 1971. (https://en.wikipedia.org/wiki/ St._Lawrence_Island)

---

[19] Ann Fienup-Riordan, Eskimo Essays 1990: 76, 186.

VI. HOW DO YOU GET TO ALASKA?[20]

WHEN we went ashore in Seattle, we knew the time had come to start thinking about how we were going to Alaska. [65]

We went to a clean hotel down near the waterfront and started on a simple program of asking everyone we saw how we could get there.

"I beg your pardon – do you know how a couple could find jobs that would take them to Alaska?"

"Hello, Sonny, if you wanted to get to Alaska, what would you do?"

"Good morning, Ma'am, can you think of any way to find a job that would take a couple to Alaska?"

Down on the waterfront we asked, "Where is your captain? Any chance of getting on your crew as stewards or cooks or deck hands?" Into the offices of the steamship companies we went. "Do you need cooks, stewards, typists, deck hands on your boats going to Alaska?"

Every person we asked made some courteous reply. Nobody was gruff or abrupt. They would scratch their heads, figuratively, anyhow, and consider the matter at more length, sometimes, than was convenient. Boys, men, women, executives, captains, sailors – they all gave the best advice they could.

One day we were walking down First Avenue when we [66] ran into a gray-haired Negro. "Good morning. Uncle, can you tell us any way to get to Alaska – get jobs that would take us there?"

The old man stood a little while in thought, then he said, "Yassir, I uz down heppin to load de ship Saturn, jist yistiddy, and I heerd de capn say dat he wuz a-lookin fur a man an his wife to teach school up on de Pribilofs. You-all schoolteachers?"

We said we could be and we hurried down to where the Saturn was tied up at the dock. The captain, a Scandinavian, was cordial and kind, but thirty minutes ago, he had hired a man and his wife for the Pribilofs. He suggested, though, that we go to see Mr Lopp of the Bureau of Education. It was late for this year, but there

---

[20] June Burn, LIVING HIGH ~ An Unconventional Autobiography. New York: Duell, Sloan and Pearce 1941.

might still be a vacancy somewhere in Alaska.

Mr Lopp interviewed us within an inch of our lives. He wanted to know all about our pasts, our beliefs, education, experience, personalities. But the upshot was that we both got jobs in his service, Farrar at $135 a month, I at $120, lasting for twelve months, with the possibility of holding them for three years, if we were good and didn't go having babies right away – for we were going into the Far North where there were few other white people.

Years later, we learned that Mr Lopp had been in a tight spot that week. The Victoria was due to sail for Nome on its last trip and he hadn't yet found teachers for St Lawrence Island. He admitted that he would have grabbed much worse prospects than we seemed to be. But the stage lost a good man when Mr Lopp went into government [67] service, for nobody would have guessed from his severe manner that we were his last hope for the year.

Tom Lopp was one of the greatest friends the Eskimos ever had. That is why, no doubt, he lost his job in the Bureau of Education during those boom years. For in our country, as in England, the procedure seems to be to take care of our primitive subjects with half an eye to them and an eye and a half to the few members of our own race who live by exploiting them. Mr Lopp worked the other way, and though he came to be regarded as the outstanding authority on Eskimo economy and was often called into consultation in later years when things got in a mess, he lost his position, and died recently, a strong, young, gusty man, still mourning his lost charges.

Farrar was to be manager of the island, the native cooperative store, the reindeer herd – a sort of governor and father combined. I was to have charge of the school, with one native assistant. Store and medical supplies had been ordered and were ready to go, Mr Lopp said, but we would have to buy our own year's food supplies and winter clothing. He advanced $300 against our salaries for that purpose.

We could hardly suppress our glee until we left the office. How much better the reality than anything we had expected! What was it that brought us such fabulous luck every step of the way? Three hundred dollars in our pockets and a first-class ticket to Nome, Alaska! We were going to St Lawrence Island, in sight of Siberia, out in Bering Sea. It was within the Arctic Circle. Nobody but Eskimos there, and we were to govern and teach a *primitive [68] people. We were filled with determination to do some really worthy work, and with exhilaration at our sheer luck. I have never been sure whether we were almost ribald honeymooners on a lark sponsored by the government, or pure missionaries burning with zeal for the work ahead. A little of both, I guess.

I don't remember what we bought in the way of clothes. Mr Lopp said that the Eskimos would make us some skin garments when we got to St Lawrence Island, but that we might need some woolens of our own. But I do remember how we splurged buying food. After a year of semi-famine, all we could think of was food. Nine sacks of clean seed wheat and a new grist mill. Five sacks of seed corn for real hand-ground cornmeal mush and spoon bread. Two sacks of steel-cut oats. Two dozen two-pound cans of butter. Powdered milk and eggs. Cans of spinach, beans, milk. Cans and cans of coffee. Sugar, candy for the children's Christmas, huge chocolate bars for use on the trail, which the sailors on the *Bear* nibbled clean out of existence before we got to St Lawrence. One day we overheard them talking about our supplies – the oddest selection any of the teachers had carried up, I expect. "What can the Reverend Burn want with these sacks of corn?" one of them said, with insinuations in his voice. Formerly it had been missionaries who had gone to Alaska to teach the Eskimos, and though they were now government-employed teachers, most of the sailors still spoke of them as "the reverend and his wife."

In a week we were ready to sail, and so was the old Victoria. With supplies for the native store, medical supplies [69] plies, school books, thirty-five tons of coal in sacks, and our own food supplies and baggage, "the teachers" for St Lawrence must have filled a pretty big hole in the hold of the ship.

Here we go, then! Cast off the lines! The old boat backs slowly out into the Sound and heads north. We are taking the outside passage, out Juan de Fuca, around Vancouver Island, straight across the Gulf of Alaska to the Aleutian Islands. Our first stop will be Akutan, Aleutian whaling station.

We found a sunny place on deck where we could sit and write letters home. Planning out loud for a year of such happiness and learning and progress for the Eskimos as they had never known before. Farrar started inventing ways to mark the reindeer, for among the many things Mr Lopp had told us, Farrar remembered that the ear markings which were then in use were not satisfactory. By the time the marks were all on, the reindeer had practically no ears left.

I began to plan reading lessons that would use Eskimo facts and situations, remembering the joke about the Eskimo who had come outside and been most surprised to find that horses had long legs and hoofs. He had seen pictures of horses in mail-order catalogues, advertising harness, and their legs had all been cut off at the knee, for lack of space. Oh, we were going to do wonderful things!

Now we sight the Aleutians off the starboard bow. We are steaming up to the whaling station. Suddenly an offshore breeze makes passengers grab their noses. We'll be [70] here only a minute, surely; we can hold our breath that long. No, we shall be here two hours or more. It seems the Victoria borrowed some oil on the last trip down and she must return it now.

Two hours in a Chicago stockyard, multiplied by the difference between the size of a cow and that of a whale. The captain says we may go ashore to gather flowers if we like. Long-stemmed wild flowers from the knee-deep grass of the rolling, treeless tundra. Many do go ashore. Farrar and I choose to stay and watch them whale.

On the long plank docks, men were stripping foot thick fat off the carcass of a ninety foot blue-back whale. One man walked down that mountain of flesh, drawing a huge knife like a long brush hook through the fat, to separate a strip from the whole. Then he fastened a big hook into the end of the strip, up at the head. The donkey engine whirred, the immense ribbon of fat peeled off the prone giant, curled back over itself, fell to the floor at the tail of the whale. Man, hook, and donkey engine returned for another strip, baring the red-black muscle flesh of the animal.

When the fat was all off, the men swarmed over the carcass to cut up the rest of it for various uses: fertilizer, dog food, and perhaps even steaks for human consumption, though it may be a smaller species from which our whale steaks come.

In the old days, the whalers saved only the fat to be rendered into oil, and the whalebone from the mouth. The rest was wasted – tons and tons. Imagine the stench then! [71]

arrival VI

There is still a good deal of waste, they say, of blood and viscera, but far less than formerly.

When this blue whale opened his mouth to take in a whole school of herring, there wasn't much of him left shut, for his head measured a third of his length and was the widest part besides. The great lower jaw was heavily furred with what they call whalebone – wide, thin, black, gristle-like slats, edged, along the upper side, with long black coarse hair. This odd timber work inside the mouth is a huge sieve; the herring lie on top of the fur mass while the water strains through. Then the whale reaches out with a hungry tongue and draws the fish in.

The donkey engine was going. Men were running about on the dock and on the carcass. There were noises on the Victoria of winches and cables and voices. We could faintly hear the cries of the flower-gatherers up on the tundra. It was not surprising, then, that a tugboat slipped up on the other side of the Victoria without our knowing it. It brought another blue whale, towed alongside, belly up. The queer, washboard-like hills and valleys of the whale's belly were all stuccoed with barnacles. This, they said, was a hundred-footer – a whale of a whale. It would be drawn up onto the dock by the donkey engine and men would set to work stripping off its blubber, cutting out its whalebone, hacking up its flesh.

A collective handkerchief still at its nose, the Victoria called its children in from play and slipped out of Akutan, heading north again. The next time we stop, we shall be at Nome.

It was early morning when we began to be put off the [72] *Victoria* and taken aboard the lighters at Nome, where the sea was too shallow to admit the big ship to the dock. It was jolly going ashore in such an informal huddle. People love that secure togetherness of shared adventure, whether of disaster or good fortune. Farrar says this human hunger to be all in the same boat together is not only an amelioration of war; it is actually a cause of war.

Nome was the whispering village. Plank houses, wooden sidewalks, muddy streets, two or three brick buildings, a few hopeful window boxes, a row of the false-front stores peculiar to frontier towns, thunder of surf at its front doorstep, dead silence of frozen wastes behind. Nome might have been built for a moving-picture set. Nothing about it seemed real. Plank hotels with typical

Bret Harte landladies, and restaurants with reindeer steaks and buxom waitresses were bits on the cutting-room floor. The people, all talking in whispers or guarded low tones, were actors. Farrar and I, apparently, were the only audience. Everybody else seemed to belong to the cast. It was the spookiest town I have ever seen.

On the Victoria we had struck up an acquaintance with one of those plain-spoken, likeable, frank girls, who was going up to the hills beyond Nome to cook for her miner father and his partner that winter, and have the time of her life in the wild, rough wilderness. A hearty girl, full of laughter and noise. We saw her a week later on her way out from the visit. She had begun to whisper. We asked about her father and she was furtive and secretive. She whispered that she could not tell us anything. Everybody was like that. [73]

But when we walked out of the village onto the endless frozen tundra toward the hills, we saw that the earth was fair up here, too. The sunsets on that strange, pale land were eerily beautiful. Bering Sea lashed the beach day and night and loped off in green rolls toward the west. The sea on the west, wide and lonely; tundra to the east, wide and lonely, and an unhappy little lonely village in between.

Down the beach the King Island Eskimos lived under their upturned skin boats, and in tents, carving ivory for the traders. Along the waterfront, a few hard-bitten miners still panned the sand for gold dust.

From Nome we were to go on to St Lawrence Island on the old Coast Guard cutter *Bear* – which Admiral Byrd now uses for his supply ship in the Antarctic. In two weeks it would return from Point Barrow and pick us up.

We were not the only ones from Nome to board the *Bear*. Every summer the King Islanders leave their cliff dwellings, and paddle their immense skin canoes across the wild waters of Bering Sea to Nome. On the mainland, they spend the summer fishing for their coming winter supplies of dog food, carving their precious winter's catch of ivory, and selling it to tourists. In the fall they return on the Coast Guard boat because by then it is too rough to paddle home in open boats. The Bear set them down at the foot of the black bluff which they called home, and the sailors hated the job. For the Eskimos smelled worse than the whaling station.

When we took them aboard, we found we had not only all

the inhabitants of the island, but also their dogs, food, [74] boats, unsold furs and ivory, dog food, reindeer sleeping skins, white leather pokes full of this and that, and a thousand other things which only a museum curator could count.

But how quiet and orderly and merry they were! Eskimo mothers gathered their possessions and their children close about them. Eskimo fathers improvised deck shelters from their skin boats and tied up the dogs. They prepared their smelly meals on primus stoves. Babies hung onto breasts most of the time. Old men sat and carved, old women worked on leather, young women did the work of the temporary camp. The young men sat and gazed out to sea.

Except for the fact that the air on deck grew heavier and heavier, we should hardly have known the Eskimos were there. They were the most perfectly behaved crowd of people we ever saw.

On the third day we sighted the perpendicular cliffs of King Island. The high plateau upthrust from the sea was covered with fog. But we could see the houses set on stilts against the side of the bluff. They looked frail, as though they might hobble off down into the sea almost any day.

The Eskimos scrambled and chattered, gathered up children and skins and dogs, and gleefully lowered themselves into their huge, open walrus skin boats and paddled for the bleak black bluff. How was it possible, we wondered, for them to have for this flat mountain top in the sea the affection we knew for our soft earth? How precarious the little houses on stilts against the wall of the bluff!

Now the Eskimos were gone, but for all the great scrubbing [75] and washing down the Bear received, their smell followed us, like the albatross, up and down the mighty waves of the storm-tossed sea.

We turned south again, to St Lawrence Island, where the Bear would leave us and go outside for its own long winter of rest in Seattle. But not yet.

The captain said that all the storms in the world are hatched in Anadir Bay, off Siberia. It was the season of the Equinox; time for the fiercest storms of the year. As though the sea weren't rough enough already.

The storms came down. The *Bear* sailed round and round St Lawrence Island, but the surf was so high we couldn't land. For one solid month we searched a lee. Twice we returned to the mainland for coal, but still no let-up in the storm.

Then one day the crown sheets of the boiler fell. The fires had to be pulled. The *Bear* wired to the Aleutians for the cutter, *Algonquin*, to come to our rescue. Meanwhile we wallowed in the waves of Bering Sea.

At last the slim-hipped *Algonquin* came rearing and plunging up from the south. They shot a thin little rope across our bow. Our sailors grabbed it, began hauling in, first the small rope, then a larger one and a larger until at last they pulled with might and main on the heavy three-inch hauser itself, inching it aboard . . . and we traveled again.

Thus ignominiously we were towed back five hundred miles to the Aleutian Islands. On the way down, we passed the Pribilof Islands, where the fur seals come at mating time and are killed for their hides. We saw St Matthew's [76] Island in the distance. Men have died on that narrow curve of land, trying to weather a winter there, hunting fox and ivory. It looked so desolate and the officers on the Bear told such tales of its danger that Farrar and I longed to tackle it. That would be pulling the ladder up after you! But later on, when the Smithsonian Institution suggested that we go back there to collect for them, we were already knee-deep in the great adventure of starting our family and thus never knew that winter of splendid isolation. Perhaps it wouldn't have been splendid, anyhow.

We were taken to Dutch Harbor, the Coast Guard's base, where, after long conferences, during which we were afraid they were going to refuse to take us back to St Lawrence, and wires to and from Washington, we were transferred, with all our goods, to the cutter *Unalga*.

North to St Lawrence Island again. The storm had not abated. For two weeks we cruised around the hundred-mile-long narrow island, hoping for a lee and a lull at the same time.

At last one morning the Captain came in and bade us get ready to land. We were off Southwest Cape,[21] some forty-odd miles from our base on the Island. But it couldn't be helped. Already one

---

[21] At SE Cape, Margaret saw rings of bear skulls: Kaka's 3 rings were by size, biggest outside; her father-in-law's 4 rings were fathers, mothers, girls, boys; prophet Yuniq turned his home into a church (Leightons 1983: 225, 351).

arrival VI

heavy snow had fallen. Soon the ice would come. If we were going ashore at all, it would have to be here and now, where there was some lee. We were to be rowed to that blizzardy bluff we saw out there – that lost land that was already covered with a foot of blue whiteness.

Boats were lowered. Sailors began unloading our stuff. And as though at a signal, Eskimo skin boats began to [77] swarm out. The people climbed aboard the Bear with happy welcoming cries. Teacher had come! "Hello, Teacher. We glad you here! More better you come ashore now."

One of the old men wore a parka made of the breasts of beautiful black and white birds. I thought it was the loveliest thing I had ever seen and later in the year I traded him out of it. It can be seen now in the collection we later sold to the Museum of the American Indian in New York City. (St. Lawrence natives always said parki with a short *i* sound; never parka.)

Back and forth the boats hurried, dumping our supplies helter-skelter onto the beach of St Lawrence. The storm might come up at any second and when it did, off the *Unalga* would go, leaving us with what stores we had, to our winter's fate. Fortunately, nearly everything had been unloaded by the time the wind came howling down out of the Arctic again and the *Unalga* steamed off down the lonely gray sea. We watched her over the hill of the horizon.

VII. THE FROZEN ISLAND[22]

THE *Unalga* went out of sight over the horizon and we turned back
to our supplies piled at the foot of a high, steep, snow-covered bluff
– tons of coal in sacks, boxes of guns, sacks of sugar, stores of
prunes, pilot bread, tea, apricots, dried apples, to say nothing of our
own personal stores. [78]

"How shall we ever get it up on the plateau?" I asked Farrar.
"How shall we get it to Gambel? And where in the world will we
live, meanwhile?"

"Oh, plenty good white-man house here," said a beaming
Eskimo. He was Oktokiyuk, and during those first helpless weeks
he took charge of us and, gracefully seeming to take orders, gave
them. "Me and my family move out that house now. You live
there."

We moved into that "plenty good white-man house" on the
bluff of Southwest Cape, forty miles from our destination on the
island. But first, Oktokiyuk and his family moved out.

What a moving it was! Out of the little twelve by fifteen
frame house, built of lumber brought from Nome by a trader, came
six people, hundreds of reindeer skins, seal skins, fox skins; bundles
of white leather, dog harness, ivory, parkas, pants, boots; tubs of
seal skins soaking in urine to tan; seal oil lamps, wooden platters,
precious [79] scraps of old papers and magazines; little bundles of
dried willow-root bark, dozens of five-gallon tins of gasoline for
their outboard motors the next spring. Eskimos in an endless line
went into the little house and came out again, laden with bundles. It
was like moving a five-and-ten.

At last it was empty and Oktokiyuk said, "Come see your
nice home."

I went up the steep, slushy bluff with him, across the windy
point of the plateau, to the forlorn little shack that was so proudly
Oktokiyok's "summer house like white man." I had had abundant
pre-sampling of the smell that awaited me inside those four walls,
but even so I was not prepared. We entered through the storm shed.
Inside the empty room shy women and children stood together. The

---

[22] June Burn, LIVING HIGH ~ An Unconventional Autobiography. New York:
Duell, Sloan and Pearce, 1941.

coal range was red hot. The unfamiliar odor that rose up bodily and rushed out to meet me was like a foul-breathed gale to blow a man down.

I smiled and spoke, shaking hands with them all – sticky, damp little hands. I took short breaths and exerted all my charm just as fast as I could so as to get outside before disgracing myself, which I did by the skin of my teeth. It would be weeks, I thought, before the house would be clean enough to endure it.

I was wrong. For, while two Eskimo women and I were scrubbing out the house, I was getting used to the odor, which was not one of filth but simply of foods and ways and garments I had not met before. In a few days I could tell by sight alone whether my house was clean. And in a [80] month or two, Farrar and I were smelling like Eskimos ourselves in our own beautiful urine-tanned skins.

It was great fun cleaning house with the Eskimo women. They were jolly companions, but inept workers. I hadn't the skill to make them do things over and over; there was nothing inept about the way they could get out of work! When I showed them that more elbow grease would make the floor look white, instead of gray, they teased me by stroking their portion and saying, "Oh, very nice!" and of my clean spot, "This place very sick," meaning pale. Then they laughed and laughed. I fell for them hard.

And so did Farrar, working with them down on the beach. For days, that first week, he and the Eskimo men toiled up the steep bluff with loads on their backs, making jokes with every puff of their breath. Fortunately, news travels fast up there, and on the day after we landed, dozens of sleds, dog teams and drivers poured over the white hills beyond Southwest Cape and everybody began to buy supplies. Everyone carried his own purchases up on to the bluff, which was a great help.

At that "store" on the beach, Farrar sat on a keg and kept records while Iwurrigan, who spoke excellent English, waited on the natives and reported their purchases to him. They sold sacks of sugar, guns, tea, pilot bread, prunes, tea, candy, tea, calico, boxes of cube sugar, tea; everything the store had brought up including tea and more tea.

Short, fat little Booshu bought a hundred-pound sack of sugar, piled it on his little sled and went back to Gambel. On the way, he had to cross a big lake which [81] had frozen over for the winter – else the Gambel people could not have come. Booshu's sled broke through the new ice and he lost his sack of sugar. The next day he came back for another, and couldn't understand why he had to pay for it. But he accepted Farrar's dictum philosophically. "Me rich man," he said. "I'm buy sugar for feeding fish."

Storekeeping went on for many days after our arrival. Gradually the supplies were brought up to the little warehouse which Iwurrigan owned. All except the coal. Long before the last of it was carried up, snow began to fall. It snowed so hard and fast that many sacks were deeply buried on the beach and may be there yet, for no teachers may, since then, have been landed at Southwest Cape.

It was a busy little community, those first weeks. Farrar and Iwurrigan kept store all day, while the other Eskimos stood around watching them and joking. Atonga, Okto-kiyok's wife, and I kept house, she faithfully standing by until windows, shelves, bunk, attic, storm shed were as clean as we could make them, the water freezing under our hands as we scrubbed.

Nearly every evening the dogs at the Cape set up a wild, yodeling howl, and presently the dark forms of sleds and teams would skim over the white slope back of us and seem to flow down into the little settlement. We thought people would never stop coming.

When the natives had bought their fill of white-man things, Farrar engaged them to haul sacks of coal to Gambel. There must be a supply for the schoolhouse and teacher's quarters before we could move. [82]

One hungry, lean, dog team could haul one sack of coal at a time. A good team could haul two. It took three days for the trip: a day to go, a day to rest the dogs, and a day to return for another sack. Farrar paid them a dollar a sack, and we employed as many teams as we could get. The Eskimos were delighted to make the money, in the form of merchandise orders to be cashed at the store.

At last, losing all patience with the slowness of the dog teams, Farrar ordered reindeer harnessed and brought from the reindeer camps to Southwest Cape. It was a revolutionary order, but the Eskimos did it cheerfully. Sled deer could carry four sacks of coal at a time, but they were not so fast and they had to stop and eat.

It was a clumsy arrangement. The only food the deer eat is reindeer-moss and the Eskimos have not yet found a method for storing it as we do hay and grain for horses. On each trip, it took so long to graze the deer that we gave it up after a few trips and returned to the dog teams. The Eskimos were delighted at the joke on Farrar.

Meanwhile, the four Eskimo women of Southwest Cape – a mother and a grandmother-in-law in each igloo – were making skin garments for Farrar and me. Immense sealskin breeches and a very tent of a reindeer skin parka for Farrar. How they laughed at the size of his garments! And they laughed because, when they made my parka hood like theirs, it stood out from my face several inches, instead of fitting snug around it. Their faces are broad, and parka hoods, made to fit over their smaller heads, are snug around their large faces and keep the cold wind from their ears. They never figured out how to make a hood [83] large enough to slip over my head and small enough to fit around my face. They thought it a splendid joke, and used to run their hands around the space between head and hood and say, "Patsarok plenty fresh air." Eskimos love a joke more even than Negroes. They are the laughingest people I ever knew. And the most loveable.

In our new skin garments we felt like conquerors, whatever we smelled like. It was good to be able to brave the elements like natives, and so win freedom to move about over the arctic land.

At last we had enough coal at Gambel to risk moving there, and school could begin. It was late October, or early November, nearly a month since we had landed. I was to take my first dog-sled ride over the vast undulating land that was hardly more than a huge, permanent iceberg. Farrar had been to Gambel several times and he was keen for me to experience that day-long journey by skimming log-sled.

On the morning of a trip, the Eskimos get up at dreadful times. It wasn't long after midnight when Oktokiyuk called us on that great day. But when we had breakfasted, cocooned ourselves into layers of warm garments, and gone out to join the party, not a soul was about.

It was fully two hours before we got under way. What was time in the Eskimo's timeless eternity? Who minded getting up at midnight when there were days on end to sleep when storms raged? Oktokiyuk was probably inside his igloo with his family, drinking hard-boiled tea, and laughing with his brothers and friends. The dogs were not harnessed, for they might eat the walrus-skin rope in their [84] eternally unappeased hunger. They were alert, though, sensing that they were to go somewhere.

Losing patience, Farrar called out the men and bade them get under way. The Eskimos laughed at his hurry. "Plenty time," they said. "Patsarok see Gambel bymby."

Just before dawn, we were ready to go. The dogs were harnessed in a fan-shaped arrangement, with the leader out in front, like the fingers of a hand with a very long middle finger. That was the St Lawrence Island style. On the mainland, dogs were harnessed tandem or in pairs.

Before the start, the three of us sat down on our sleds, Farrar alone on his, Oktokiyuk and I on the other. Farrar was a veteran by now and could drive his own. He was, in any case, too big to ride double. Oktokiyuk sat in front on his six-foot-long, eighteen-inch-wide sled, his legs going off sidewise, up forward, mine going off the other side behind him. Nothing to hold up my legs. Try it, sometime, for a day.

The dogs were not straining at their leashes, raring to go. They sat down, as we did, and snarled unhappily at each other, or chewed at their harness and had to be cuffed.

Now we are ready. Oktokiyuk strikes the ground with his whip. "Huh! Huh! Huh!" he shouts. "Hooh! Hooh! Hooh!" shouts Farrar, never quite getting the exact sound of the Eskimo "Get up!" The lean beasts strike out up the rise behind Southwest Cape and we are off.

Behind us the villagers stand outside the two igloos to watch us leave. But they are not saying unfriendly things [85] behind our backs. Just little chuckly things, laughing together.

Behind us, the sea was pale green under the new ice edging out from shore. Eskimos call it green ice, meaning that it is not solid yet. When the sun came up, the cliffs of Siberia would rise beyond the forty-mile stretch of sea.

Before us rolled hill after white hill, so much alike that I had no sense of direction or of progress. Under the cold dawn the land was palely gray.

Then, after a while, the sun came up. By a chance turning of our way, it was behind us as it rolled up over the horizon, making the snow blush like a rose, and all the white hills were vivid pink.

When the sun was higher and the rose color had faded, the snow began to take on blue lights. Under the eaves of immense drifts, the shadows were a rich sapphire.

We put on our dark glasses, but still the glint of snow was painful, coming in from the sides. We hadn't gone many miles before I began to fidget. A little more and I could no longer maintain my position.

"Aren't your legs getting tired, Oktokiyuk?" I knew a hint would be enough for him.

He laughed. It would have been a joke on him if they were. "Oh, no," he said, "my legs got bone in him all same stick. You legs no got bone?"

"Yes, but my feet seem to be getting heavy, all same rock. What shall I do about that?"

"More better you get off and run little bit," and without stopping the dogs, Oktokiyuk hopped nimbly off the eight-inch-high sled and began to run alongside. I rolled off [86] into the snow, pushed and pulled at the bundle of skins which was myself, and sure enough, I could run, too. For though it looks clumsy and heavy, the skin clothing of the Eskimo is surprisingly light. But without our weight, the dogs could run much faster, and in no time I was left far behind.

I don't remember any way of stopping those dogs. The driver has no lines, only a whip to make them go, and once they are off, he depends on himself to keep up with them. But there must have been a way to stop them, for when I was tired of running, I dropped down on the sled again and rode the rest of the way to Gambel.

We skimmed those frozen hills in four or five hours. When we topped the last high bluff above Gambel, we had passed no sign of human habitation.

Below the bluff, only three or four miles from our destination, we must cross the frozen lake where Booshu had lost his sugar. The wind had blown it free of snow. The ice was strong and thick, now, and as slick as glass. The dogs' feet skidded as they flew across it, the sleds swinging from side to side, faster and faster, making at last considerably more than a semi-circle. The dogs smelled the end of the trip and nobody could have stopped them now; we clung on for dear life.

Beyond the lake, at the very edge of the ocean, on a low, out-jutting sand spit, the igloos of Gambel huddled together. We could hear the dogs of the village, and ours gathered still more speed for the last mile or so, whimpering hungrily as they flew along. Now we saw that all [87] the people stood outside their houses in solemn rows, like penguins, waiting to welcome "the teachers."

How the Eskimos welcomed us that bitter cold day! Not that their welcome took any such practical form as having cleaned the schoolhouse, or even having built a fire for us in our living quarters. They were as passive as children. But we felt welcome, for all that. And when the whole village followed us into the house and stood around while we shook off snow and set about building a fire, we felt flattered.

Silook, a meek young man, was the assistant teacher at Gambol. He assumed gentle authority over the crowd of visitors, pushed them back when they threatened to swarm over us, advised us to serve them tea and at last dismissed them for us, so that we could unpack a few things for the night and be ready to open school next day.

After our supper that first night in Gambel, Farrar and I went outside to look around. We knew, from the weeks at Southwest Cape, that the Eskimos would already be inside for the night. We would not ourselves be objects of attention. Snow was falling again – earnestly, steadily falling. It snowed with all its heart.

I wish I could find the quiet words that would be a picture of evening, night, and dawn in the Arctic. Eskimo children are quiet, even at play. But their soft noises abate at early twilight when they go indoors. The men have all returned from hunting or setting fox traps. They are indoors, too. Women have gathered in whatever they had hanging out on the whale-rib and walrus rope fences. [88]

Some of them have been to the deep cave in which they store their "rotten meat," and brought up what they needed for the night. Outside, nobody moves about.

Even the dogs are as still as the snowbanks they resemble, for they are curled up in the snow and it drifts over them.

The village of rounded walrus skin igloos is utterly silent. The gray sky darkens. The line of sea, far out on the point, is black silence. Snow falls on snow, quiet as thought. Night comes down.

arrival VII

There are no stars. Now the falling flakes are no longer visible against the white darkness. Nothing can be seen except the dark forms of houses which might be sounds, so much do sight and hearing seem one, up here.

Inside the igloos, one imagines the family group sitting, naked or almost, on the walrus-skin floor of their hot inner skin living room. They are drinking tea. Or they may be gathered around a huge wooden platter, eating hunks of meat – seal, fish, walrus from last year which has become exceedingly "high," duck, or even seagull if the family is poor. They may be eating half-boiled prunes and pilot bread in celebration of teacher-come; white-man food is doled out sparingly and only on rare occasions. If it is a wealthy family, they may be playing the phonograph with an unchanged needle, on a dusty, scratched record.

When the food is eaten and everything cleared away; when the children have all used the little wooden chamber pots in which urine is carefully saved to be dumped into the tanning tub; when the little fund of jokes from the [89] day's happenings is exhausted, the family and visitors are ready to sleep.

The Eskimo woman brings out the roll of skins, spreads them over the floor up to a log which lies across the entrance of the living room, and which is the common pillow. Eskimos lie side by side in a row, heads on the log, naked bodies on the long-haired, soft skins of reindeer, killed in mid-winter. They lie sardine fashion, fathers and brothers outside their own women, visitors beyond them. The old grandmother, or some dependent, watches the seal-oil lamp so that it will not go out all night and the sleepers grow cold. There are skins for cover, too, but they are not always needed, unless the lamp goes out, or the inner skin house is so old and thin and worn that it is not complete protection against the air in the outer igloo.

There is no ventilation except for one small hole in the skin flap which is the door of this inner house. Steam continually pours out of this hole, as though from the spout of a kettle. It is the steam from breathing, from the lamp, and from cooking.

Morning breaks slowly, even in the fall. If you are up before dawn, you look out into the smother of white darkness that is falling snow, and see nothing. Then, after breakfast, the snowflakes are separate things, coming down onto visible drifts. Day has wedged in through a crack somewhere.

Outside, the dogs budge their little hills, erupt from them, shake themselves, stand at their chains looking forlorn and hungry. After awhile, each dog will curl down again in a tight roll, like a caterpillar when you touch it [90] with a stick. Then the day snow covers them again with its light warmth and they sleep in lieu of eating. Once a day, except in lean times, they get food – generally one salmon each from the whale-rib racks high out of their reach where the dried fish are kept.

After awhile, you will see a man crawl through the little square door of his outer igloo and stand there. His arms are folded inside his parka, against his bare, warm belly, his sleeves hanging limp. If he is a lazy man who does not work hard enough to soften the skin sleeves, they will stand out stiff from his parka when his arms are folded inside. The Eskimo expression for a lazy man is "He got stiff sleeves."

A man or a woman or a child will come out with a vessel in his hands. He is going out to chop some frozen snow to be melted for tea. Early in the morning, they must have tea.

Tea-drinking is the great indoor sport of the St Lawrence Island Eskimo. Boiled over and over, tea is their water, beer, confection. They drink it continually. And though they ruin it in the making, they buy the very best to start with.

When Eskimos come to call, one serves them tea, or else. (Or else they will ask for it.) When you visit them, they serve it as a matter of course. Eskimos drink tea scalding hot, sweetening it by letting it slip down past a lump of sugar held in the jaw. They learned this, no doubt, from Russian or Scandinavian sailors. It accounts for their demand for cube sugar.

Old Agooiki used to come to our house, grinning [91] toothlessly, his feather-filled pipe going full blast. He would sit flat on the floor, his short legs stretched out in front of him, arms and body so completely relaxed and motionless that he might have been molded from putty. He spoke little English, but he could ask for tea. And he would drink it hour after hour. He was the oldest man on the island and the only one who remembered clearly the first white man's ship stopping there.

"My little boy when big ship come here," he would say. "I'm think bird coming. Bymby, go out that big white bird. Lalurumkit (white man), Bump arm, not hit."

arrival VII

What had impressed him most, he meant, was that these strange white men did not fight like dogs at the slightest provocation. If they bumped against each other, they did not turn and rend one another, savagely.

I think it is the most interesting thing I have ever heard about the Eskimos. It meant that, within the memory of one man, the Eskimos themselves had come up from snarling dogmen, fighting each other, to being the peaceable, happy-natured children we knew.

Yet how strange that they could so completely have changed. It is true that the wildest and fiercest animals can be tamed by removing the conditions under which they fought, namely, trouble in getting enough to eat. Perhaps it means that human beings can be tamed when they make the sweet discovery that food and safety can be had without dog fights. Eskimos never lift their hands against one another now, whatever must be said of their brutal treatment of dogs.

VIII. WE MEET THREE SHIPWRECKED MEN[23]

ONE day, before we moved from the Cape up to Gambel
[92], a sled arrived with two passengers, one of them a white man –
an immensely big, very bald, ominous-looking white man – who
plunged at once into an account of his troubles. He and two
companions had been shipwrecked upon the Island during the storm
which had kept us circling round it for so many weeks. It was his
companions who were the source of all his trouble. They were in
Gambel, awaiting our arrival, he said, without enough spirit to run
with the Eskimo dogs, as he had done, to meet us. Anyhow, he
wanted to get to us first with his version of the quarrel, for the leader
of the expedition, he warned us, was a slick proposition and would
tell everything his way.

We were destined to hear versions of that shipwreck and that
quarrel all year. But the first consideration now, was where the man
could sleep. We had no extra bedding, and he none at all. When he
saw that it was impossible for us to put him up, he decided to bunk
in with the Eskimos – he said he often had, in Nome, and didn't
mind. He would have his meals with us, though, he said blandly, for
he didn't relish Eskimo food except as a last resort, and he knew
from the look of her that the little missus was a good cook,
whereupon he gave me a great toothy leer. If there ever was a
forbidding-looking man, he was. [93]

But before the year was out we knew that his looks did not
tell a fair story of him; he had many good faults.

We never really grasped the story of those three men except
in the vaguest outline. So far as we could gather, a doctor, a very
tall, thin man, something of a mystic, had decided that he was called
by God to go to Russia to stay the Revolution – or help it on – we
were never sure which. The Bible had prophesied that the second
coming of Christ would be out of the north, and he would come in a
time of world trouble. This was the north. This was such a time.
Was this, then, Christ again? He never came right out and said so.

The Doctor had a round disc of elephant hide about the size
of a dollar which, he said, would admit him to the forbidden land of

---

[23] June Burn, LIVING HIGH ~ An Unconventional Autobiography. New York:
Duell, Sloan and Pearce, 1941.

Tibet. He was financed by some religious zealot in Los Angeles. He had with him several thousand-dollar bills, one of which Farrar was able to change from the Eskimos' co-operative-store cash. From Los Angeles, the Doctor had come to Nome, early in the summer, where he bought a small boat and persuaded the big old prospector and a young Russian to join him. The Prospector was to navigate him to Siberia in exchange for free passage there to prospect for gold. That was what the Doctor said. The Prospector said it was to be in exchange for the boat, which he would navigate back to Nome. The Russian was to go on with the Doctor, acting as interpreter and guide through Siberia, up the Amur River and so to Moscow – America was not then recognizing Russia, and it was illegal for Americans to go there. Hence this back-door entry. [94]

When the three men got out into Bering Sea, it became apparent that the old Prospector knew nothing at all about boats. He had four-flushed his way into the party. The storm which sent the big ship Bear marching around and around St Lawrence for a month had driven this small boat all over the sea before it came to rest. With the Prospector prostrate with seasickness, the Doctor and the Russian had made a storm anchor of oars and a piece of canvas, and so loped the waves in comparative safety. The wind blew them north to King Island. Then it shifted and blew them south to St Lawrence and piled them onto a beach where they had been rescued by the Eskimos – seasick, frightened, and hungry.

Here they were, our major problem for the year. Farrar assigned them the only other white-man house in Gambel, but the old Prospector stiffly refused to live with the Doctor and the Russian, and spent most of his time going from one Eskimo igloo to another, finally coming to rest in a little frame shack belonging to one of them. We let him alone and he went about his lonely way, un-befriended by us all. The Doctor bought his food. I wish we had been kinder to him in spite of his surliness.[24]

That winter the Doctor spent endless, sometimes tiresome evenings at our house, talking politics, religion, mysticism, biblical prophesies, the right and wrong of the quarrel. All year he gave generously what help we needed in the treatment of illness. He was a good man.

---

[24] Dell Bishop (Leightons 1983: 338), See p235 for tiny last note from Bruning.

Our house at Gambel was an unnecessarily large, roomy, porous board structure, thrown together as though [95] for use in the tropics instead of the Arctic. It was not triple-sealed against the elements. Weather made itself right at home with us. In no time we were on intimate terms with snow drifts. With our short supply of coal, we had to confine ourselves to a single room – the kitchen. Here, with coal for the range, we cooked, ate, slept, and entertained the Doctor and the Eskimos.

The other rooms of the house were ghost chambers, bitter-cold, bleak, empty. After our year of homesteading on Puget Sound, we didn't mind the cracks and crannies. In fact, we thought it great fun, huddling together in the very innermost room of the big old empty house. Nowadays, the teachers have better quarters.

The schoolroom was part of our house. It too was un-arctic in construction. But the Eskimo children came to school in their furs and needed no air-tight house. Those nearest the big-bellied stove nearly cooked, and we had to rotate them there.

On the first day of school, children tumbled in like puppies. Silook introduced them to me and gave them their seats. He knew each child's grade and place. We passed out the books, some of them bright and new, some old and tattered.

The most advanced children had reached the sixth grade. I gave Silook the three upper grades, on the theory that he could do the least harm there. I took the young ones, and all the reading classes, and sometimes I had to take over Sixth Grade Arithmetic. But, on the whole, Silook was capable.[25] He was earnest, quiet, and, if a little lazy, he did his work as long as I was there. When our [96] coal would give out and we had to return to Southwest Cape until another surplus could accumulate (for we used it faster than the men hauled it), Silook shirked a bit, but there was no help for it.

Lessons went smoothly on. If you had come into our warm old barn of a room full of skin-clad children and teachers, the stench would probably have sent you outside again to catch your breath. But in school as at home we couldn't smell ourselves. We were as happy as snowbirds – all of us. I never loved teaching so much, never loved any children more. Yet there was one little boy who kicked the dogs whenever he got a chance. Just as the dogs

---

[25] See p251 for his family's fame.

themselves would tear to pieces one of their number who was sick or weak, so these boys seemed to despise hungry or whining dogs and delighted in tormenting them.

One day I saw this child kick a dying dog. It was lucky for him that the schoolroom was very long. By the time I reached him, I had reminded myself what his upbringing had been, how little he could feel for helpless creatures. But I lectured him and all the rest of the children. I gave Silook a tongue-lashing for not having taught them better. And I made Farrar call a council about it a few nights later, and there I stormed again, and so did Farrar in his milder, merrier way. But except for their treatment of dogs, I found no fault with my children.

Meanwhile, Farrar and Oningayu, the storekeeper at Gambel, were arranging goods in the little frame building that was the co-operative store. And before long, Farrar [97] went over the snowy hills and far away to see the reindeer herders who lived some fifty miles down island and were his special charges. I was left alone in the great, loose-joined, empty, roomy house. The Doctor spent the evenings with me, generally getting there in time for supper. I got awfully tired of him, poor fellow. And by night, the snow came sneaking in through all the cracks and had to be swept and shoveled out next morning.

When Farrar returned from Reindeer Camp that first time, he was a chastened man. I ran out to meet him. "Keep away from me," he said. "Bring me some clean things and a can of gasoline and heat some water on the stove – I will wait here in the shed."

It seems he had caught lice from a blanket which one of the Eskimos had lent him to sleep in. The shed was nearly full of snow, icicles hung down through its cracks. But there he stayed until I had heated water and fixed him up. Then he washed his garments in gasoline and I took them outside to hang on whatever whale ribs I could find sticking up near our house. The wind froze them at once and we later beat them until everything living or dead must have fallen to the ground. It was surely the most thorough delousing anybody ever had.

Farrar had had another adventure. He had eaten seagull. He said it was far from palatable and very tough. The dirty old woman at whose igloo he had stopped on his way, eager to serve him, grabbed a cup at her feet, a filthy rag from a corner to wipe it, and poured him some tea. Then she pushed the family platter towards him and [98] bade him help himself to the bird. He took a piece and chewed and chewed, his stomach protesting at the taste. But he downed it.

One evening after school, Farrar and I took a walk out to the beach, about a mile away. The sea hadn't begun to freeze over at this out-thrust, wind-swept point. The surf still beat there, night and day. We wondered whether there would be any agates here, and there were. We were walking along bent nearly double, peering into the gravel, not talking for a wonder because the noise of the surf was too great, when a big wave rolled in from Siberia and knocked us both down. We had been twenty feet above the highest wave and now we were sitting down in a froth of water, a determined undertow tugging at us.

Farrar struggled to his feet, grabbed my hand, and we lit out from there as fast as our high, water-filled boots would carry us. By the time we got home, our garments were frozen stiff. That was the last time we ever hunted agates on St Lawrence beaches.

In time we settled down to the steady routine of our work: school five days a week, sewing classes for the women on Saturdays – which turned into story-telling festivals and ended as scrubbing bees, all of us on our hands and knees trying to get the week's dirt out of the place. Each woman was paid, of course. Catch an Eskimo doing work for nothing! On Sundays we held a sort of community sing and council meeting at which we discussed our problems of living.

Once a week [99], Farrar held another meeting, in the evening. The people loved meeting to sing and to talk. If there was nothing to settle, they made up something, I expect. They were capable of it.

Christmas found us at Southwest Cape. We celebrated there with candies and gifts for everybody, found, somehow, among our things. There was a gale blowing. Risking going off the bluff in a sudden gust, Farrar crept out with the gifts and returned with the many thank-yous from people who lived in the two houses. They would all come to tea with us that evening, they said.

When the gale blew away to Japan, we returned to Gambel and had another Christmas there. With our buckets of candy and whatever there was in the store we could buy – prunes, cube sugar, and so on – we managed something for each person in Gambel, but it was a tight squeeze. Nobody had prepared us for this Eskimo greed for gifts.

Still, we reflected, we could not alternately exploit them and bestow beneficent largesse without creating this cunning rapacity in them. One minute we found ourselves hotly championing them against what had been done to hem, and the next ruefully defending ourselves against what they were doing to us.

Wherever you find primitive people looked after like children by some benevolent and alien white government, you also find this servile demandingness – a hateful paradox. How long would it take some wise administrator to set them firmly on their own spiritual and physical legs, [100] make proud adults of them on all levels of their being? Perhaps one generation? If we have brought them so quickly from an almost barbarous existence, we could take them on the rest of the way.

IX WINTER OF SPLENDID ISOLATION[26]

ST. LAWRENCE ISLAND is a hundred miles long by about thirty wide. It is within the Arctic Circle but almost the length of California from the North Pole. It is a hundred and fifty miles west of Nome, but only forty miles east of Siberia. [101]

In winter, when the sun is given to making only polite little party calls, life on St Lawrence goes on just as usual. The Eskimos do not huddle in their igloos and say, "Now long night come. More better we sleep now." They pay no more attention to the grayness that passes for daylight than we, outside, to the shorter days of our winter. They go out hunting every day except when there is a gale blowing. For St Lawrence Island is whipped by stinging winds so violent that they will literally blow you off the island if you don't look out. When children go out in those gales, their mothers tie them to the igloos by walrus-skin ropes. In the big blows, grown men sometimes go on hands and knees.

We kept our lamps going all day and felt curiously separated from the world, but it was not really dark – not with all that snow-whiteness with its stored light.

On the shortest day of the year, the sun came above the horizon about a foot, rode across a little arc of sky for perhaps two hours, and went down again. On the longest [102] day of summer, the blazing wheel ran around the full circle, slowly edged down toward the horizon at midnight, took a dip for about an hour, emerged again, and rolled up and on to light the blinding white world for another twenty-three hours. But we could read small print all night, long before that longest day arrived.

The lowest temperature which our minimum thermometer registered before it froze and burst was minus 55° – no colder than it gets in Minnesota. In summer – in mid-August – the temperature may go up to sixty or seventy or more on still, sunny days, mosquitoes hovering in clouds over the thawed-out swamps.

The loose gravel that passes for land on St Lawrence is frozen clear to China, I expect. In summer it thaws about two feet down. But that is enough to turn the land between mountains into

---

[26] June Burn, LIVING HIGH ~ An Unconventional Autobiography. New York: Duell, Sloan and Pearce, 1941.

lakes which can be crossed only by birds. Travel is by boat, around the island, and Eskimos who have none are water-bound in their own villages.

Before I saw it, I imagined the frozen sea to be smooth, and I thought what fun it would be to cross to Asia by dog-sled. That would be about as easy to do as crossing the roofs of a city in a horse and buggy. For the ice is like a hodge-podge of wrecked buildings. Wind and current push it together, jumble it, open sudden channels down into the cold watery depths, heap up blocks nearly as high as the pyramids. Even on short hunting trips, it is hard for the Eskimo dogs to find any passage through the rectangular ice hills to the dead animals which they must haul home.

Then there are the icebergs which come sailing down [103] from the Arctic to settle on the St Lawrence shore for the winter. They are pale green, beautiful, almost translucent. They are the last things to melt in summer, and they are hardly gone when the first snow falls and it is time for them to come again.

If some epidemic should destroy the people of St Lawrence Island, I would like to write their epitaph. I would say that life was fun for them. The Eskimos don't need our manufactured pleasures; everything they do is recreation. It is rare fun to gather beach wood to build the base of their skin houses – to watch for the chunks or logs or planks drifting in out of the sea from Japan and Alaska and Russia – to run and pull them from the surf. The hard jobs are hunting, fishing, trapping, making white leather, building houses and boats and sleds – but they are fun, too, and it is evident that the Eskimos enjoy them.

They are a small-bodied people, seldom fat, though their broad faces and the swaddle of skins they wear make them look so. But they are strong. The men think nothing of running beside their dog-sleds all day long. I've known them to do it for forty-five miles at a stretch. A man will take gun and harpoon, and sit all day on a hummock beside a hole in the ocean's ice, waiting for a seal, and pity himself no more than a man who sits at his desk all day. If there is any meat or food left in his igloo before he sets out to hunt, he will take some with him. But if there is none, he will sit and watch that deep blue [104] lake rimmed with pale green ice, thinking – who knows what?

They think nothing of physical hardship. But then, most

improvident people regard mere physical hardship a good deal as the provident ones regard monotonous routine – as an inescapable part of the way they live. Nobody works monotonously hard on St Lawrence Island. They take time out for what we call laziness. Perhaps we were too long misled by pioneer necessity into calling laziness a fault; we have undervalued this gentle virtue. In a good life, a right life, all people would have as much sheer joy of living as the Eskimos have.

Perhaps it is more fun for the men to hunt seals than it is for the women to skin, dress, cook, tan, and sew them. But the women laugh at their work too and seem contented – if a shade too quiet about it.

For the children life is a continual festival. They run about, helping or not, as they choose, quickly learning the skills, playing quietly, laughing easily.

Seal hunting lasts all winter. Wherever the wind has blown the ice away from some tiny hole of water, you will see from one or two to a dozen hunters sitting with their guns, watching for a seal to poke its head up. If food is scarce in the village and water-holes as well, all the men may huddle around one hole all day without catching a single seal. That is a great joke. No food. All mans hunt one hole. Not one man got one seal. Very funny.

Seals are found in the open water-holes because they must come up to breathe. When one of the slick, dark, [105] doglike heads slips up through the blue water, the Eskimo waits until the seal has breathed his fill. Then, pop! goes one of the surest guns in the world. Whiz! goes the ivory harpoon into the flesh of the seal. Whish! goes the long walrus-skin rope, if the seal was not shot in a vital spot. Firrp! go the sealskin floats as they strike the water and are jerked partly under.

The blue water is stained with red, now. The floats ride it like big toy balloons as the seal thrashes about. They are so buoyant no seal can long outplay them. After awhile they are still as dreaming seagulls on the water. The seal is dead.

The hunter begins to coil his line. The floats come to shore and are taken in. The line is coiled onto the end of the ivory harpoon, and there is a helpless floppy seal secure on the hook. He is drawn out onto the ice and the Eskimo laughs.

While the fight was going on between seal and white floats,

somebody was sent to the village for dogs and sled. If hunting has been good and food is not at the famine stage, only the one team and sled sent for will come, and the hunter will put his seal aboard and haul it home with some dignity.

But if it has been a hungry time, many sleds will come lolloping over the rough ice. Women and children come, too, laughing and chattering. They are given pieces of the seal and their sleds will go racing back to the village with a pound or so of meat aboard. When the hungry ones reach home, they cut the meat into hunks about the size of a fist, boil it a little, and fall to. Three meals a day do [106] not mean as much to an Eskimo as they do to us. But a meal any day means something to him. And how much gusto they put into eating it – all sitting on the floor around the big wooden platter or the pot in which the meat was cooked over the never-dying flame of their seal-oil lamps.

If several seals are caught at once, there may be a waste of meat. Even the dogs may be given a scrap each. Farrar and I occasionally bought a piece of red-black tenderloin of seal which we broiled in butter and liked.

The common hair seal, weighing a hundred pounds and more for the larger kinds, is probably the most valuable product the Eskimos have. From its strong, smooth-haired hide they make water-proof pants, mittens, and – from the hide of the very large varieties – boots. By rotting off the hair, first, and freezing the skins, they also turn them into harpoon floats, using them whole; or into white leather which they cut up for trimming for their garments. The flesh, liver, and heart of the seal are standard food, and the fat is rendered into oil for their lamps.

Next in importance to the seal is the walrus. It is hunted in spring when the ice is breaking up. Herds will be sighted, miles away, on drifting ice floes. Eskimos go out in boats to hunt them, invariably killing more than they can possibly bring home. They leave whole mountains of flesh behind them for the polar bears. Some day there will be a shortage of walrus there. But perhaps, by that time, it will matter no more than our wanton waste of buffalo mattered by the time we had exterminated them.

Walrus skins are used to make the roofs of the outer [107] igloos, the floors of the inner living rooms, and, when they are cut into strips, ropes for dog harness and other uses. But their most valuable use is for the long, deep, canoe-like boats, up to forty and fifty feet long, with a carrying capacity of forty people.

Walrus intestines are cleaned, flattened, and sewn together for raincoats. The tusks are carved into trade articles. And the stomachs are treasured most of all for the undigested fresh clams sometimes found in them.

All the flesh is eaten, but we did not like it, though we found the liver very good. It is this meat which they store away in their underground caves literally to rot. But the modern Eskimo does not like this high meat as much as his ancestors did.

Reindeer herding has grown to be an important business on the Island. Since the days of Mr Lopp, many of the Eskimos have owned reindeer. There is a little community of herders on St Lawrence who see that the herd of some five thousand deer is driven to good feeding places, who corral and mark them once a year, and watch out for the does at fawning time.

From the reindeer the Eskimos get their beds and the walls of their inner living rooms, which are made from the winter skin with hair four to six inches long, and very strong. The summer skins are used for inside trousers, inside boots, mittens, and outer parkas. Fawn skins make inside parkas and all the children's garments. The tendons of the legs are used for thread.

Every year the herders sell a few hundred carcasses for cash. They seldom eat the deer themselves; just as farmers [108] outside sell cream and use skim milk for their own families.

Farrar and I ate nine reindeer while we were there. The carcass would freeze solid and we would use a hack saw to cut off thick steaks which, broiled quickly, were tender as butter. Reindeer stew is good, too.

Nearly all the men trap white and blue fox, getting two or three hundred beautiful pelts a year. But they do not wear them. The only fur they use as decoration is wolverine, with its harsh, snow-rejecting hairs. They sew bands of wolverine around parka hoods to keep out the snow, and around the bottoms of the parkas for decorations. As there is no wolverine on St Lawrence, the natives traded with the Siberian Eskimos for it once a year. Now, however, the Soviets keep the Siberians at home.

No whales were caught the year we were there, but polar bear is sometimes killed. The flesh is eaten, but it was too strong for us. The strong, heavily furred skin is much prized for sled seats.

When the wind blows too hard for hunting or trapping, the men help the women with the tanning or carve ivory. They make napkin rings, salt cellars, paper knives, cribbage boards, and all manner of trade articles which have been taught them. Sometimes they can be induced to turn out a long necklace of ivory lace, each link a fragile medallion fastened to the next by ivory rings, with slits in them which can be sprung.

Sled building, house building, boat building, tanning; making intestine raincoats and parkas of bird breasts and white leather of whole seal skins; carving, skinning fox, [109] and drying the skins; gathering driftwood for houses and sleds and knees for the boats; herding, hunting, fishing in summer, gathering willow roots and dry wild grass for boots – there is not a dull job in the lot.

But while the daily activities were enjoyable in themselves, the Eskimos have story-telling to beguile long winter evenings. They will gather into a little cluster anywhere, any time, and start telling stories, their voices rambling along in a sing-song fashion, without any colorful inflections to mark the periods. To indicate the end of the tale, the story-teller puts his little finger in his mouth and blows hard. It is the only way you can tell the story is finished. From our standpoint, the stories are not interesting; they have no crisis, no theme, not a resolved ending among them.

A raven, wanting to show off, bragged that he would jump into the fire. His neighbors built a fire for him, he jumped in and was burned up. A blind man, mistreated at home, ran away to the moon. There, too, he was mistreated. An old woman reached the age when it was customary to be killed by the younger people. She did not want to die just yet. She ran away and got into so much trouble you'd think the moral must be that she would return home and say, "Yes, my people have wisdom. It is, after all, time for me to die." But no such thing – she just went on having trouble. Thus their stories are the closest approximation to realism we have found in literature.

Eskimo dancing is like strenuous setting-up exercises. Drums and sticks beat the complicated, broken rhythm, voices sing, and one or more individuals stand in a cleared [110] space and dance. They do not move about the space but keep their feet in the same position all the time. In the heat of their contortions, shrieks, and yowls, they may leap into the air, but they always come down in the same place.

The women dance more quietly. They neither leap nor yell. Theirs is more a dance of the torso and arms, their feet together on the floor, never leaving their position. But they too get more and more excited as the drummers increase their tempo and the singers whoop it up, and they are exhausted at the end.

The St Lawrence Island drum is a reindeer stomach stretched over a hoop. It is roughly the shape of a palm-leaf fan, with a handle about as long as the fan's handle. It is beaten on the rim with a stick, the skin head giving out a shallow, booming sound. The rhythm is impossible to reproduce. It is not syncopation; it has its own plan or continuity, each dancer or singer making up his own tune and tempo. The air pulsates with the living tide-rip of sound. It is tremendously exciting.

Running foot races seems to be the chief outdoor sport. Of course, they used to have many others, but as this was the one white teachers could best understand, it has persisted. They practice with weights on their feet, increasing the weights as the time of the contest approaches. "Suppose run fast, load on feet. Run fa-a-st, suppose take load off."

There were fewer women than men on St Lawrence, but this seemed to give them no particular advantage. As in biblical times, the young man works for his wife, joining [111] the family, helping with hunting, building, trapping. He is a prized addition to the family. He works a year – sometimes two, for his wife. When his time is up and the bridal night comes, the ceremony of taking a wife is very simple; the father moves over one place, leaving his daughter outside the family line and she sleeps next to the young man who, with her, now constitutes a new family.

If the young man is well-to-do, the couple may move to a skin house which he has built. Or they may live with either family, for an extra man means more food for everybody, particularly if he is a good hunter; and an extra woman means less work for the women in the mother-in-law's house.

Occasionally there is a shrewd old Eskimo who will overdo this business of exploiting a son-in-law. Old Shu-look, one of the wealthiest men on the Island, had a beautiful daughter. She was Amamunga who worked for us. She was about twenty-five and quite lovely, with hair that reached the ground. And she was sweet.

One day she told me shyly that she wished Nanook (Farrar) would speak to Shulook about marrying her off. "More better I'm marry now," she said. "All time womans laugh me, for not marry." Farrar did speak to old Shulook, and Amamunga was being worked for once more when we left. I hope she married, at last, and lived happily ever after.

The Eskimo morals are different from ours, but they stick to their code as well or better than we do. They easily lie. They tell you whatever you want to hear. They will cheat you in trading if they can. Their hands are [112] always out for gifts. But all that is conditioning from their exposure to some of the less moral individuals and groups among the whites – ignorant or unscrupulous traders – and others.

Polygamy used to flourish on St Lawrence Island. While we were there, one man still had two wives. But changing conditions, and the fact that it is now illegal – to say nothing of the shortage of women – have gradually let the custom die out. It is not for moral reasons, however, that the Eskimos are not polygamous. It is a matter of economy. They are children of nature and could as easily reason that polygamy is right because the seals have more than one mate, as that it is wrong because their favorite duck has only one. They have a legend about the faithful, monogamous duck. Once we were driven past a lake where a lone drake swam round and round. "That duck never marry again," our guide said. "Him love wife ve-ery much all same Eskimo."

Before our government took charge of them, the Eskimos of St Lawrence Island buried their dead on a ledge of the high bluff behind Gambel. They could not dig graves in solid ice. Even in summer, they can dig only two feet down. So bodies were laid out in the open – and there were times when things happened to the bodies and other arrangements had to be made. It seems to us that water burial is the only solution. They are a sea-living people. They should be given the seaman's funeral. Even in winter, there are water holes. But, fortunately, we did not have to face that problem.

In the old days, the St Lawrence natives killed their [113] old who had outlived usefulness – when their teeth were worn through the gums from chewing leather, when they could not see to sew or carve ivory, or even to tend the lamp. That custom, too, has been outlawed. It would have gone anyhow, when greater security for all came to the Island.

We found no indication that the Eskimos ever lived communally. Their stories, which go back to their earliest traditions, tell of the rich and the poor, the kind and the cruel, the haves and the have-nots.

When, as occasionally happens, an Eskimo woman is coerced into relations with some white sailor, the tribe is bitterly ashamed and angered, and the half-breed child is hated. But in the spring some of the Eskimos trade wives among themselves. This is not a breach of their own moral code; it grew out of their love for and need of children. When one brother's wife was found to be barren, another brother would lend his wife so that there might be small folk in that igloo, too. So many of the women are barren, indeed, that it seems inevitable that if the natives are to survive, new blood from the mainland will be necessary.

There seemed to be no sexual delinquency between young people. People lived together so intimately; there was so little mystery about bodies, everybody going naked inside the hot skin living rooms; getting married was such a simple affair that there was neither opportunity, necessity, nor desire for pre-marital relations between the young folk.

We never knew whether or not the Eskimos were clean, according to our standards. Amamunga declared that they [114] bathed in melted snow water just as we did; that the women often washed their hair. They washed it with urine sometimes, as it kept down lice, was a good tonic, and made the hair shine. She also said they rubbed their bodies in oil. But while I believed the part about the urine and the oil, I never knew whether or not to believe in the water baths. The women, Amamunga said, use moss for their personal needs.

Sanitary cleanliness was rare among them. They drank melted snow from any source, casually fishing out the undrinkables. When our water boy, Iyu, brought us blocks of snow-ice chopped closer to the village than the bank we had chosen as apt to be free of foreign matter, we would find hair, a lost mitten, and nameless other things in it when it was melted. Iyu could not understand why we didn't simply fish them out and use the water. We had to watch him on every trip to the ice bank.

The disposal of human refuse offers no problem. The dogs eat it. Then the ravens eat the dog refuse. There is an Eskimo song, wondering what becomes of the raven droppings.

The Eskimos are subject to skin disease, venereal disease, tuberculosis, sore eyes, and – since sugar and prunes – tooth decay. They are not outstandingly healthy or long-lived. But while they do live, they make a wonderful job of it.

X. A FEW STIFF SLEEVES LIMBER UP[27]

MORE than anything else, Farrar and I wanted to leave St Lawrence Island better off than we had found it. We wanted to manage so well that every human being on the Island would have enough to eat, would improve his status, and make some progress toward adult living without sacrificing the values and good customs already obtaining. [115]

Part of our job was to raise the price level of Eskimo goods and lower that of the trader's goods, so as to make it more worth while for the Eskimos to work. All Eskimos are easy-going, but some of them are so lazy that their families are reduced to extreme poverty, hunger and disease. These live off the bounty of others – for there is little margin in a primitive society, even among the wealthy.

Our task, then, was to find some way to persuade the laziest ones to work. We tried preaching, scolding, shaming, cajoling them off to the hunting and trapping grounds, the white-leather making – all with little success. They agreed to everything we suggested graciously, admitted their laziness humbly, resolved to improve themselves earnestly – and went right on behaving as before.

Then one day we saw the laziest man on the Island running a race with his dogs, apparently just for fun. He won the race. [116]

"We'll try turning the work into play," we said, and knew we had the answer.

So, early in the year we decided to hold an Eskimo fair. It seemed the made-to-order answer to all our problems. It would encourage productivity, even among the laziest, and provide them with goods which they could exchange for the supplies they would need for the coming year. And they would have fun doing it.

Before Christmas, I typed twenty copies of a "Proclamation" telling about the fair, which we sent by messengers to every group on the island, explaining what fun it would be and what a lot everybody would have to eat.

It took time to work up any enthusiasm. At first everyone thought how much work it would be to make boots fancy enough to

---

[27] June Burn, LIVING HIGH ~ An Unconventional Autobiography. New York: Duell, Sloan and Pearce, 1941.

compete for prizes, to carve ivory lace, trap fox until the choicest pelt on the island was caught. We had to emphasize the fun, the prizes, and the "plenty grub."

At last we began to get a flicker of interest here and there. The idlest old man on the Island, as it happened, was also the best carver. By a campaign of flattery we finally got him stirred up, and after that things ran along with more spirit.

The Siberian Eskimos, who came in the spring, were always entertained with races, dances, and "big time." That, then, would be just the time for the fair. No one knew, of course, exactly when they would come, but we set the date for the fair for some time in March or April – I cannot remember exact dates from our year in this timeless land. That would be before the land ice had [117] begun to thaw, but after the days had begun to get long and bright. By then there would be good hunting, too; the Eskimos at Gambel would have food for their guests from Siberia as well as for those from all the other parts of St Lawrence Island.

Early in the fair month, Farrar went to the reindeer village to select a couple of fine government bucks, which were to be our contribution as hosts-in chief. By that time the co-operative store, and we too, were running short of food. We still had a hundred-pound sack of steel-cut oats left. It would make washtubs and boilers full of oat-reindeer stew for our three hundred guests. And thereby hangs a tale.

The great day came. Eskimos began arriving in their dog-sleds. There was dog-pandemonium on the little sand spit on which our cluster of igloos and frame shacks sprawled. The great tea-drinking began. Everyone came to pay respects to us. Fortunately we had plenty of tea, plenty of snow to melt for water, plenty of sugar and hardtack. But not plenty of pots in which to boil the water; everything was filled with reindeer stew. However, we managed to serve tea just the same. To fail in that would doom the festivities at the outset.

Silook and I had decorated the schoolroom with maps and drawings which the children had made. Now we added the fair exhibits: soft, strong-haired, great snowy fox pelts; ivory chains intricately carved; beautiful hair-seal boots, decorated with finely cut white leather; gloves, parkas, pants, ivory toys, rare old ivory in many colors, harpoons, miniature walrus-skin boats, miniature houses, perfect [118] facsimiles of the big ones. Everything Eskimos use was represented at that fair – proof that they could do sustained work over a long period of time if there was incentive enough. I doubt if any of them thought that by working now they would have food next winter. They worked for the fun of competing – "I'm get prize. I'm plenty laugh for big time in March."

In spite of all our cajoling it was the wealthiest, least needy Eskimos who made the greatest number of fine articles for trade after all. But every man and woman had done something, and we saw that there would be a money surplus for all of them. They could buy what the store had left now, and still have money left for fall when they would be more in need of it. I felt like asking them all to stand up, hands inside parkas, to see whether there was a stiff sleeve left among them.

First we elected the judges. The Doctor was chosen by acclamation, for he was popular on the island; Silook, who, at our request, had entered nothing in the fair; Sepillu, the wealthiest and most intelligent man on the island; and me, to make sure that everyone got some sort of prize, if only a stick of candy for the little boots fashioned so clumsily by Maskin's sickly girl-wife. We kept Farrar off the judge's bench to act as supreme court in case we couldn't agree.

The display exceeded all our hopes for it. With what patience old men had sat and carved all winter that these blackened tables should hold delicate ivory chains! Farrar and I bought every prize-winning object, at top prices, partly because we wanted them, partly to show them – as [119] nothing else could – that there were prunes and sugar and calico and tea to be had by all, if they would work for them.

In one of our private financial depressions – so frequent that Farrar calls them our status quo – we sold this collection, and they can now be seen at the Museum of the American Indian in New York City.

On that first day of the fair, the Siberian Eskimos did not arrive. But the weather was calm and sunny and the ice floes well-broken as far as we could see; they were sure to come the next day. Meanwhile those merry people were immensely enjoying their first fair.

At noon we served our tubs and boilers of reindeer stew.

arrival X

The Eskimos brought their own plates, cups, buckets, pie pans, lids, wooden platters, on which to receive their helpings. One little boy had an old rusty tin can. I lent him one of our plates, and after that had much trouble not to lend all the rest of them to people with shallow bucket lids or too-deep buckets. There was plenty for everybody.

With singular bad judgment, we gave second and third helpings of that rich food to those who wanted it – the hungriest or the greediest. That day the Doctor dined with us, and the stew was so good that the three of us ate too much of it, too.

Then, to cap our foolishness after that heavy meal, we held the preliminary races. Without the weights which they had worn in practicing, the men ran, losers eliminating themselves for the big races with the Siberians later. Between stakes or ice blocks or natural hummocks, they [120] ran, nimble and fleet. They wore only their soft light skin boots and one pair of skin pants, and nothing on their upper bodies. Their feet seemed barely to touch the snow as they flew, their coarse hair lifting and falling on their heads. The middle-aged men were the best runners, easily outdistancing lads and old men. The women, too, were surprisingly fleet runners. Before that day was over, everybody had run. No one was winded. No one needed a rub-down. They ran as simply as they laughed, and thought no more of it.

But that night nearly three hundred persons – including ourselves – paid for eating too rich food after abstemiousness, and too much exercise after eating. Every single one of us had diarrhea.

Next morning, Silook came in, looking limp and wan. He wanted some medicine.

"Oh, everybody plenty sick," he said. "My father, he go outside, inside, outside, inside. Bymby he just stay outside."

Farrar and I nearly finished ourselves off laughing, though we were frightened, too. Presently the Doctor arrived to prescribe for us all. He had been sick, too.

On the second day of the fair we went right on with the contests and games. The Eskimos are a hardy lot. They aren't particularly Spartan; it simply wouldn't occur to them to miss anything interesting by being sick.

We had a rifle match, using powerful thirty-thirties, and I won second place. It must have been an accident for I wasn't used to such a heavy gun, but the generous Eskimos [121] crowded around, patting me on the back. "Patsarok fine shoot," they said.

The dog races were next. Scrubby, dirty, scrawny, hungry, sullen dogs in teams of three or eight or nine were hitched to sleds, leaders out in front. The sleds were lined up, drivers sat ready to shout the first "Huh!" when Farrar should give the signal.

"One – two – three – go!" said Farrar.

"Huh! Huh! Huh!" screamed the drivers, slashing their whips on the ground, now on one side, now on the other side of their teams to direct them along the course.

The dogs ran belly-low, straining out. The sleds flew over the hard trail. We watched them sail over the last snowbank onto the lake ice, swing around the far edge of the lake and start on the homeward stretch. By that time, Farrar and I had shouted so much we had begun to get up some excitement among the imitative Eskimos, but it all turned into shouts of laughter when young orphan Iyu's three mangy dogs came in trailing the pack. Iyu was carrying one of the dogs in his lap, the other two pulling them. "Him not keep up," Iyu said, perfectly cheerful. The fun was the thing.

It was late in the afternoon. The scheduled games were over. Callers from other parts of the Island had come in to have tea with us and had gone again. Farrar and I were thankful for a little quiet beside our kitchen range.

Suddenly Silook ran down the hall, poked his head in and shouted that the Siberians were in sight. We grabbed up our parkas and ran with him down to the beach – or [122] to the massed shore-ice that served as a beach at this time of year; it was about a quarter of a mile beyond the summer beach.

A huge walrus-skin boat had slipped into the open channel to our shore, and presently some forty smelly, cheery, casual individuals tumbled out of the deep, open craft onto the pale green ice. They pulled their boat up onto the shore-ice to make room for the one behind. And then they turned to greet us. Silook stood near by to act as interpreter for the visitors. By this time the second boatload had come ashore, and we were proudly presented by our Eskimo names – Nanook and Patsarok. The Siberians laughed at our names, gazing appreciatively up at Nanook, the polar bear, as though they thought he had been well named, and at me, the little weed, and thought that funnier still. Everybody beamed.

arrival X

Now we streamed back along the ice trails, over the dirty snow, homeward. The seventy-odd Siberians were so much like our own Eskimos that I couldn't tell them apart at a little distance.

That night we had a dance in the outer chamber of Shulook's big igloo. It lasted nearly all night. The Siberians were much dirtier than our Eskimos. They didn't laugh as much or as happily. But how they could turn themselves loose in the dance!

Lanterns stood about on boxes or hung from the roof. The air was close and strong. Small children lay on reindeer furs in the corners. The larger ones were given places of vantage around the dancing ring. The drummers sat in a row on boxes, close about the dancing space. Everyone [123] was silent, waiting. Waiting for some dancer's spirit to urge him out into the ring.

Presently one of our men came, then one of the Siberians, another, another, until there were six or eight naked men in the ring. They wore loincloths, beads, fringed bands around their calves, white reindeer skin mittens to accentuate the rhythm, for it was a hand, not a foot dance. They danced their wild, shrieking, leaping, writhing, contortion dances, each according to his own impulses, but, to our untrained eyes, all looking the same.

Amamunga danced, her long dark hair loose, sweeping the floor. She wore her daytime clothes, dropping everything down around her hips to leave arms and shoulders naked and free. Another girl came into the ring with her. There seemed to be rivalry between them. Without moving their feet from their place, the two girls bent at knee, hip, shoulders. They turned and twisted from the ankles up. Their hair flew about. The drums went faster and faster. They danced so violently and with such swift movements that I began to fear they would kill themselves. And when I could bear no more, they stopped in the middle of a drum tap, walked calmly out of the ring, out of sight behind the crowd.

On and on into the night the drummers beat, the howls and shrieks burst open the skies. Then – out of a dark corner, a white woman came to dance! We had not seen her before. Where had she been hiding? I asked Silook.

She was a half-breed, he said. "Him not like to be seen. Sailors come ashore at Siberia, too," he said.

The woman's eyes were blue, her hair and skin fair, [124] her expression one of infinite pathos, as though she felt completely outside life. But when she danced, she flung herself into it as though it were the only way she had ever found to say, "I live, too – I am."

Next day, there was trading between the natives from across Bering Sea and our own. They had brought soft fawn skins, for they had more reindeer than we and no government regulations to say how many should be killed each season. They had brought wolverine, beautiful brass samovars in which they made their own tea en route, and which they didn't want to trade. Silook got one, however, which he later traded to me for my best boots. He no doubt had that in mind when he wangled the samovar.

From us the Siberians wanted sugar, tea, calico, and white-man things in general, including fine guns. Our men were the sharpest traders, having had more dealings with white men, and the poor Siberians came out at the short end of the horn, but everybody was happy.

In the afternoon of the third day, we held the long-awaited foot races. Our Maskin won first place – and the fair was over. Soon the Siberians would go back and life would fall into a new pattern for the Eskimo spring.

XI. WE TOSS A COIN[28]

SPRING comes with a rush and a roar on St Lawrence Island. [125] Ocean ice begins to crack like cannon. Winds blow the floes about, opening up long blue channels to tempt the natives out in their whaling and walrus-hunting boats. The sun glares down on the eye-blistering snow. The pale green icebergs, like a city of skyscrapers along the shore, begin to look uneasy, as though they knew their time had come. Sapphire shadows underneath the curling eaves of snowdrifts darken to a rich purple in contrast to the dazzling whiteness around them.

Immense flocks of birds ride the winds from the south, settle on the rocks and bluffs of their summer home. They fill the air with happy, homecoming cries. The days have lengthened rapidly and amazingly. Even in March, night has receded so far beyond our bedtime we never know when it comes down any more.

But spring really comes when the Eskimos take off their heavy winter reindeer parkas and don white-man clothes. One night we went to bed in a land of people we knew. Next morning we looked out to find a flock of scarecrows over the landscape. It was the Island's Easter parade. The women seemed to have lost twenty or thirty pounds overnight. Their calico parkas hung limp without the padding of heavy fur underneath. [126]

But the men! They were unbelievable in coats and trousers bought in Nome or traded from former teachers. Silook walked solemnly up and down in a khaki officer's uniform which Farrar had traded him for something or other, and the pair of boots for which I had got the samovar.

Farrar is on the biggish side and Silook was small, even for an Eskimo. The trousers were tight below the knee, puttee style. The bloused portion came nearly to Silook's ankles, and the tight leggings were rolled up. The coat hung far below his hips and the sleeves were doubled back to the elbows. The cap came down over his ears and eyes. But Silook was the envy of the Island. And when Farrar complimented him on his appearance, he nearly burst with pride.

---

[28] June Burn, LIVING HIGH ~ An Unconventional Autobiography. New York: Duell, Sloan and Pearce, 1941.

The reindeer fawn in the spring. Farrar and I went to the reindeer camp for a month, I to give the dozen children of the herders some schooling, Farrar to superintend the counting of the herd and its new additions.

It was a crazy beach-wood, whale-rib, walrus-rope corral into which the milling deer were gathered. The Eskimo lariat is a walrus-skin rope, pliable and easily thrown. But they weren't cut out to be cowboys. Farrar lost all patience with them and would come in at night fuming at their ineptness. They ran a deer down instead of lassoing it. That seemed a good way to me, if they could catch it, but he said it ran off too much fat, was bad for the mother deer, and anyhow wasn't good cowboy.

At reindeer camp we lived in a tent. Sepillu, chief [127] herder, and the only man on the island of whom we made a real friend, had fixed it up for us. He had put up a tiny ship's stove in one corner, railed off a space at the back for our bed in which he had spread down all his own cherished supply of boot grass – a strong grass which they gather in summer and save to pad their boots with, for it is springy and breaks the hardness of ice underfoot.

There was a box for a table and two whale vertebrae for seats. The floor was frozen ground, of course, and the unbearable glare of the sun on snow outside was scarcely dimmed by those thin canvas walls, but we loved it. After a winter of living in a house it felt like adventure and freedom. There is something exciting about a tent. A sense of impermanence, as though one weren't committed to this forever. The closeness of air and sky and ground – all the outer world. In a tent one has the delight of camping in the open beside a fire, plus the thrill of being hidden in a cave.

The reindeer-camp children hung around so hungrily, in their eagerness to learn to read and do sums, that I rang the school bell – or rather beat on the frying pan with a stick – as soon as we had had breakfast and Farrar had gone out to the herding. The children sat flat on the snow outside the little tent, and I on a sack of coal. I wore sun-glasses but they didn't seem to mind the snow. We had few books – only those that could be spared from Gambel – but it seemed riches to them.

We read and wrote and sang, and I told them stories, made up on the spot, about the things they knew. Once upon a time there was a young seal that decided it would [128] rather be a little

Eskimo boy than a seal and so it went off to school to learn how it could be done ... on and on, not knowing where the next word would lead, the children motionless as long as I kept going. Never was there a jollier school, or pupils so eager to learn – or a teacher gladder when the term ended. For they nearly exhausted me that month.

In the spring the women have their inning. With the children they go to the "woods" to gather bitter tonic willow bark from the roots of the six-inch high shrubs that grow wherever there is soil. Later in the summer they gather the boot grass, too. And with their families they go to the lakes and streams to scoop up hordes of spawning salmon to be dried for their dogs the next winter.

Spring is walrus-hunting time. All winter long, occasional herds of walrus are watched as they move slowly up or down on the currents, dark masses on the white ice floes. But even during semi-starvation, the Eskimos dare not go out to hunt them so far from shore. A sudden wind might come up, break off the floor of ice on which the hunter travels, and sweep him to Japan. That happened to Athelingok's father once. Before he got there he had 1 eaten everything he had along with him, even the dog harness. And he is not sure it was Japan he reached. All he knows is that it was a long way south, and that, three years later, when he was again out hunting off the shore of his new home, he was blown away once more – northwards this time – and actually landed on St Lawrence Island. He lived many years to tell that unbelievable tale. [129]

But when the boat channels are safely open and the calm weather has come, how quickly the hunters get under way! All over the Island, men get out their outboard motors and prime them for the start with ether.

"Suppose see walrus this day, we hunt," Sepillu said one morning while we were at breakfast in the tent.

Out over the sea, long ribbons of blue wound about among the ice floes. No wind threatened. It was ideal walrus-hunting weather. Men stood on their roofs and searched the ice fields with their long spyglasses.

"Ievuk! Ievuk!" they said after awhile. "Walrus! walrus!"

They had sighted a big herd. Everyone hurried into winter clothes again, for it would be cold out in the boats with ice all around.

Eight or ten of us equipped with big thirty-thirties piled into Sepillu's whaleboat. The outboard was attached and off we sputtered, the noise shattering the winter-long silence.

The herd was miles away. In and out of cul-de-sac channels we wound, finally approaching so close to the herd that engines must be shut off and paddles broken out. Silently, then, we crept up on it, approaching on the lea.

At first the brown beasts had been a thin dark line on the ice floe. Then they were black hummocks. Now they began to stir, to lift their two-tined, clam-digging heads. They were very mountains of flesh. "You shoot first walrus, Nanook," the Eskimos urged Farrar. [130]

He protested he might miss and cause them to lose all the walrus. But our polite hosts insisted. Farrar stood up in the boat and aimed a gun that all but had buck fever. The gun roared. A half-dozen Eskimo guns echoed it.

A dozen walrus slipped off the ice into the blue water and we saw them no more. Two great wounded fellows thrashed about, making a red sea around them, roaring out defiance. They were dangerous. Shots rang out to silence them.

We turned, then, to the kill. Nine dark forms, some as big as draft horses, one a baby walrus, lay on the bloody ice. Sepillu pointed out the biggest one as Farrar's kill and laughed in delight at Nanook's prowess.

Now to the butchering. It is impossible to take back all this meat. The heads are saved for the tusks, the pair of baby tusks given to us. The guts are piled out in a huge mass, stripped of their contents and loaded in the boats to be further cleaned in the village and made into raincoats. The stomachs are carefully felt for clams, and those that have them put into the boats. The skins are hacked and ripped off for houses, boats, ropes, harness. Livers and hearts are saved and as much of the tons and tons of flesh as we can pile into the boats.

We had a tea-party there on the iceberg. The butchering took hours. We had all brought lunches. At noon, Sepillu got out the ubiquitous primus stove, boiled some snow cut from the top of the ice floe and made tea. We ate and drank sitting on carcasses and ice hummocks.

When we left the floe, the sun was swinging down over

Siberia. We traveled in its glittering path all the way back [131] and I saw setting suns in my eyes for days afterwards. The whole village met us at the shore. That is one of the things I like best about the Eskimos – they make a celebration of everything.

In those days, the great event of the spring was the coming of the trader, usually in early June. One day, shortly after the close of school, we saw a flock of children running toward our house. Something had happened. We ran out to meet them.

"Pederson come! Pederson come!" they said, pointing out to sea where, tangled up with icebergs, the masts of a ship could be seen. Already dog-sleds had been harnessed and were skimming down the worn trail toward the beach. People were streaming out of the houses, some of them plopping down on the sleds as they shot off, some running in their clumsy boots. We joined the crowd flowing toward the big ship.

Over the ice blocks, through puddles of slush, around icebergs, along fairly good trails over level ice, Farrar and I hurried. The ship was jammed up against the shore-ice so that we could walk to the foot of the ladder against her side and climb aboard.

Pederson had been coming here for years from a house in San Francisco. He was on his way to Point Barrow where the year before he had married the station's nurse. She was with him now. Farrar and I stayed for lunch on shipboard – a lunch of canned foods, prepared by one of those inevitable oriental cooks favored by ships' captains but not by us. After a winter of fresh reindeer and our [132] own hand-ground wheat bread, we were spoiled. But the captain was so solicitous of what he believed to be our semi-starved condition that we had to pretend we thought it a feast.

After lunch we watched the trading. The natives swarmed all over the boat, fingering things, delaying trading for very joy of the business. They loved Pederson, for though he was canny he dealt more fairly with them than other traders had done. And he was genial and friendly. He brought them the best of trade goods, too, not trying to palm off cheap tea or guns on them. He respected their desire for oh-plenty-fine-thing.

Then, too, since Mr Lopp had set up the government cooperative stores the natives had discovered what standard prices were, so if they were willing to sacrifice something in every deal for the fun of trading on shipboard, Farrar thought they were justified in the name of romance and adventure. Nowadays, the natives have both the romance of trading aboard and the security of not being cheated, for the government Bureau of Education ship takes things up to them.

Pederson stayed three days. By that time the dog-sleds had worn a sloppy brown path over the ice to the ship. The Doctor offered the captain five thousand dollars to set him and the Russian across on the Asiatic shore and was refused. And one morning early, the ship slipped away from its ice-moorings and glided off through the dark green channels to the North. Nearly three hundred persons stood on the pale green ice banks and watched it go. [133]

That very day the Doctor and the Russian began to load their whaleboat which they had hired for their trip on to Siberia. Cans of gasoline, boxes of food, bundles of garments, trade goods which they had got from Pederson who had changed another of the thousand-dollar bills – everything was easily stowed away in the big open boat. The Doctor covered everything with canvas. His Eskimos were ready. They left next morning.

Earlier in the spring the Doctor had offered to pay our way to Russia and clean on around the world, back through New York and on to Puget Sound, if we would only go with him across that fearful Bering Sea, with Farrar navigating the boat. The Doctor wasn't afraid. But he was in earnest about his mission and wanted to make sure that he got there. He felt that Farrar, just out of the Navy, would take care of that, and that if he and the Russian undertook it alone they might come to grief again.

We were tempted by his offer. But it was an illegal venture and we were taking government pay. Moreover, we wanted to start our family, because it seemed a shame not to wait for the children so they could enjoy our adventures, too.

On the one side lay danger and uncertainty and, perhaps, loss of standing with the government, but it was tempting. On the other lay safety, legality, security, our first child. Farrar tossed a coin. Heads, we'd stay safely in America and start the family; tails, we'd go to Russia and maybe never see America again. Luckily, the coin came up heads. If it hadn't, though, I expect Farrar would have kept pitching until it did. [134]

On St Lawrence Island, people announce a new addition to their family as soon as they are sure of pregnancy. By the time we had come back from Reindeer Camp, we were sure that our first-born was on its way and had proudly made the announcement. Everybody was greatly excited, and I felt like some kind of sacred cow. Women would come up and say, "Patsarok got baby inside. Fi-i-ne!"

I like that custom. Somehow your child seems more real to you, acknowledged and talked about like that. To the poor Doctor, the baby spelled the doom of his hopes. He took it gracefully enough. But from that time his restlessness increased. He was all for starting right away. Farrar had difficulty in persuading him to wait for a time when the ice was more nearly gone and there was less danger of getting cracked between floes in a sudden wind. Now, that time had come.

It was a calm sunburst of a day, the light from the ice splintering off in our eyes, when he finally left. How near the bluffs of Siberia – surely not more than an hour's paddle away!

At last everything was ready. The Eskimos pushed the boat into the water. They primed the outboard motor. It would start at the first turn. The immensely tall, lean Doctor shook hands with all of us and stepped in. The stocky, short Russian followed. We pushed them out into the channel. The sputtering roar of the outboard was their final word as they moved swiftly out along the winding blue passage toward Russia. When the Eskimos returned, they brought us a pitiful little note[29] that said, "When you [135] see the face of the world change, you will know that I have accomplished my mission."

Poor Doctor – kind and humorous, strange and a little befuddled. A year later we heard that the young Russian, who had been so eager to return to the land where everything was now for men like him, had been killed by the Bolsheviki; that the Doctor had been robbed of his money and sent back home, broken and defeated.

Now, our good Doctor and the silent Russian were gone. School was out. Our reports were all written. Farrar and I had compiled a sort of census-taker's survey of the Island, listing every inhabitant and describing him fully with all relevant matter concerning him. He had written down the Eskimo names for things, the stories we had heard. We had set down all the legends and

---

[29] See p235 for the full note on a tiny notebook page.

superstitions and rites we could persuade them to tell us. We had given the schoolhouse a final cleaning, made out the order for books, medicines, store supplies for the following year, and were waiting for the Bear to come and get us, to take us back to Nome.

Then good old Sepillu arrived from Reindeer Camp to tell us that the men from there were going to Nome in Sepillu's whaleboat and we could go with them if we liked. Go a hundred and fifty miles between ice floes in a thirty-foot boat, with a wind as likely as not to come up and crush us like an egg shell? We didn't hesitate. It might be a month before the Bear arrived, and we had had enough of that ship. The old Prospector was going back on the Bear and we had had enough of him, too.

We had set our hearts on the baby being born on [136] Sentinel; we didn't want to stay on St Lawrence Island another year. We hurried our packing. Willing Eskimos – their hands out for parting gifts – took our bundles and ran with them out to Sepillu's tiny boat, invisible from shore behind the ice blocks. Trunks, boxes, bedding, suitcases went off on sleds or backs, and we followed.

No wind blew. The ice lay in great, still, broken fields over the sea, leaving winding channels between the floes. Sepillu steered his boat back to Reindeer Camp to pick up the rest of the party and then straight east to Nome, on a gamble that for two days the wind would not come up.

As we rounded a point below the highest mountain on St Lawrence, Sepillu told us that the Eskimos used to worship up there. He said there was a perfect, three-tusk walrus head there – one of their old objects of worship. Farrar offered him twenty-five dollars to get it for us. Sepillu ordered the anchor overboard and set off with one companion up the mountain. After what seemed hours, they returned bearing the huge head with three, long, perfect tusks. It can now be seen in Dr Hornaday's famous collection of heads at the Bronx Zoo. It is, he told us, the most perfect three-tusker he ever saw, perhaps the most perfect one in existence.

We were off again – thirteen of us. There were no sleeping accommodations, no conveniences of any kind. We sat or half-lay on bales of reindeer skins. The men took turns atop the dinky little mast looking out for open channels, but even so we had to back up and try again, time after time. We stopped for lunch on an ice floe, got out to [137] stretch our legs, made tea on the primus stove, and thoroughly enjoyed ourselves.

The Punuk Islands lie not far off the eastern end of St Lawrence. They are famous for the enormous flocks of waterfowl that nest there. Sepillu wanted to stop and gather bird eggs for dinner. We went ashore on the long beach of the largest island and Eskimos began running up and down the beach like wild things, stooping down every now and then to pick up something.

Sepillu alone behaved with his usual dignity and restraint. He said the men were gathering old ivory. "Sea wash him up all winter. You look, too," he bade us, and we did. And there on that beach we found a gunny sackful of rare treasure which the Smithsonian Institution later pronounced to be prehistoric ivory. There was a half tusk of solid black – the rarest piece we ever saw. One fine whole tusk of a rich deep rusty rose. We found blunt, broken tusks of beautiful amber, one tiny point of a baby walrus tusk, yellow as gold all through.

When we had picked up all the ivory that showed itself above the water line, the men turned their attention to egg gathering, and soon they were scattered all over the perpendicular bluff, holding on to inch-wide ledges.

It was supper time before we left Punuk. We broke out the primus stove again and scrambled two or three dozen of the white shag eggs, as good as hens' eggs ever were, and ate them with hard-tack and tea.

Now to sea again, the sun still riding high. At midnight it took its brief dip, rose again a foot or so away, the sky a radiant yellow all around it. We were going east. But [138] the sun had gone down straight in front of us and was still in front of us when it came up again.

It was early morning, and the sun was straight overhead, when we left the ice and went galloping out into open choppy water off the mainland. Fifty miles of this. And now for seasickness. I kept my head low against the hides and was completely miserable all day until the man on the mast called out, "Land ho!"

We had made it. Cramped, weary, and nauseated, we went ashore on the bleak beach of Nome and not long afterwards took passage for the Outside.

Three-Tusked Walrus Skull
Information Pertaining To

1 It was found on St Lawrence Island, Alaska
2 St Lawrence Island is about 120 nautical miles south of Bering Strait. 120 miles west of Alaska Mainland and 40 miles east of Siberia.
3 St Lawrence Island is a government reindeer reserve
4 Three hundred Eskimos live on St Lawrence Island
5 No white people live there excepting government representatives
6 The natives are of the Siberian Eskimo stock
7 The three tusked skill was taken from the top of a hill where it had been placed many years ago according to Sepillu the chief reindeer herder.
8 The old people were very superstitious abut it he said and used to worship it
9 Many of the present natives were superstitious about it
10 They supposed it was possessed by the devil or something of that nature
11 Sepillu said that he did not know when it was killed
12 Sepillu is the least superstitious native I came in contact with
13 He did not appear to regard the head with awe
14 I think the skull to the National Museum in Washington, DC, several weeks ago
15 It remained there for several days in the office of Dr Merrill
16 Several scientist saw it there
17 None of them had ever seen nor heard of a specimen of its kind
18 I believe they came to the conclusion that it is a freak of nature
19 I brought the head to New York a few days ago
20 Dr Kuntz of Tiffany's put me in touch with Dr Honaday of the New York Zoological Society
21 Dr Honaday purchased it from me for the collection of Heads & Horns at the New York Zoological Society

FIRST IMPRESSIONS OF THE ESKIMOS

Of course, the <u>very</u> first impression I had of the Eskimo was one of a disagreeable odor. An odor of urine tanned skins sweating bodies, unwashed hair, wet cotton over parkas, stiff with dirt. Filth and an odor. But so adaptable has kindly nature made the nose of the human, at leas of the Americas, that I merely remember that a few days ago something smelled unpleasant. It is no longer noticeable even when I crowd with many Eskimos in a skin house.

The next impression I can recall from the dim past of a few weeks ago is one of simple kindliness and cordiality. That is remarkable because I had been repeatedly warned to go slowly with the Eskimo and to watch him. That he was slick, shrewd, untruthful. I was on guard against being taken in. and folks usually find what they expect. It may be, tho, that down underneath the fortifications lay a deeper desire to find them simple, kindly, friendly. Anyhow, that is what we have found. The first thing that happened to us that was pleasant on our long, tiresome, nerve wracking voyage here, was he finding of an Eskimo down in the hold of the ship, repairing a broken box of or freight which careless white men had left to the rats. [1b]

When out ship finally landed us here on St Lawrence Island, with what tact and thotfulness did the swarming, eager, curious natives restrain themselves from pressing upon us. It could not have been learned politeness. It was that instructive culture of unspoiled children. Tho goodness knows the Eskimo is not unspoiled.
One man, who came aboard our ship before we were off, instantly offered us his "lumber" house where his family was then living. It is true he did it for pay, but no word was said about price. His wife and other women cheerfully began moving when we arrived and by nightfall the empty odorous house was ours. Another and another came to offer their ~ his services. Out of curiosity to see us, and a desire to insinuate themselves into our favor but what white man would have come at all? Perhaps that is not fair. A white man in so isolated a country would do the same and without thot of pay or obligation, and so I am sure would the Eskimos in the days before

notes

the traders. But they are so much more naïve, direct, childlike in their offers and curiosity that somehow one likes it better than the same article "outside"

Of course, it is very early to say "The Eskimo is so" but it is good to say what I think now and learn how I change. I think, however, we have chanced to land in a nest of exceptionally unspoiled natives. They live far from the settlement. Boats land here but seldom. They work or starve and have not learned the ugliness which the Gambell people know. So here goes for generalization to my heart's content. Perhaps I deny them all some day, but first impressions are as important as last ones and who knows [2a] But that they are true? Sine time may render on indifferent to some qualities and sharply sensitive of others, only medium between the two ends cold give a true picture.

Well then: the Eskimos are naturally cooperative. I have never seen really cooperative people before. If an Eskimo needs a new boat, he and all the men around who are not engaged in anything else, set to building one of walrus skins tied with seal skin ropes onto a frame made of what tough pieces of wood they can find on the beaches. If one man is a good hunter and catches many seals for his winter use, all his brothers and in-laws and relatives and friends may share with him. The families here on this island scatter about over the 1600 square miles along the water front, some of them killing much food, trapping many fox, digging much ivory and carving it, others "sitting" and eating from the plentiful stores of the workers, nobody reproving the lazy ones. The Bureau of Education has established a cooperative store on the island which can be made to do much good to the natives if one good man would be allowed to stay long enough to get it out of debt and actually to paying dividends. That store is a source of much fun to us to see how the Eskimos think of it. We asked one of the most intelligent men if all the families trade with the story. He said No, only some of them. Others too poor. We then asked if the poor ones lived without bread and sugar as the Eskimos did long time ago. He replied simply that the poor ones get them others.

The spirit of cooperation extends only among themselves, however. The store is an alien to be got the best of, if possible. No matter how much they like the teacher, he also is an alien against whom they all unconsciously combine. Not to [2b blank] [3a] harm

notes

him nor even deliberately to cheat him but certainly to get as much from him as possible. Is he not a white man from the government which is so rich and give so much to the Eskimo? I do not know how the think of the teachers and the government, but I have a sneaking suspicion that they take us rather too much for granted as their just dues. They have no idea of our word "obligations." Eskimo psychology is "different." To make a simple class of whites such as remote mountaineers appreciate and care for any gift, make them pay for it in the way they will feel most. I can not think how to make the Eskimo properly appreciate & feel some obligations to the government for a school teachers, help, a store, and medical aid. Do not misunderstand me. I have no pious idea of gratitude for the sake of the government or teachers or the overzealous missionary, only for the Eskimo himself. He is being spoiled. Spoiled. It is a shame.

Many would be cynics and nature worshiper have said to me "The government is spoiling them. It ought to get out and let them alone. Why, when I was up here 30 years ago, they were healthy, happy, and increasing. Now they are tubercular, syphilitic paupers." They are right partly and wrong mostly. The crux of the matter is in that misused little statement, "When I was up her 30 years ago." That is just it. They and others were up here many years ago trading, exploiting the wholly unprotected natives. They brot white man's diseases, foolishly introduced white man's food, wickedly planted the idea of white man's superiority, grew fat and rich in the process and now because the Eskimo in imitation of the white men whom he knows, has become less [3b] Gullible, more shrewd, suspicious, untruthful, believing in the great high gospel of buying for little and selling for much, they scoff at a "sentimental" government for pampering a happy, work loving people into pauperism. I agree heartily with them that the chief duty of the US government to the Eskimos is to leave them alone. But under one condition. That traders and missionaries and scientists and prospectors and adventurers and all manner of white men also be forever banished from their country. So long as the lowest type of white men come with their venereal diseases and their white plague, so long as smarter, perhaps cleaver [clever], white men come for their furs and ivory and the gold in their land, so long also is the government of the country which bought with money the Eskimo's land – bound by all that is human and decent to sent counteracting influences to a helpless people. It is all a tremendous mistake, this gobbling up of the simpler races by the shrewder white race. How infinitely stupid would be a world wholly commercial, wholly "efficient," wholly controlled and governed by that divinely superior creature – the white man! How too bad to think that the isolate people are disappearing as has the American Indian.

But I can not forecast a future for the Eskimo. When I think of the far future at all and of the corrupting and exterminating of the Indian in our own country, and of how unequal is the struggle for existence between the Eskimo and the effect of white man's food and diseases and customs and ideas, I am overwhelmed with a feeling of the unworthiness of any effort. The birth rate runs a losing race with the death rate. The greedy whiles are upon them. Let them alone. It is a losing fight. Then I look out a tiny four-paned window of my shack and I see two women dressing a seal each, two tiny boys keeping off the dogs, a larger boy running here and there bringing empty vessels [4a] and taking away vessels filled with seal feet, hearts & entrails, dark red seal meat, white seal fat, and a horrible bloody head. One man splitting into two lines a long ¼ inch thick walrus skin rope, another man starting off to hunt, his gun strung over his shoulder by a walrus skin rope, yet another man arriving on the run with his dogs and sled, and to more "young big seals" or young mukluk, little girls and women inside the house, working, working, and I love them and want them to live and never to grow dependent on money which is the worst form of pauperism and never to go the way of the Indian. Effort seems more worthwhile. Instruction, medical relief, visiting among them, health talks everything becomes important and worth trying.

But I set out to talk about the Eskimo as I see him now and not my relation to him.

He is naturally kind and thotful. He is always so to his own kind and knows very soon which white man he will trust and favor. He takes a mild but permanent dislike to any white man who promises & does not fulfill, who seems to favor a well fixed Eskimo ahead of the poor (or lazy) one, but although he will beat anybody in a trade, he will be a mild and permanent friend to one who keeps his promises. There is a certain trader who comes up here every year from San Francisco whom the natives like exceedingly. "Oh, veeeery good man. He speak Eskimo, bring stove, he bring. Very good man." The natives reward this man's faithfulness with the best they have, and from all I hear, he is equally fair with them. But the kindness of a man is measured by his thot for those of his own kind and in [4b] his regard for his fellow the Eskimo is surely unexcelled. He is kind to his children, never shouting to them, nor shooing them from under his feet. Indeed, The Eskimo children so early become men and women in their work because the grownup so tolerantly allow them to hang around under foot doing whatever they can to help. Nobody ever hurried so it does not matter that the child is a mite slower than his father in accomplishing his task.

There is a crippled child at this camp. His back was broken in play two years ago. It is charming to see the patience and pleasant care with which every person treat little Oobistak, and to see the cheerfulness of him all day long. Every morning I inquire of him. He always replies with the one word "better". On sunny days or every day, when the wind is not sharp, someone gathers him up and take him outside to his sled where he sits all day a sort of center of everything. This morning Iwurrigan, his father, stretched a walrus skin line from one house to another and laboriously split it in two. Oobistak sat out with him. Whenever Iwurrigan progressed a few feet beyond the boy, he stopped and brought his son up with him. He kept it up all morning, the two talking in the Eskimo's extremely low tones about goodness knows what. Whenever visitors come, which is all the time, just now upon the arrival of the supplies at his place, every man spends much time with the little crippled child. Whether he does it thotfully or because Oobistak is actually more intelligent than most of the grown men and therefore interesting to talk with, I have no idea. Whenever Oobistak speaks, all listen.

The men and women seem much attached to each other, also, [4b] occasionally giving an impulsive caress. Our "brother," Oktokiyuk, as he calls himself, is more than usually fond of his wife and family. His wife, little Atonga, is the prettiest, smartest woman we have seen, a wife and happy worker, quiet, cleaner, than most, and as appealing as a baby. I have seen Oktokiyuk suddenly put his hand to her hair and say "little Edna". He knows whenever she is doing something in my house of which he proud. Once he touched her like that with some Eskimo phrase. I asked what he said. He replies, "I speak, my wife, my little wife." It is true that the women work very hard but the work they do seems to fall so naturally to them that even I, arch feminist, can find no fault. The men do not sit idly around while their women work, nor do they "boss" their wives. They take the initiative in outside matters but the opinion of the women seems to be valued highly. Indeed, they are smarter. As, perhaps, nature intended they should be, since they are the mothers and first teachers. They have stores of philosophy and advice which their husband proudly translate to me on occasions. A man & his wife were in here one day "visiting." They were telling me how very, very much they love us, when the woman, who speaks no English, broke out in a long speech, her husband translating. It amounted to this: "Some teachers come. Lover very much three days. Maybe seven days. After that no love all the time." I reminded that it was pretty early to be professing love for me in as much as I had been her only seven days myself! They saw they had trapped themselves. They made many quick words and left me quite satisfied. As Farrar says, it is gladsome to be told you are loved even it is just taffy.

I have not learned just what ceremony is gone thru when the Eskimos marry, but I do observe that they are as much married as anybody. There is a shortage of women on St Lawrence Island so that, no matter what his instincts, each man can have only one wife. So that the law of the country to which the Eskimo has be brought is fulfilled. What more have we the right to demand? How silly, almost nasty, to come flaunting papers and licenses and especially "qualified" men to marry Eskimo boys and girls. If a man goes to another's house, asks for a girl, takes her home with him, and makes a home with her, the spirit of every marriage law under the sun is fulfilled. There was a funny Captain on one of the Coast Guard ships on which we spent some time who is licensed to marry natives. He described one of his ceremonies to us. He naively said that the certificate part of it to comply with the law was the only part that mattered so he thot and decided to have some fun. He gathered his crew around so as to have an admiring audience, took a Sears & Roebuck catalog, announced as text "It is a wise rooster who knows his own chickens" and proceeded to discourse on married life in the old state, supposedly funny manner, ending with a toast of imitation beer all around. He thot it very funny and we thot it perfectly harmless, but I did not know in what that lawful ceremony was superior to the native's own.

There is one man on the island with two wives. The women age fast and die young. His first wife had grown old and no doubt ugly, so he took himself a young one like unto Jacob. But they say he is the most henpecked man on the [5a] face of the globe. The old wife running the household completely. Dominating both her husband and her successor. The natives think it a great joke and despise him in their mild, friendly fashion, which is more punishment than jails. On account of the scarcity of women, he is considered greedy.

Girl babies are welcomed most heartily here, naturally, and a man says "my daughter" in the same low, proud tones one of another race would say "my son". How his eyes shine when he tells you that his new baby is a little girl. It is too bad they let their women work themselves old so fast. Every man ^of all races^ could outlive two wives if he worked outside and she inside all the time. Nature seems to have made a slip somehow when she started out the human race or else humans began early to violate her laws. By and by, I fix, as Oktokiyuk says when I need anything in my shack [done].

The Eskimo is not kind to his dogs in any thotful fashion. He gives them food and rest as scrimpily as possible and looks upon them in much the same way as he regards seals for his food – simply part of his life and nothing more. He takes very little pride in his dogs, building them no shelters, taking no thot in their comfort. I thot when I heard another say the native is unkind to animals that I should be hurt to see his neglect, but somehow I am not. Everything seems so to dovetail together that to change or upset any existing custom would involve so much change that one shrinks from attempting it. The means, however, to study the dogs and see if the Eskimo would not be served better if he took more thot of them & their food & breeding & houses. Such puny, scrawny, expressionless curs as they do drive! A great man riding 40 miles in the day, behind 3, 5, 7 scrawny dogs! [5b] However, in that as in all other things the Eskimos resemble us. In a rocky hilly farming country, where living is as difficult as it is up her, most of the animals are thin, rawboned, unhappy looking creatures while one man, the most progressive and heartiest usually will have sleek horses , clean cows, and fat hogs. Oktokiyuk the Eskimo in whose house we live, who seems the good Samaritan of the island, has twenty fat, large, swift dogs. He builds snow house for them in the bitterest weather and he feeds them more than the winter ration of a fish a day. Still, even his dogs are not what they might be with intelligent care. How hungrily they all gather around a seal when one is sleded up from the beach to suck blood that drips from the seal's mouth. How persistently they hang around while Atonga or Yahonga are dressing the seal, crowding up to steal a lick whenever she turns her back to sharpen her big knife on a smooth black rock or for any other reason. One of the, an ill-natured black mongrel, sits whining most of the time from a kick delivered or merely casually aimed in his direction. A red brown slut keeps him company. They secure but few stolen morsels. Most of these dogs, however, bear pain, abuse, cold, hunger, and weariness in absolute silence. There is not even the barking for joy that one hears from "civilized" dogs. No tail wagging. Only sometimes a chorus of peculiar songs and moans when the whiff of a new set of dogs is caught from the trail over the hill. Then every dog, no matter how he may be engaged, sits up, lifts his head, opens his mouth [6a] and "sings" each his own tune. Nor do the mouths close until the newcomers are near enough to be met, when every dog bounds up the hill and escorts the visitors down to the camp with yelping & trembling and fighting and such great confusions that the lone man on the sled is completely lost sight of. He reaches out with his whip, but there are times in the experience all dogs & men when those commands to which we indulgently obey usually are not longer of ay interest or consequence to us. Victory after war with Germany for instance and the arrival of seven dog friends from Gambell forty five miles away! But the lone man triumphs at last. When the dogs abruptly stop and he gets out to take off the harness, every dog fellow becomes quiet until that is done and when all are loosened the crowd disperses in little friendly groups of twos or threes and an occasional lone dog, too tired to play, for all the world like boys.

The Eskimos are as smart as they be, learning English words much more easily than I can learn theirs, quickly taking up little customs of the white man, some of them instantly catching up a mechanical idea and correctly executing it. Oktokiyuk wanted a "lumber" house. He says, "I think more better I go Nome. Bynby ship come.

notes

I go. All time I watch house in Nome. Measure too. Roof, side, everything. Little house just like this one. Then I come home. I make one." It is well made, too. Double walls. Staunchly built throughout with four tiny nailed in windows, a storm shed and a hole in the roof for ventilation, that hole [6b] is not despised either. From somewhere, cracks around doors & windows & in walls, so strong a current of wind travels thru & up that ventilating pipe as almost to suck one's hand up. There are two quaint "closets" in the back of the room consisting of a lower portion entered by two small doors & two upper open arched affairs, a little on the idea of ships bunk. They are too short for us, but might have been meant for Eskimo beds. Anyhow they are ingenious. Oktokiyuk is full of clever ideas from a lid for my water bucket to managing people. All of them are quick to catch changed of moods, openings, and so wide and free if they think one is wholly in sympathy, closing so swiftly if one shows the slightest sign of disapproval or lack of sympathy.

They are smart traders, too. They assume so innocent and helpless an expression when they present their articles of trade, shrewdly putting on a childlike appearance if expecting praise and appreciations, that no person not born a heartless trader can coldly examine the article for possible flaws. He can only explain & admire – and pay the extra price his admiration has added! On the other hand, they examine with the minutest care every smallest article they contemplate buying. Not by words or many protestations, such as Jewish or American traders use to overwhelm their victims, but by mute turning over & over a garment or a gun silently pointing out flaws, do they shame you that you perpetuate so worthless an article on the helpless Eskimo! [7a]

It is not a studied shrewdness. That is to say, they have no books on "The Psychology of Trading," nor does a sale manager, meaning a head of a house, gather his young aspirants around him and discourse on "selling points" , "getting a hearing" and so on. But it is a <u>learned</u> shrewdness. Each man has learned, for himself, that the skilled white trader can get anything from him for valueless articles. He observes how he himself is separated from a fox skin or an old ivory chain with only a few yards of red striped calico, a few pounds of cube sugar, a package of tea, and some candy & chewing gum pile together loose in a sack or a box to bring home in place of the skin and ivory. It therefore behooves him to turn the trick on the next person who come his way. It evens things up for him. And that next person happens to be not only a profoundly unskilled trader, but also a philosopher who observes the double process and is therefore bound in the interest of poetic justice to be a willing victim. The Eskimo comes out rather on top in the long run.

Shortly after we landed, people from the village of Gambell, forty five miles away, began coming for supplies from the store. One old woman, Popogak came along to ostensibly visit her daughter who lives here at Southwest Cape, really to see the new teachers and to do a little petty trading. She came down to our shack immediately upon arrival. She could speak no word of English, so she merely sat on a bog and "looked" until I had someone tell her we wanted to have our own dinner. We had evidently looked like good game, for in the afternoon, she returned with an old sack in her hand. I was afraid she had come to beg, for that is a problem up here, but when I found some [7b] one to interpret, she dug up a tiny, soiled par of slipper with no claim to beauty, saying that a little girl had made them & wanted to sell them to me. The little girl part of it was sheer trade-lying, I am sure. I made a joke about their size and the size of my feet and sent her off laughing on her face but cursing in her shrewd old heart, I'll be bound.

Shortly after that, a boy came down wanting to show us some of his father's ivory carvings, which he had brot from Gambell. Father very old. Hoped we would buy. Our endless harangue on our mission up here, that it was to teach the Eskimos to make prettier things and to sell more wisely and not to buy for ourselves – evidently ended the procession of which they two formed the head, for nobody else has been her with anything to trade. I am no end glad, for every encounter is a stain on our huge store on yielding propensities.

While the Coast Guard Cutter stole every opportunity to run up the hill to trade, I saw Yahonga, a charming little chatterbox wife of Iwurrigan "next door," exchange a lousy, worn birdskin parka for then good dollars, a few bits of old ivory worth very little, for cash and expensive jack knives. I saw her scornfully refuse some of the offers of the sailors who came out losers every time. On board the ship, officers were buying seal skins from the Eskimo men in more than the market price more than they could have bought identical skins in Seattle.

notes

There is something about trading on board a ship that intoxicates white & Eskimo alike. The white pays too much for the Eskimo things. The Eskimo accepts in payment worthless nothing that catches his eye. They come out even, perhaps, after all. Only the hardened trader grows rich at that game. And I think he grows rich more & more slowly as the Eskimo "catches on." [8a]

The Eskimo is both a Philosopher and a keen judge of people. He can tell in words very little of this impressions of persons. That some on promised a rifle and no bring. That another sweat and get mad. That another talk oh [too] much. But by watching him, one can see how correctly he has estimated the white man's nature and how incorrectly and shrewdly he trades on this nature. Of course, when one writes or reads of the characteristics in unfamiliar people, one is like to regard all as strange and alien and to be remarked. One should remember every sentence or so, to look inside and find kindred qualities. A homogeneous race, such as the Eskimo ,, has kindly stayed in one part of the world, living in one unchanging fashion so that it is easy to pigeon hole characteristics, but even in our conglomerate America, every one of those "Eskimo" qualities, can be found by the mere act of looking inside or, at lest, close about. For instance, by a quarter of a century's experience, the Eskimo has learned that the white man's friendship can soonest be earned by allowing the white man to "help" him. Not a ship nor a teacher nor any white man of consequence comes about but that the Eskimos swarm around to be "doctored". They have had coughs, usually, since experience has taught them that cough medicine is pleasantest to take, and they give generous demonstrations. Whereupon to ship's doctors, or whoever the "good" man may be, takes them all to his stateroom, doctors them heartily, sends labeled boxes full of cough drops & aspirin and cathartic pills ashore with them. But more to the point, this good white man, no matter how he deplores the "spoiling of the natives" nor how he exalts nature's slow processes, has put out his hand to help the poor natives. Shall it stop with medicine? Has he not lockers bursting with sweaters and [8b] wristlets and helmets and mufflers and mittens and socks which to generous (over stocked) Red Cross has sent to the poor natives? He takes out huge bundles of these futile white man's garments to send to the skin clad Eskimos, who joyfully & curiously put them on over three skin parkas & hoods & parade a little while and then forget about it. But what is the point. The doctor's hand was opened by service. He over did it which is exactly what that smart Irrogoo meant he should do. Besides that, except for the pills actually taken in the doctor's preserve, no medicine will be used which is one blessing, anyhow.

In the same manner, they come to me for medicine and I confess I feel all glowing and sort of worthwhile to be sending argyrole to Nunreelas's wife, whose eyes are sore and phenantine to Sikwaka's mother with the rheumatism and headache and vomiting and cough and goodness knows what else. I do not stop with medicine, either. I corner Mr Eskimo and talk & talk & talk to him about his TB and his syphilis and his influenza. I tell him the many things a white man would do if he were sick like that and the very few precaution which it is possible for the Eskimo to take and I warn him to work very hard at those few getting well jobs since he can't do the others. In fact, I talk till I have repeated all I have learned from that invaluable Public Health book when I unbar the door and let the weary fellow escape. He has left with me more germs of disease than all the medicines of my slender stock could kill for him in a thousand years. Last night I found a cootie in Farrar's neck!

Now I call that pretty smart. Farrar reminds me that it the same thing a white merchant does when he goes to church and professes religion for the sake of the preacher's trade or when a criminal gets converted to keep out of jail by the preacher intervention and so on.

When the "Reindeer Boys," men who own and herd reindeer on St Lawrence, were in Nome, they made some sort of an appeal to the Lomen druggists there for medicine. Coughs and a long list of ailments. The Lomen bros were members of the group who had brot reindeer from these boys so naturally felt some interest in them. The idea of their being over here without a doctor or any medical aid! They made up a drug kit to send to the camp. A generous one according to Periyuh, one of the herders. When we arrived, we learned that there was an excellent doctor marooned on our island, who had been giving medical aid all summer and ho had the government's supply of drugs at Gambell as well as his own to draw from. Furthermore, this same Periyuh was one of the first to come to me for medicine! They have the "getting uplifted" bug very badly. More & sterner teaching and less giving would cure more consumption. For the sake of their health and their morale and their hope of any independence at all in the next generations, they should be required to pay for medical aid. The money could be turned back into their own pockets indirectly, but they should be made to pay, even tho it is undeniable right that a white man's government should give a thousand times more freely to them to cure white man's diseases among them. A pitiful teacher her and there knowing too little and caring less about their permanent [9a] wellbeing, a skeptical doctor on a seldom seen government boat to dole out pills with no explanations nor, to him, troublesome teaching is too little. Unless, of course, we have scientifically decided that the Eskimo is a dying people, destined to die and that our job is to ease the death pangs, and our delicate consciences, there should be an extensive health campaign carried on up her backed, not by twenty five thousand poor dollars, but by as many hundreds of thousands. Such a campaign as Gorgas carried out in Panama in the Canal Zone. How stingy we are in some things.

I think the Eskimos are exceedingly pretty. Some of the women. And he men are strong, well built, shapely. Their bodies, in spite of the straight meat diet, are "healthy" looking, smooth and shining. They sleep naked. I often see the little square doorlet of Iwurirgan's house where two families of five members each, an extra old man and just now, one of the marooned white man, live to say good night or to go in and chat a minute. If it is after dark, I always find seven or eight heads and glistening shoulder stuck out from under the heavy skin curtain that surround the sleeping room. Sometimes, Atonga will hand up her beautiful naked baby to me. It is hard to resist this temptation to kiss its little unwashed arms and legs and dimpled shoulder. If I had that child now and could rear it, what a ravishing would she would make! Great brown eyes, glassy black hair, firm brown skin, and tiny Eskimo hands and feet. Little Matiktuk. Her mother is also very attractive in spite of, or perhaps partly because of the three pairs of lines tattooed on [10a] her chin from lip to throat, three parallel lines following the curve of he cheek from the temple to the neck and a long blue line running down each side of the nose, beginning at the edge of her hair. Her face is heavy with thick lips and fleshy cheeks, but her eyes and expression are so merry and untroubled that she *tout ensemble* is please to look at. Her hands and feet are about the size of a white child of ten or

ST. LAWRENCE ISLAND

Not at all because you do not know, but because I certainly had no idea of its location before going up there, I shall tell you first where is St Lawrence Island. Just within the International boundary line, a hundred and fifty miles west of Nome and only forty miles from the coast of Siberia, whose white mountains are plainly visible on clear days, from our Island, St Lawrence Island, Alaska is located. Somewhat warmed by the Japanese current which is said to sweep around it, altho we never had any direct proof of the fact that we could have been any colder, St Lawrence Island is not so bitter cold as the mainland. The snow and ice are as plentiful and the winds are more violent, but the thermometer whose nose does not need to take into account the fact that wind more than makes up for actual Fahrenheit degrees below, does not register more than twenty five or thirty degrees below zero which is not ~~nearly~~ so cold as Montana sometimes becomes. The Nome temperature is considerably lower, but the winds on St Lawrence Island, which must be the winter home of Boreas, act as giant needles for injecting the cold well under the skin. Sometimes they are so strong that children are not allowed outside the door for fear of being swept into the ocean, which is not far from any house. And the grown people go about on their hands and knees when they must be outside, which is certainly not often, there being very few musts among Eskimos. Sometimes, when papa [2] Eskimo must go out for a block of snow, which he cuts from any drift not too near the village, he fastens a rope around his body and is paid out by someone inside and pulled in again like a kite when he gives the signal. But on such windy days, Brother Eskimo usually bides within, having no more robust or venturesome disposition than the rest of us. Indeed, I think he likes the winds much as children love rainy days when they may scrooch up in a corner and read without having to run out on errands. They give him an excuse to lounge inside his oven house, beating his odd drum, telling stories, singing, dancing or rarely mending his dog harness or carving ivory. Moreover they break up the ice pack out on the frozen sea so that if next day should be calm he will have 'plenty hunt'. Early in the morning on a calm day after wind, every hunter in every village will be out with his glass, some of which are of the finest, peeping out for seals lying on the edges of the black pools which the wind has obligingly opened especially for the mutual benefit of seals and Eskimo that the one may come up for a fresh breath and that the other may shoot him while he is up. If it is a good day there will be one or two grunts of satisfaction as the men go about getting ready gun, seal hook end harpoon. If nothing is in sight, every man of them will laugh as if it were a joke which Nature had gone to the trouble to play on them. Nothing in sight, however, does not mean that nobody goes hunting, for altho there may be no seals lying about on the ice, they are sure to be bobbing up and under in some of the holes. One day just after a wind that had lasted a week, and [3] consequently after a famine which had lasted a week, twenty men went out to hunt off the shore of Gambell Point. There was one fruitful hole. The twenty men sat all day around this one lakelet, and Silook shot one seal which he divided with his wife's nearest relative. They all came home laughing at the big joke. Quietly laughing, as they also talk, play and quarrel quietly. I suppose every family dug a little deeper into its precious store of white-man-food for supper that night, except those families who could boast a good beggar woman in the lot who would call on Silook while his wife was skinning the seal and wheedle him out of a hunk about the size of a double fist. An Eskimo family can live on as nearly nothing as possible. One good mouthful of meat can pass for a dinner when times are hard.

St Lawrence Island is ice bound ten months of the year. There is nothing so silent as a still day in the winter when by a super effort the sun tops the horizon, rolls sluggishly across a dirty sky, and falls dejectedly behind the Siberian mountains about two oclock PM. On such days, white folks think about daisy meadows, sunny singing awake brooks, and other things as sentimentally as Brown folks think about, well, I don't know what they think about and I doubt if anybody else knows. At any rate, the men folks go hunting if there are any pools visible and the women folks sit all day beside the seal oil lamps sewing, or scraping hides, or often luxuriating in pure idleness, and the children play quietly at sliding down snow banks or just standing out with their hands inside their sleeves hugged against naked breasts. A surprisingly large number of men thus spend their time also – But 1 was talking about the silentness of an ice bound island. It was the year of the election of [4] Harding and we used to spend hours learnedly analyzing the political situation, alternately deciding that McAdoo and Hoover would be the next President. The old marooned Doctor who was handed us by fate for the year always declared that Christianson would be the next President. He had dreamed of him one night which was proof conclusive. How quickly every person white and brown on the island threw down whatever he was doing that June morning when word came from the beach that Pedersen was coming! It meant the end of the ten months of ice. He was the first trader up in the …

notes

DEPARTMENT OF THE INTERIOR
BUREAU OF EDUCATION, ALASKA DIVISION
ALASKA NATIVE SCHOOL, MEDICAL, AND REINDEER SERVICE

Gambell, St. Lawrence Island;

June 30, 1921.

To the US Commissioner of Education, Washington, D.C.

Sir,

We submit herewith the annual report for the year ending June 30, 1921.

The general story of St Lawrence Island has been frequently told. We shall therefore outline briefly conditions as we have seen them and make what recommendation seen to us practical. We have written briefly under the following general headings:

RESOURCES .. MOVING THE VILLAGE .. GOVERNMENT BUILDINGS .. GOVERNMENT FUEL .. TRANSPORTATION .. MEDICAL .. RESTITUTES .. WEATHER .. MAROONED MEN .. NATIVE HOUSES .. AND WRECKED SCHOONER

And have attached more specific reports under the following special headings:

REINDEER .. SCHOOL .. REPORT OF MEDICAL AID BY DR BRUNING .. FAIR .. DETAILS FOR FUTURE TEACHERS .. and STORE

We have had a delightful and, certainly to us, profitable year up here and we have tried to give you such information as will enable you to help the persons following us to enter upon a plan of work from the beginning. Certain bad habits of the natives, such as deliberately deceiving new teachers should be known to newcomers and the guilty ones made to feel that the head office knows each one personally and is following out one consistent plan with them. Other faithful and helpful natives should have the reward of recognition from the new arrivals. This simple precaution would at the outset help to insure a more successful year. The natives trade on the ignorance of the new teachers to impose on both them and the Government. This explains the native desire for a constant change of teachers. A notebook containing particular information about each person on the island, somewhat on the plan of the Resources chapter personnel book, would be neither difficult nor impossible for this isolated place. We have included this information with the report to the future teachers. The natives would be tremendously impressed to perceive that they are not strangers to the head office.

There is another thing which would help to familiarize the new teachers with his field. It has taken us the entire year to understand the natives' method of living, and to learn what resources he has at his command. This difficulty could be largely overcome by a general survey of the island. It can only be done in summer time, in common with any other activities, but it would be a big help to have a survey showing the shore line with its harbors and deposits of driftwood, the locations of lakes and streams, the best feeing places for the reindeer – this is particularly important, for even the best of herders have a tendency to move to the best hunting places rather than the best feeding places and they too depend on the ignorance of [2] the teachers – the locations of the camps and the routes of travel between them.

A small wireless station is needed here. The genius for mechanics among some of the natives would soon furnish a permanent operator.

It would have been both a blessing and a calamity this year if I had had some legal authority to deal with white people so that I might have put an end to the boat controversy. A blessing to the natives who have been considerably disturbed over the matter and a calamity to me who would have been between the Devil and the deep sea. I am therefore doubtful whether some sort of legal commission should be given the Superintendent of this Island.

We have done little this year, outside the regularly required activities, than to get acquainted with conditions. But we have made a serious study of practical things capable of factual accomplishment, and it is with these plans for the future that this report is concerned. We know that you will not regard as impertinent the suggestions and criticisms we offer.

RESOURCES

There is no longer an abundance of wild foxes on this island and the yearly catch is decreasing alarmingly. I have made an effort to cause the natives to anticipate the disappearance of foxes by talking to them in the night classes and elsewhere on the desirability of farms. I have doubted, however, whether they would ever learn to give the foxes the necessary care since they have not yet learned how to take decent care of their dogs. They are willing for the Government to buy the materials for constructing an experimental farm and would be glad to assist in the work provided they received pay for their labor! Sepillu has expressed intelligent interest in the fox farming idea. His training as herder would help him to understand than certain care must be taken. He is perhaps the leader on this island in progressive matters. If a small amount of fencing and other necessary materials could be sent up and an experimental farm started at Sepillu's camp, I believe we could secure sufficient cooperation from the natives without further expenditure by the Government. The reindeer camp men are the ones to work with. They have availed themselves of the Government's help and everyday realize the actual gain they have made. A man stationed with them to look after the reindeer interests and to institute gradually what practical things seem most needed would do more good that [than] a general Superintendent of everything with nothing especial to achieve. At least this particular man could do so.

A very few men on this island do good ivory carving. All of them have a great deal of time which they utilize for the most part, standing outside their houses looking out for open water. We have attempted to interest some of them in carving and in making new designs in chains and bracelets and pendants and also to make them realize the importance of depending more on the quality of their work and less on the ignorance of the buyer. I wish there might be sent up an illustrated book on ivory carving for the library here. Pictures of what men of other countries carve would inspire them more than words.

Little more than half of the men here are good hunters. The remainder either make a half hearted attempt or beg from those that are successful. It is not a question of supply, but of industry. There has been no serious shortage of food on the island this year. Walrus and seal are not so plentiful as they once were, but the reindeer industry will offset this disadvantage if it is properly managed. The reason for meat shortage when it does occur is not that there has been an insufficient supply killed, but that they have no place for it.

In the spring, when the walrus are plentiful, the men kill for pure lust [3] of filling saving only the heads for the ivory. Then winter comes, the poorer ones suffer want, the others, of course, eating white man's food when meat is scarce. They have rude cellars or holes in the ground, which they fill with meat, but the new generation seems not so fond of rotten meat as the old. This is one difficulty, at least, that can be easily and permanently overcome. Large ice houses, three or four, built at the best hunting camps where surplus meat could be stored and kept frozen would forever prevent all danger of famine. There is constant travelling back and forth on the island. There is weekly, and during the winter, daily communication between all camps. When there is a surplus of meat caught 40 mile a from Gambell, a regular caravan of dog teams hastens thither. How easy to see the advantages of ice houses. These could be built of driftwood principally and the first one placed at North Cape where there is the best year round hunting. There is always open water somewhere on the island and a team of hunters could be gathered which would keep the ice houses full all the time. But this, nor any other long time job, cannot be accomplished by one entrusted with the entire supervision of the island. He must be constantly on the job, working himself, urging, encouraging; and he should collect the most wide awake group of men to center his efforts on. An idea, if it is adaptable to their needs, will spread rapidly enough.

There has been a sufficiency of animal oil for heating the native houses this winter. We have been able to buy all the drift wood here that we needed and all industrious houses have their wood piles which do not seem to diminish. Along the beach a few miles from Gambell there is plenty of driftwood to heat what lumber houses are here. The coal vein which was reported to be here is under water. It cannot be investigated save in the summer time.

There are sand and gravel all around the island, of good quality for concrete work. I believe concrete could be used to good advantage for building purposes. At least in building a government house for the teachers which is greatly needed.

There is no soil at or near Gambell, but there are many places on the island where grass grows abundantly and where the soil appears to be of the beat. Some experimenting with cold frames would be interesting. The natives are exceedingly fond of greens, of fresh onions, lettuce and such things. I am sure they would eagerly learn how to raise them. A few square feet of glass would be enough to start with. Such experimenting as that would not be a long time job, either, and I believe the ultimate result would be little green gardens under glass dotted about all over this island.

Whaling is the most lucrative pursuit here. These Natives kill on the average of one whale a season. They are on the whole less skillfull, because less bold, than are the natives of other whaling countries. Whales are plentiful and there seems no good reason why they should not kill several every year. Their superstitious custom may have something to do with their timidity. Or the crews lack training in concerted action, or the men have lost the art of leadership since the coming of more forceful leaders. At any rate, the boats come in every day to report whales sighted, missed, gone off with paraphernalia sticking all over them, but not killed. However, one whale a season is sufficient to keep them out of debt, and until they learn more about how to spend their money, they are not greatly in need of more to spend. Several beluga whales are caught about the island but they make no commercial use of the skin and I do not know enough about it to advise them. (We need an encyclopedia!)

In fact, the resources of this island are so numerous that one cannot help building air castles of wonderful things that might be accomplished but when one wakes up to the fact that it is not the resources alone [4]

THE FAIR

Early in the year, we began to think of a fair as the best way of getting acquainted with all the people on St Lawrence Island and of finding out what handiwork they were capable of. Every native to whom we spoke of the matter seemed to think it a good plan to have a "big time" but few of them were sufficiently enthusiastic to satisfy us so that we almost persuaded ourselves many times that we too little understood their natures to succeed in such an attempt the first year. Little by little, however, the enthusiasm increased.

A committee of Eskimos and myself completed the plans towards the end of the year and in January I sent out the letter a copy of which is attached to this report. I sent forty three, one to every family on the island. Pretty soon, we began to hear of boots, sleds, parkies, harness, or rain coats being made all over the island. They were very secretive about what they were making, at the same time wanting the reward of our appreciation that they were preparing. It seemed that some member of every family on the island was making something for the Fair. Excitement began at last to grow among those whom we had thot to be wholly phlegmatic. As the time of the fair drew near, a severe spell of bad weather set in and lasted for two weeks holding us at SW Cape when we needed to be in Gambell getting ready. The Eskimos began to be uneasy that we were going to be late. At last, on the 5th of March, we moved permanently to Gambell, the Gambell people having promised to keep hauling coal until we had sufficient for the rest of the year.

The weather remained ideal – warm, sunny and windless from the 5th till the 19th of March. We could not have had better weather if we had made it ourselves.

A few days before the fair, people began to arrive in Gambell. Entire families who would have come a month later, anyhow, for the whaling, moved here. The day before the fair almost everybody on the island had arrived. Their exhibits were brot to the schoolhouse for Silook and me to arrange.

I was agreeably surprised at the number of articles entered, but not at their quality. There were handsome boots and some well made sleds, and one or two beautiful carvings, but the parkies, furs, cut leather work, harness, gloves and many other things were mediocre. The present day American Indian does better work. Altogether, there were eighty-seven entries including all the different articles mentioned in the fair letter. We bought the prize winning snow boots for the Seattle office so that you may see what can be done here, tho it seldom is done!

Seventeen dog teams raced for the dollar prize, fifty two men entered the shooting race, eight young men ran in the foot race and, eight boys in the potato race. No reindeer were brot. [5]

Every man, woman and child in Gambell entered and won in what Dr Brunig called the reindeer race which was an epidemic of diarrhoea following the two tubfulls of reindeer and oatmeal stew which were consumed on the second day of the fair and which continues to furnish fun.

The house was packed at ten o'clock in the morning of the fifteenth. We sang many songs, talked a little, appointed the three white marooned men as judges and set everybody free to inspect the exhibits. Many of the people went around the room to see the Perry pictures we had tacked up for the occasion, but few of them evidenced any curiosity about the articles made by themselves. They are very different from white folks in the things they "take on" over. Perhaps they had all seen everybody's exhibits.

In the afternoon we had races. The shooting match aroused most interest, but none of the races created any of the sort of excitement one sees outside. Everybody crowded on top of their houses to see, but not one shout or word of encouragement was uttered. They laughed a great deal, but nothing else. It was decidedly different! At night, Dr Brunig spoke to the men on his pet theme of evaporation. He asked for the evening and we gave it willingly for he has been fair and just with the natives and the Government, but his theories are fanciful and as little understood by the Eskimos as they were by us. He imagines he has planted seed which will one day sprout and grow into a flourishing tree of knowledge.

The morning of the sixteenth was devoted to giving out prizes. Then everybody went home for a cup, a bowl and a spoon, to return and form a line outside the entrance to our house. Sepillu and Otiyohok marched them in, children first. Everybody was served in a reasonably short time with stew made from the largest deer in the herd, and afterwards with all the tea and bread everybody could eat. Almost every woman slyly filled her snow shirt apron with left over bread. I had done nothing but make bread for a week before the fair.

After lunch, we were supposed to sing and have some Eskimo dances, but we were too full and stupid. Farrar offered a personal prize of five dollars to the best Eskimo dancer, but it was no use. Not even money could rouse us now. Next day, everybody was blue around the lips and as careless of the future as any tired army. Old Agoolki, the oldest man on the island, ate not less than five pounds of the stew which contained one whole sack of steel cut oats, and drank seven cups of tea with uncounted muffins and lumps of sugar. He was one sick old man next day. He is sure the stew was "old". We ate the remains for a month afterwards, however with no unpleasant results.

In spite of the reindeer race, the first annual fair of St

Lawrence Island – if it were the first, which I doubt – was a success from every standpoint. We all had a good time. The tone of the community was improved. The visiting children packed the play room from daylight until we ran them out at night.

On the next page there is a list of the winners of the prizes. The rewards seem absurdly small, but we were giving any at all at a risk and we reasoned that the amount was of little importance compared to the spirit of the competition. They seemed as proud as the winners of any contest to receive the little Government slips to be exchanged at the store for candy and gum which we had saved for this. [5]

The total expense of the fair to the Government including one sack of flour and twenty one pounds of cube sugar, eighteen one dollar [bills] and seven fifty cent prizes was thirty three dollars and ten cents. We furnished one forty-five sack of oats and the small items such as tea and labor.

One sack flour	5.00
21 # sugar	6.60
Toota prize (bird parki)	1.00
Toota prize (parki)....	1.00
Yochkotak prize (dogs)	1.00
Maskin prize (shooting)	1.00
Apata best carving......	1.00
Kingonga snow boots....	1.00
Tootmatolik dog harness	.50
Sepillu deer sled	1.00
Okiyaka wrestlers pants	1.00
Obeyaka water boots	1.00
Annogiyak the largest kill of mukluks	1.00
Yahonga fancy belt	1.00
Athelingok largest catch of fox of any man present at fair	1.00
Koonoku largest number of seals of any man	1.00
Iknakinuk summer shoes	1.00
Okwahani fancy slippers	1.00

Pungewiyi dog sled	1.00
Okwoolu fancy rain coat	1.00
Okwoolu fancy gloves	.50
Napowatuk foot race	.50
Owhowin white leather	.50
Sepillu deer harness	.50
Numolug cartridge case	.50
Tootmatolik fox skin	1.00
Oovookitak potato race	.50
Total	33.10

THE STORE. EB & LA

Supplies for the store arrived at the beach at SW Cape without damage or loss save for a half barrel of toast eaten little at a time by the *Bear* crew and everything slightly damaged by rain during the transfer of the supplies from the *Bear* to the *Unalga* at Unalaska. The supplies were carried up the steep bluff to the house at a cost of sixty five dollars to the store.

Before the store was put in order dog teams began to arrive from all camps for supplies. We had, from the beginning, to attempt an equal division of things so that the rich ones might not get it all. It seemed that every man had ordered a gun. It was impossible to know who needed a rifle most, so I tried to give them to the men who were sure of paying. I made some mistakes.

Everybody had questions to ask which I could not answer. I was too ignorant to get the information I needed at the Seattle office. We came up with last year's teacher but the information he could give me was confusing. I could secure no information from the district Superintendent's office and I dared not rely on the scattering things I had heard by way of mouth. A story of the store, how it began, what it seeks to accomplish in the way of cooperation, how it stands outside, whether it is in debt, whether it has money in the bank, and if so what is to be done with it for the natives, what disposition should be made of the native produce – whether ever to be sold to traders or always to be shipped out, whether the rules on ivory permit our shipping out so that we will not have that puzzle every year, and the market prices for the year before each yea, together with a list of prices the head office thinks we would be safe in giving here so as to get the skins most of which are going to Pedersen who does not give more but only charges more for his stuff so that they think they are getting more. All these things would clear up a deal of confusion at this end. All these questions are asked immediately by the natives as well as definite demands to know what has been done with each man's skins and when he will receive his rebate.

There were too little of all the supplies. Flour, sugar, dried fruits, candy, gum, bread, calico, and guns were all gone by the first of the year. We were forced to buy from Pedersen to the amount of a little over four hundred dollars much of which cost us more than we had sold for during the year. Many of the natives, and all the richer ones hoarded their skins for Pedersen and bought from him supplies for next year which we might have sold if we had had them. He did more business during the two days he was here than we did all the year. Of the staple supplies it would be hard to send too much and there needs to be added a great many items to the list of things sent. In the order this year, I am not allowing the store keeper to include anything which has not been many times called for during the year nor to order for those who are still in debt or who may not be able to pay. The only risk this order will take is a small list of children's toys [2] which I have been requested by many to order, but which I am not sure will be purchased. There will not be so much money available next year as there was this, both because the reindeer men have spent all their moneys this year and because so many have stocked heavily with Pedersen, but the store can do a good business if we change the policy somewhat. These people are aristocrats when it comes to buying. They do not ask the price, but the quality. We have on hand now seven hundred and forty six dollars worth of two articles – 516 pounds of cheap tobacco and six hundred and eighty eight pounds of poor quality Java tea – which the store will sell only in dribbles and will never get entirely rid of. We are ordering heavily of good tobacco and good tea for they will not buy this. Every body buys tea by the case and they want the best. I believe our policy could be improved by taking example from Pedersen who gets their trade. He sells high of good quality stuff and pays good prices for their things. This is far more impressive to then than the store's way of selling low and paying low. For example, Pedersen charged one dollar fifty for a box of gum – they buy gum by the box – and pays seventeen fifty for a number one fox skin. We charge one dollar for a box of gum and pay ten dollars for the same fox skin. Now we have paid within two and a half of the same price if they bought wholly in gum and they have still another chance of getting more for their skin. But they do not see this. They only see that Pedersen pays almost twice as much for the skin as the store. Do not you think we might also have high quality stuff, sell high – even higher than Petersen since I doubt if he can buy as cheaply – and pay more than he for their skins? I am afraid that is the only way the store will ever come to really belong to them all. Now it is a store for the convenience of the poor and the mid winter convenience of those whose supplies have run out.

If we are to realize actual profit on this business the little leaks must be stopped. Granulated sugar should be shipped so as to prevent its absorption of moisture. Candy should be included in other packages so as to prevent its being eaten en route. Everything should be more carefully packed so that the thotless young fellows on the ships will not be tempted to investigate and consume them. Our forty five pounds of personal candy and other things which could be eaten raw, including two cases of canned peas disappeared on the *Bear*. Coal oil and gasoline should be sent in drums. The thin cans live short lives in this moist salt air and their patent spouts leak badly. The produce at this end should be packed so that it cannot be easily opened en route to Seattle. I have tried this year to pack things with extra care so that the weights can be checked upon arrival without the necessity of checking each separate article. The bundles have been sewed in burlap, numbered and weighed so that if they are tampered with while en route it can be seen at once, and checked against the receipt. The natives object very much to having the skins opened in the district superintendent's office. They all prefer that they be sent to Seattle. I was very glad to learn from Petersen that the Bureau actually has its own boat this year. I hope it will prove successful enough to warrant its permanent continuance. This will eliminate most of our troubles, we believe. The natives have complete confidence in whatever Mr Lopp does.

Soon after my arrival, I set to work on the books. I had nothing to work with but the little perforated counter books and a statement which Aningayu had made out of the indebtedness hanging over from last year. It was not difficult to set up a simple system of book-keeping for James which he easily understood and to get all the accounts entered into the ledger. I found that there was owing on the island [3] a little over four thousand dollars including the amounts purchased during this year in October and November. I made a statement of the debt of each man and included the whole list in a circular letter which we sent to every man on the island. I enclose a copy of that letter. Some of them professed to be much astonished at the amount of their bill, which is not unusual. In one case we found we had made a mistake of fifty dollars! The majority of the men reacted immediately to the letter and began to pay their bills in cash, skins or ivory.

I raised the prices we were paying for skins and ivory a small amount. There were a few, however, who had to be reminded constantly of their bills before they would pay, and there are a few who have not yet responded. Some of these are trying and paying little at a time but others are indifferent having hoarded their skins for Pedersen. The reindeer boys have all paid by signing statements to Mr Lopp authorizing him to deduct their bills from their reindeer money which we were informed by the District Superintendent that he would hold. Silook's, the Government's and our personal bill will also be paid in this way. The store will have this year, including these amounts and a low estimates on the skins, about four thousand dollars. I hope that a complete statement in writing may be sent up so that the Eskimos will know exactly how they stand. The cooperative idea is still formless in their minds and therefore they yet do not feel any pride of ownership in the store. The intelligent and prosperous ones would be able to understand a full statement if it were explained clearly to them many times over. They could explain it to the others. There is no story of the store here showing how it started with the history of its activities and from what sources the funds have been derived. On this account, I found it very hard to be able to talk intelligently about it to the natives.

I was told that James had agreed to turn his stock of goods into the cooperative store on condition of his being made store-keeper. I had no written statement concerning this and he denies that any such arrangement was made. He says he will consent to sell out if we desire him to do so. He is therefore at present conductings two stores, his on, however, amounting to almost nothing. I would suggest that we do not buy his stock but allow him to sell it all out himself since it is almost worthless, and not large enough in quantity to bother with transferring.

Aningayu is a good store keeper. Typical, in fact. He has the store keeper's belly and disinclination for any form of violent exercise. I gave him a simple system of bookkeeping which he mastered without difficulty, but I found it impossible to get him to keep the books up to date by making the entries daily, and I always found them just where I had left off. At the close of the year, it took us almost a week to get them straightened out again. I explained to him that if he did not keep the books he did not earn his salary of 25.00 per month. He also desires to be given his supplies at cost in addition to this, the wisdom of which I am doubtful of. He says it was done last year and I have given him a discount on his bill this year, but I would like to have a written statement about this. He seems more interested in getting what is coming to him than in the general welfare of the store, but he is probably the best man on the island for the job. I do not know why the store was taken from Ozeevooseuk, unless it was because he is soft hearted. Last year this little stock of goods boasted of two store keepers from the middle of October to the first of June, Oozeevooseuk at a salary of sixteen dollars and Aningayu at a salary of twenty five dollars per month. Oozeevooseuk says that he was promised three dollars per day for escorting the [5] local superintendent over the Island over the island [sic] while taking the census and that the 120.00 salary he received from the store was for the census work. There are no records here of such an arrangement only there is a record of his having received the salary. I an unable to explain this to the natives. It would seem that the US Census Dept. is indebted to the EB & LA to the amount of 120.00.

While Aningayu was the official store keeper last year, he was not entrusted with its management. He complains that he did not see the bills and that the local superintendent kept the store cash and used from it constantly during the year without entering on the books the amounts he had spent and without leaving a receipt in the store for the amount of cash taken and that he announced at the end when he was repeatedly questioned that he had six hundred dollars in cash to take outside. Sepillu says that he alone paid five hundred dollars in cash for supplies. The amount of six hundred dollars does not seem unreasonable, says that some store supplies were purchased from Pedersen and the *Bear*, but there are no receipted bills among the store papers to show for this expenditure, so that we cannot explain the discrepancy. Many of the natives are skeptical. It is account of this and other stories I have heard that I have published freely among them every transaction of the store this year. I believe every native should know or [be] given an opportunity to know the details of every transaction including wholesale cost, freight, store profit, selling; price of skins and ivory outside, cash on hand and outstanding debts. There can be no harm in this and there will be many advantages. The store will gain in the confidence of the natives in direct proportion to its frankness. They are suspicious, but they have enough intelligence to understand what is thoroughly explained. I have included a hectograph in the Government order this year which I hope to use frequently in publishing news among other things. I wanted very much to establish a sort of advisory counsel to regulate store matters, but I knew too little about the store and the Bureau's plan to institute it this year. If I can set the matter straight in my own mind, I shall organize such a counsel next year so that the natives may gradually come to realize that the store belongs to them and not to the Government. I have already turned the whole management over to Aningayu as fast as he has been able to assume it. I refer everything to him so that the natives may begin to rely on him. I gave him a copy of the bills and let him dictate the selling prices of the goods. The confidence in the store has increased this year because of the serious efforts we have made to get clear of debt. I have told them positively that if they pay their debts and keep clear of large debts in the future that the store can and will order for them whatever they want. I have promised that those who pay their debts will be given first chance next year and that those who are able and have not paid will be given no future credit. I hope that if the management of the store falls into other hands next year this policy will be carried out. Nobody should be allowed to get deeply into debt for it is not necessary. Those who buy heavily have plenty of money and the poor ones do not buy much anyhow. A policy of allowing no man's debt to go above fifty dollars could be easily followed. The only object in allowing them to get in debt at all is to give them time to bring in their skins and ivory if they do not want to pay in cash. Most of the wealthy are in debt to Pedersen and he encourages them to remain so. I have found it hard to convince them that their own store has the first claim on them. But there is one thing to be said about Pedersen. He brings what they want. If any native orders a whale boat, darting gun, bomb, sewing machine, pianola or porch swing, he [6] brings it. He charges big prices, but it is the article they want and they are not concerned about its price. I have told them that their store cannot bring everything as he can for they do not furnish sufficient money and the store has problems of transportation which Pedersen has not.

There is another thing which I think should be changed and about which I would like to have your opinion. Many of the natives have been accustomed to ordering definite articles such as boats, masts – we have an unsold one here which was ordered and never called for – without making any advance payments. The store is not able to carry such things in its general stock and sometimes the native finds himself unable to purchase what he has ordered. I think it unadvisable to order any especial article for an individual without an advance payment of half its estimated cost.

What do you think id a fair per cent of profit for the store to ask above the cost of supplies, freight and running expenses. I think a certain per cent should be determined upon so that every new teacher will not have to puzzle over this. I did not know enough about the policy that [had] been pursued before me to make any statement this year to the natives. We sold for too little above cost this year owing to the high prices of everything. This was about ten per cent. It was the least we felt safe in adding. Should the teachers receive the profit discount from their bill at the store? A written statement should be sent. We have no precedent to follow. I think it unsafe to discount any bills, the store keeper's included. The store has been accustomed to sell its ivory and fox skins to teachers and sometimes to natives at the same price it had paid. I put a stop to that custom for it might lead to all manner of evils. The store should make a profit on everything it handles. I am attaching the auditing report for which you asked together with a statement of the present outstanding bills.

The store has had an unusually good year and I believe another one like i with a complete explanation to the natives of its standing and policy will root it finally. Thee sensible ones see its value. It has been a great deal of trouble to me but some pleasure also. I love to straighten out messes. It was lucky for us during this somewhat difficult year, that the store which the US Marshall of Nome intended to establish here did not arrive. I do not know whether the wrecked schooner was bringing that store or not. Should we have a rival next year, we are on our feet and if the order is filled with first class goods we can compete with them. The store with the best tea, the finest guns, and the brightest best calico will get the trade.

Respectfully,
Farrar Burn
Local Superintendent
St Lawrence Island Alaska

THE SCHOOL

We moved to Gumboil from SW Cape the first week in November. Mr Burn remained to have a meeting with the village people before going on to the reindeer camp for the marking.

Silook and I unpacked and put the schoolroom in order, selected books from the dank, moldy shelves and made ready for school. I had to rely on Silook's memory for the grading of the children and for the selecting of books for temporary use. Few of the texts were familiar to me.

I found boxes piled on boxes of kindergarten material which had been ordered year after year and which nobody had had the time to use. The dreary piles of stuff, the green molded books with stuck leaves, piano covered with snow, every window broken, not one joint of whole stovepipe, a cracked lifeless bell – if I hadn't already acquired the reputation of a happy person, I should have sat down and given up the ghost. Silook confessed that his order for this year had been copied from that of the year before. We had that which we could not use and lacked that which we needed. However, we had enough pencils and tablets, a large amount of blackboard space, a large fairly well lighted room, numberless maps, charts, and mechanical contrivances, and best of all, when Monday morning came, a host of unclean ill-smelling but eager pupils who from the first day to the last learned with all their mights. Nothing else much mattered. The man who said that all it takes to make a good school is a log with a pupil at one end and a teacher at the other was about right.

On Monday morning, the eighth of November, we rang the dismal bell whose dead clack was always a surprise. About forty bundles of skins tumbled into the room. They had been waiting outside to tumble in for some time. We sang awhile, had oral examinations to see where each child belonged, and distributed books. There were only two boys who had been to school long enough to require advanced work. The others all were little beyond the first or second grade as the schools are graded outside. No child of school age was absent that first day. The later increase in attendance was due to the constant arrival of new families.

Since I was unable to be in Gambell long at first nor continually until the spring, I did not arrange the program for two teachers. I spent one hour of every morning with the larger children and one hour of the afternoon session with the beginners working on English only and teaching them songs. When I was here, I also took the reading classes, hygiene, and some of the beginning number classes. Those subjects which I felt hopeless that they would master anyhow, I turned over to Silook whose method of teaching consisted at first of sitting in state at his desk and hearing his pupils drone out all their lessons as reading lessons. [2]

Before I left Gambell each time it was necessary to go over the work of each day with Silook, urging him to be more alert, more interested. I told him that the examinations I gave the children on my returns were not their tests but his. But he was hard to arouse, and may not be aroused yet for all I know, tho he seems better to me.

With the exception of seven children, these have been the easiest pupils to teach I have ever known. I mean easy to interest. There was no problem of discipline when I was there. Silook complained once but he learned that I blamed him and not the children for their misbehavior whereupon his complaints ceased. I tried to make him see the object of discipline – that it is not to display the authority of the teacher but to secure the best working conditions for every body. We allowed them brief intervals of chatter between all the classes. I told them a hundred times or so that I wanted them to talk, to have fun, to laugh. They need only keep still when others were trying to learn.

In reading, everybody "beats". I never saw such little

parrots. But when I learned that neither the school children nor any other person on the island read with understanding of the words they so glibly turned off their tongues, I instituted a slow and painful process of learning to read. Every lesson was required to be translated into Eskimo. This took the time of both Silook and me. Even he had trouble to translate many passages after they had been simplified by me. Not much book space was covered but we did not mind. By the way, that little book, "Eskimo Land" by Hawkes is a jewel for beginners. I wish we had every text as adaptable.

Somebody has done some good teaching in arithmetic back in the dark ages some time, but I could not imitate their example. The children are quick in number work and the mechanics of arithmetic but I could not get any response to the most elementary problem save from the two large boys and I could not possibly claim any credit for their ability to master it. It was delightful to observe how quickly they learned to add, subtract, multiply and divide, but disheartening to have as reply to the question "How many seals will Savlu have if he kills three and gives one to Kastevek? the eternal "saa-a" (I don't know). It is true that towards the last the children and Silook seemed more able to think ample problems thru, but teaching Eskimos to reason is certainly not my long suit.

We all greatly enjoyed the work in physiology. The texts were not at all suitable. I used the charts and board. We had illustrated lessons whenever we could. No, I mean we had them when I thot about it. (It is so easy to make a report sound as if one had been the most wide-awake, interested untiring teacher ever sent up, but I slept as late as anybody and accomplished really almost nothing at all. Do not form the impression that I am trying to make a busy sounding report.)

Geography and history were taught by Silook. He did very well and I think perhaps his slow quiet method is after all as effective, if not more so, than the white teacher's hurry and noise. He taught all the classes of course when I was not here. [3]

There were a great many absences among a few children. Iyakitan, Apata, Amagoo, Yawakseuk, Yaghak, and Massiu kept their children out on many excuses. I did not insist on their attendance. At a parents' meeting, I told them I loved to teach their children and that there was a law which I could use to compel them to send regularly but that I had no intention of adding to an already full time job the bother of running after absent pupils. If they did not want to send their children to school, there would be just so much less work for Silook and me. It was the attitude which seemed right to me in view of their tendency to shift all responsibility. Instead of saying, "You must send your children to school except when they are stoic and the weather is bad", I wish I had said right at first, "I am glad to have your children come every day for they learn very fast when they are not absent, but you must not send them when they have colds or when the weather is too bad for the little ones". The reaction to these two remarks ia vastly different and it is the latter remark which produces the healthier reaction. The fathers take more interest in the progress of the children than do the mothers. When I called a parents' meeting – everybody was present and I announced that we would have one every month, but that is the only one we have had to date, June fourths! Only the fathers came. They told me that they had never before heard that they should take to their children about their school work or ask questions about what they had learned each day. I don't believe it. No lie is quite so popular up here as that one of "You do this first time. We never hear before". They imagine it is pleasing, and so it was until I stopped believing them. How they strive to master the delicate art of saying pleasant things. Aningayu said he had never asked any of his children a question about what he did in school. Even after that one meeting in January attendance was noticeably improved.

At first, Silook seemed the most hopeless proposition I ever saw. Slow, half-awake, timid, and assertive only in asking for "his share" of the supplies sent up. He had taken no care of the Government property. He had made no preparations for the coming of the next teachers. He is too insignificant a person in Eskimo land to act as watchman for anything. He seemed utterly indifferent whether school kept or not and his slow, uninteresting monotone in the schoolroom produced no more effect on the hubbub in the mornings before I went into the room than if he had not been there. Gradually, however, he improved or further acquaintance made him tolerable. He was willing, desirous of increasing his own knowledge and his teaching ability, the I never observed him reading any of the things I recommended to him. Once after an absence of almost a month in December when Mr Burn had been ill, we found all manner of small evidences of abuse to the property.

report

We called a meeting to which we commanded every man come. Mr Burn rebuked them all pretty sternly for allowing their children to abuse that which they should protect. Silook received the largest share of the rebuke and Mr Burn told him we would not continue him even thru this year if he did not take his responsibility more seriously than that. Silook came to us after the meeting and apologized and promised that such neglect would not occur again. Nor has it so far as he has been able to prevent it, but he comes from a family every member of which is despised here on this island for reasons we cannot find out, and his word carries little weight. So long as we are here to back him up he does things well, but he can do nothing without someone behind him.

I have talked frankly to him about his teaching. Perhaps it is because I have worked so hard with him that I have grown to love him. At any rate I have. I wish that he might be continued another year as teacher. He really has had little opportunity before to show what he will do. He seems to us to be the best there is available. He has an intelligent father tho he lives apart from his neighbors, and an uncommonly intelligent wife. A native teacher in necessary. Silook was taken from the reindeer business to be made teacher. It has unfitted him for anything else and unless he forfeits any claim on the Bureau by neglecting his work, it seems hardly fair to drop him now. He is the sole dependent of his large family. His inability to take advantage of all good hunting weather forces him to pay the high prices for white man's food and often he is unable to buy all of that he needs because of the small store supply. He saves but little. Indeed, I have heard it said that he cares nothing whether he saves or not, and that he makes debts with other natives and never pays them. I cannot verify such tales, of course. His bill at the store now is almost a thousand dollars with last years and this years purchases.

Of course I do not mean that Silook should be retained out of charity. What he needs personally should not be considered in his appointment. I only mean to say that if he continues to take care, these things might be considered in the question. He is not the brightest man on the island. Far from it! Nor is he forceful, nor influential in the slightest degree nor a good linguist either in English or his own language, but he is the only man who reads for self improvement, who writes for the love of writing, or who takes an interest in any children beside his own. I have asked him to write in his own words uncorrected by me, a story of the school year. I am enclosing it with this report. It speaks for itself in broken English!

Every night in the school week, from the beginning of the year until Spring, we held a men's night class. I began them and held the classes until Mr Burn returned from the reindeer camps when he kindly took them off my hands. That class was a joy. We had English one night and arithmetic the next. The twenty-one most progressive young and middle-aged men in Gamball came regularly. On the very first night of our return to Gambell each time after an absence at SW Cape a delegation from the men's class would wait upon Mr Burn to learn if the class would be held that night. There was no problem of regular attendance with them. The men asked questions about everything they wanted to know. They had elementary exercises in letter composition, reading, translating, and quite advanced work in practical arithmetic. When the two hours were up, I would go in to drill them in songs. They learned "Good of the Nations", "The Spacious Firmament On High" in parts and other less difficult songs. How well they sang and how they did enjoy it. I envied Mr Burn that class. We held it nightly because we were so much absent. Nobody tired. When the days grew longer and the men were out till past our bedtime hunting, we stopped the night class so that it might not peter out as did my sewing class.

I started a sewing class the first week also. I had some tables made to replace those burned last year and made great preparations. Fifteen women came regularly, only two of whom could speak English. We began with songs and lessons in English until I could think of something for them to begin on. I had them each hem a towel and initial it from a bolt of towelling I found here. The five or six who had cloth were set cutting and sewing, but how to get materials for the poor ones who came, like as not, that they might get materials free, was a problem. [5]

I was determined that the Government should not furnish these materials. I believe it is wrong to give so much to them. At last, I called Aningayu and told him to ask some of the leading men if the store would not furnish material for the poor women in the sewing class to make a garment for the smallest child in her family. He reported that the store would [do] so we were all happy.

It was a merry little party of women with children sitting

contentedly astride their necks while mothers sewed. We had a good time while it lasted. Three women made white man dresses and the rest made snow shirts. We learned songs. The sewing class sang "Onward Christian Soldiers" at the Christmas celebration. When our material was gone, we turned ourselves into a storytelling English class. By and by that gave out because the poor ones left when they found they had gotten all the free stuff they were going to get and the rest of us grew tired of so much work. I tried to interest them in sanitation and home nursing, but they told me in grandmotherly fashion that they had been taking care of babies before I was born. We drank tea a few times in my house and some time after Christmas we died. I had used up our huge music chart for patterns. There was no other paper on the island larger than footscap.

The social life of the village so far as we were admitted into it was centered around us. We held meetings to sing and talk in a friendly fashion and many times we had two dozen young men around the piano singing till ten o'clock. They love to sing. Next to drinking tea, that is their favorite past time. But they drank little tea at our house. We had plenty and it was fun to make it for them and see how they can hold a wee corner of a cube of sugar in one cheek and allow each swallow of tea a brief glimpse of it as it goes down, thus sweetening three cups with one cube. But we have done our best in every way we know how at great expense to our personal popularity to stop this begging in any form. Those who came to drink tea and for no other reason were not hard to find. We believe that giving to them even in the most social and personal way has hurt them and we have told them so. Of course, I do not mean that we always denied ourselves the glow of giving pleasure, but we allowed ourselves a holiday only on the most legitimate occasions. We gave several dinners to friends and had frequent "big times" during the year.

But the social triumph was the opening of the play room. Shortly after we came, I observed that the children had nowhere to play on bad days. They might only sit in a too warm unaired crowded Eskimo winter house. At one of the general meetings, I spoke of the matter and said that I believed the children would enjoy a place to play. There were "Ah-hs" all over the house. Then I said the Government would furnish the room and the playthings if they would give the work needed to fix things up. We needed only low benches and tables. Not an "ah". I was disgusted and told them so. They would like to be paid to help fix up something for their own children. If they did not come to me and offer to work an hour in the playroom there would be no playroom. Would you believe it? Not one came. I cannot understand how they could ever have been allowed to become so selfish and greedy. It is revolting and constantly reacts on them for harm by causing the teachers to despise them. I know nothing that can be done about it save by slow process. We should certainly require a return for every gift. Not for the Government, but for their sakes. If we did that our giving would enrich them as well as ourselves. [6]

THE PEOPLE OF ST LAWRENCE ISLAND

Everybody told us before we came that it would take one year for us really to understand the Eskimos and to know the Who's Who of the Islands (305 people). We have found that to be the truth, but it does not seem to me that it need be so for every teacher if the information each gathers were passed on from year to year. At first, for instance, the ordinary provincial American such as we were, is apt to think this a hard life, full of trials and suffering with small reward. The Eskimos know this and you bet they trade on it. There is not one man, woman or child on this little island who has no one to care for him or who is so poor that he needs to beg from the teachers. With the exception of four families in Gambell all of whom have wealthy relatives, there is no person who is not far more prosperous than any mere school teacher I ever saw. They have their living with little expense to them in labor, sacrifice or money. They all have house, skins, more guns than the most enthusiastic white hunter ever thinks of accumulating, ammunition, stores of white man's food which they hoard like squirrels and pretend to be always in want of, boats which cost them a thousand dollars each, white man's clothes, phonographs, fine pipes – everything they want – and more actual cash than they know what to do with. No white man knows or ever will know how much money they have. From little dabs of things which the faster white would not bother with, they accumulate thousands every year. The traders beat them and pay them too little for their produce, but the trader lives the complicated life of the outside and makes far less out of his ill gotten gain than they from the small prices he pays them. Men who would be called young outside, are worth in goods and money from five to twenty-five thousand dollars. Disagreeable as it sounds, their trait of bagging, if it were natural with them, has been fostered. Many beg outright. Many beg by subtler means, and no person whom we have met, which includes every person on the island except a few old women in far camps, is above accepting "presents" which he knows the exact value of and purpose of its presentation.

Contrary to the custom of the white man, the Eskimo finds it most to his advantage to appear poor as possible instead of as rich as possible. We have had several funny experiences of being fooled by them. The man whom we have only this week found to be the wealthiest man on the island, we have been helping all year by giving him work, encouraging him, being as lenient with him as we could in fairness to our principles. One old woman whose husband is an invalid and who has had a great deal of help from former teachers sent us a note shortly after our arrival saying that she was not glad for our coming because we had sent her no tea and sugar and she was poor and had a sick husband and no sons to help her. We were quite downcast to receive such a letter when we had never even heard of her before, but we did not send her any presents. Instead we went to Gambell and told her among the others that we would give work to the poor ones and nothing else. She rallied immediately and has been all year the best and most cheerful worker we have had. I have lately found that she has wealthy relatives who help her all the time and that she wants for nothing at all ever. There are no destitutes at all here. Beggars are not destitutes no matter now sweetly they can say in their broken English that their babies are crying for food and they have "big think" what to do.

The characteristics which I have listed here under the names of the men on this Island are all of them comparative. When I say "honest", I mean that he is not a downright liar, but none of them are honest in the Christian meaning of the term. They will not be able to tell the truth about the values of their things unless they think you already know. They cannot help putting a per cent onto the cost price of something they desire to sell to you. They do not seem even to know that an unpleasant truth is ever expected from them. They will tell many fine tales of how [2] "you best every teacher" and "first time I hear about that" and "we never learn that before" and such stuff that they have learner somewhere or other. If they must say no to any request of the teacher's, you may be sure you will never get any unpleasant reason for the refusal. When I say superstitious, I mean that they are of the old time group who do things or refrain from doing them at certain times for religious reasons. The younger generation of men are growing out of it, but none of them are wholly fearless of offending their old customary gods whatever they are. Some; like Sepillu and Aningayu say they are not superstitious at all, but they too have streaks of it. But the really superstitious ones to an offensive degree are few and old, and fast losing their hold on the island, tho the number and forms of worships do not seem to diminish or change much as far as we can observe. By superstition, I do not mean their religion, either; just as many Christians are superstitious about Friday and a thousand little things, these people are afraid of moving old rocks, building fires in whaling time and such things. But I cannot hope to make you really understand the people with words. I only hope to give you enough information to start on so that you may come to an understanding of them and how to deal with them sooner than we did. We have been very cleverly "strung" many times. (I need a book of synonyms! I positively cannot find another word that means the same thing as strung.) It is not conducive to tolerance nor good work nor friendly feelings to know that one is ignorant and apt to do foolish things every minute of the day. One does not like nor love people before whom one has been ridiculous and it is important that we like the Eskimos if we are to work with them.

GAMBELL   Five families in lumber houses
                 Fifteen families in skin houses

Massiu. (I spell all the names as they sound with the English sounds of the letters. "a" of course varies from the long & short to the "a" as in "what". "I" and "e", "^o" and "u" have only the long and short sounds. I will not burden you with vowel markings. You will learn their names soon enough. They like their Eskimo names better than the English ones which some of them have, tho they often speak to a white person using the English name of the person spoken of.)

report camps

Massiu. Called an old man here. Hunts little. Carves a little. Skin house. Only one 15 year son living with him. No wife. One girl living with his brother. Son poor in school, much absent. Iyakitan is his only brother. Poor in cash but rich in Eskimo things. No education. Non progressive. No influence. Remains away from the teachers save to borrow picture books occasionally. Dirty. Of the group of most superstitious men.

Apata. One skin house. Three occupants. Two little girls in school. Not good attendance. Little girl bright. Older one getting more stupid every day. Has one married daughter who is an idiot. We fear he abuses his daughters as they grow older, but we have found no way of ascertaining our fears. No wife. Oldest and therefore boss of three other brothers, two living in Gambell, one at a far camp. Hunts little. Called old, Good carver but lazy and dishonest. No artistic sense. No English. Fairly prosperous. Beggar. Comes first thing to bring "present" to teachers. No influence. Would be friendly to teachers if petted. Did not like us.

Yaghak. Skin house. Four occupants. Wife. Daughter in school. Much absent. Not bright as some. Grown brother, Blassi, living with him. Apata his brother. Fair hunter. Fairly prosperous and progressive. Blassi, the bachelor brother speaks English well and attended men's night class. Not of superstitious element. Never comes around the teachers except to attend called meetings. Not a beggar like Apata. No English. [3]

Iyakitan. Skin house. Seven occupants. One old wife and one young one who is the worst beggar on the Island. Sorcerer. Most superstitious man here. One daughter and one son in school. Much absent. Not good in scholarship. Two small children. Massiu's daughter living with him and going to school. Fair hunter, fairly industrious, fairly prosperous. Pretends to be always in want. Begs from everybody. Dirty house. Dishonest family. Aloof from teachers. Sends to school only on compulsion. Perhaps the lowest family altogether that we have. Cheerful as everybody is. No English. No relatives save his brother Massiu. Young wife a good worker if not spoiled by gifts for no return. She did some excellent scrubbing for me.

Owhowin. Woman. Husband invalid with TB. Skin house. Three occupants. This is the old woman who wrote us the unpleasant note soon after our arrival. She is now a good friend and she is adorable. Good worker. Cheerful. Fine mimic. Good story teller. Two married daughters who are the wives of Athelingok, brother to Timkaroo. One grandson living with her going to school. Good attendance. Fair scholarship. This old woman was once a notorious character here, drinking, and all manner of things not done in the best of families, but she is good now. No English. Her daughters are among the few good sewers on the island.

Amagoo. Lumber house just built. One wife. (Had another but he turned her out in Siberia! She was a Siberian woman). One son who affects the company of older fellows and refuses to come to school without coercion. One half blind adopted son regular in school and excellent in scholarship. One daughter. Five in house. Good hunter. Fairly prosperous. They say he would have plenty but that he gives too much away. He and the beggar Iyakitan have lived together till this Springs. They made a good combination – one loving to receive and the other loving to give. No English. Industrious, but not of the progressives. Less superstitious than Iyakitan with whom he lived. One married sister.

Yawakseuk. Skin house. Five in house. Two children in school. Much absent and poor scholarship. This ends the little group living in the "North End" who are superstitious, aloof, beggars, nonprogressive, and who neither speak English nor send their children regularly to school. They have all huddled together in one section of the village, and save for Owhowin, are not much good. They believe that the US Bureau of Education exists to be begged from and they have no realization of any benefits the efforts it makes brings to them. They trade little at the store save for a few staple groceries. They come to none of the meetings unless sent for. They are not friendly, but neither are they surly or disagreeable. This man has a grown son who speaks English – Pasquatak – and who is working for Iyakitan's daughter. Another son who is reindeer apprentice in Peniu's camp. Wealthy. Good hunter. Industrious.

report camps

No English.

Montowkoli. Skin house. Five in house. Intelligent wife who came to sewing class. One frying sized son, Anangti, who is this year out of school for the first time. Anangti came to men's night class. One little son regular at school. Two small children, one of them born this year. Wealthy. Good hunter. Industrious. Dirty house. Little English. Progressive. Friendly to teachers tho he never comes around. Not a beggar tho any of them could easily be made beggars. They were frightened off this year. We told them it was a disgrace to beg and that white people who begged were no good. [4]

Timakaroo. Clean skin house. Six occupants. Two wives. No children. His niece, her husband and baby live with him. Another sorcerer, but much higher class than Iyakitan. Dignified old man. Does no work. No English. Not in any sense a beggar, at least to us. Wives good sewers. Relatives of Owhowin. Athelingok his brother. Wealthy. Progressive in spite of his superstition. Hard to become acquainted with. His brother speaks English.

Aningayu. The dirtiest house on the island. Lumber. Seven occupants. This is the storekeeper. Three children in school. Perfect attendance but too slow or lazy to learn much. Beautiful children. Wife a model of filth. Mother and. two small children besides. This man is extremely wealthy, shrewd, intelligent, ambitious, progressive, adopts white man's ways and foods as fast as he learns them. Has been many times converted. No superstition. Men's night class. Poor hunter. As honest as any. Has been the interpreter a long time. Not such good English as Sepillu of the reindeer camp, however. He it was who bought the boat about which we had so much trouble this year. Friendly, of course, to the teachers. A likeable person.

Booshu. Lumber house fairly clean. Four occupants. No wife, tho the rumor was spread this year that he had married the widow, Aganachlokuk, who is the village scold, but she told me that he was a no good husband and she had left him. Two sons in school. Good attendance, fair scholarship. One grown son, Iuwikson, who speaks English and attended the men's night class. Superstitious, but progressive. Head of a house of five progressive men all of whom live in other camps. Best whale hunter. They say he has the strongest prayers and that the whales follow his boat. Industrious. Little English. His brothers are Otiyohok, Tattoowi, Kinoko, and Aginaloo. They all speak better English than he. His son working for Shulook's youngest daughter, Agaanangarak.

Ozeevooseuk. Clean, lumber house. Nine in house. Wife who speaks some English, three children in school, one of whom will not attend next year, probably, having gone as far as any of them ever go. Good attendance, and fair scholarship. Two smaller children, mother, grown brother and uncle who is oldest man on the island all living in house. Mother named Weyu. She came with Owhowin every Saturday to scrub the schoolhouse. She is a good worker and the dearest old soul on the island. Grown brother, Kapunga, working for one of Shulook's daughters and therefore not much help in supporting Ozeevooseuk's family. Both men were constant attendants at men's night class. This man Ozeevooseuk is the former storekeeper. He is one of the four really poor families. He has a very hard time to make ends meet. He trades conscientiously with the store, is friendly to the teachers, ambitious, industrious and progressive, but he just does not get ahead. None of his family save the old old man who lives with him ever begs. They are a sweet clean beautiful family and I wish they might be helped in some way besides charity. He owes a large debt at the store Mid may never be able to pay it. We allowed him to get more in debt this year. Has one married brother, Rakok, herder in Peniu's reindeer camp, but he is not of much assistance to him save in sharing meat with him when hunting is bad. He conducted the last year teacher about over the island, with only promises as reward according to him.

hw: Next to Tangyun, this little crippled man is the best carver. Unlike Tangyun he will make anything, or try.[30]

Oitillan. Skin house. Seven occupants. Wife in sewing class. Two children in school, one of them getting too big to attend perhaps. Little one the brightest child in school. Perfect attendance. Son, Silook, the school teacher. Son's beautiful wife and fat baby living

---

[30] hw: = hand written text.

with him, or rather he and his family live with Silook's family, for
Silook makes the living. Industrious. Poor. Little English.
Progressive. One brother at Sepillu's reindeer camp who will be a
herder next year, tho a very unpopular one. This family is the
hardest to understand of any I have known. They are extremely
unpopular with their own people, being almost outcasts in a quiet
sort of way, nobody ever mentioning them in any way. They have
no friends that I know except the man, Mugayok, who married
Oitillan's daughter. Silook is friendly, willing, fairly capable, and
lovable after a great while of getting accustomed to him, but he
lacks force, or belief in himself. Something is wrong. I wish I could
understand it. Perhaps you will get closer to the people than I have
been able to do and find out just what their relations are to each
other. Tungitoo is the name of Oitillan's brother. He is as unpopular
as Oitillan.

Kaningok. Skin house. Dirty. Seven occupants. Three exceedingly
bright children in school. Good attendance. Oldest boy, Ifgachlak,
will not be in school next year. He has gone to Sepillu's camp to be
apprentice. Wife, chattering, laughing, dirty Yagho, member of
sewing class. One small boy, Maskin, his son-in-law and his
daughter live with him. Poorest man, perhaps. Industrious, always
trying, but never fortunate. Even in a son-in-law, he did not get a
helper. Maskin is one of the boys the Gambells reared. He is
intelligent and alert in some things, but he does not seem to fit
anywhere. He has lived too long in the white man's way to be able
to be happy where he is. He is fond of his wife, but her father will
not let her go away with him and he is forced to live in that very
dirty, poor house to whose support he renders nothing. Kaningok
speaks no English, but he is ambitious. Not a beggar, but his wife
would be one if she had any encouragement. It is the wives who
take over that disagreeable task anyhow. Maskin and Tokoya had
twins this year but they both died.

Aganachlokuk. "The widow". Skin house. Five occupants. Three
children in school. Good attendance and good scholarship save with
the baby who has attended only a few weeks. This woman [is]
sister-in-law to wealthy Shulook. But she is such a scold and foolish
woman that nobody seems to love to help her. She has all she wants

however from her brother-in-law and her son-in-law at Southwest Cape. She is a constant and whining beggar refusing to work. I offered to find her something to do every week – enough to buy her coveted sugar and tea – but she preferred to risk her begging qualities. She was not rewarded however. I gave her not one cube of sugar the whole year. She came with a note one time asking for one spoonful of tea and one piece of sugar. I set her to grinding flour for us and gave her sufficient to last her some time. She never came back after that.

Shulook. Skin house. Eleven occupants. Two grown sons moving away with their wives soon. One wife. Four married sons – Wamkon, who with his wife, two daughters and son live with him; Noongwook, herder at Sepillu's camp; Apitiki, recently married to one of Athelingok's daughters, and Ovi also recently married. These two last live with him now, but will gradually move away. Two grown daughters whom he uses as market produce to bring him in wealth. Amamunga, an old maid (*rara avis* here), pretty, clean, tidy, a good worker for teachers, and Iknakinuk living with Konahak. Boolowan is working for Amamunga. He is the sixth man to try to get her. He is wealthy and will probably succeed. Kapunga, brother to Ozeevooseuk has been working for several years for Iknakinuk. He is poor and will be likely worked a long time and then refused. He has one [6] daughter in school who will not be there next year perhaps. Booshu's son is working for her. This family is wealthy, progressive, ambitious, only moderately superstitious, educated. The chiitdren are good in school and never miss one day. Wamkon, Apitiki and Ovi came to men's night class and Amamunga and Iknakinuk came to sewing class. They all speak English. Tangyun, the best ivory carver is his brother. Shulook good whale hunter. Friendly to teachers and nearest neighbors. They are a loveable family but somewhat stingy and very likely to overcharge if not watched. Wamkon, the oldest son who lives with him has one daughter in school and two small children at home. His wife was also in sewing class.

Konahak. Skin house. Dirty. Eight occupants. Two wives, one of them young and prone to beg. Three children in school, one of them to be reindeer apprentice in Sepillu's camp next year. Good attendance. Mother always comes with baby astride her neck to see that her little boy learns fast. Old man is Konahak and unable to care for himself. Kapunga, the boy who is working for Iknakinuk who lives with him, is his only dependence for food except Sepillu, his nephew forty miles away. Poor. Superstitious. No English. Relation to Shulook. Has plenty, tho sometimes they get out of meat entirely. Sepillu takes care of them really and sends them food every day or so.

Ongwaluk. Skin house. Three occupants part of the time, tho some of the year two of his nephews and all their families live with him. Wife and one adopted son in school. Bright and good attendance. Wealthy. Always trying to learn. He is uncle to the SW Cape outfit. He is a good carver, but it is hard to persuade him to do it. Indeed, it is hard to get any of them to make things. He will charge high prices if he is not helped. He belongs to the same shrewd stock from which the SW Cape people spring.

Tangyun. Old man. Best carver. Brother to Shulook, brother-in-law to Sepillu. One bright little girl always in school. Two grown sons, Oovookitak at home and Yochkotak married and living with Timakroo's family. Oovookitak came to men's night class. One married daughter, wife of Napowatuk. This old man altho he is the best carver can not be persuaded to undertake anything besides paper knives, napkin rings and walrus teeth chains. He does these exquisitely compared to the rest of the work on the island but nobody's work can compare with the Chinese carvings of course. Industrious, cheerful. A sweet old man much like Shulook tho he [has] no English at all. He should have had the prize for the best carving at the Fair according to everybody's opinion. Lives in Seplll's lumber house.

Khkagak. Skin house and lumber house also. However nearly everybody has a lumber house beside his skin one which he uses in summer to live and in winter for a tool and store house. They are very proud of their lumber houses but their construction will never allow them to live comfortably in them. They have been built for style's sake and to please the vanity of themselves and the Government. This picturesque man has a wife and one child given to him by his nephew Napowatuk. Napowatuk with his wife and baby live with him and also Boolowan in the winter months, tho Boolowan has a very pretentious camp all his own over by the coal beds. He is working for Amamunga now, I hope he gets her. Extremely wealthy. Makes believe to be poor. Industrious, shrewd, no English. Napowatuk in translator for the family. Boolowan came to men's night class but he did not learn much. This is the man who has fooled us so completely about his prosperity. We thot they were poor until just lately. [7]

This completes the list of Gambell inhabitants. It is the largest settlement on the island and the poorest. However it is always so that poor people are found in clusters. Not all these people are poor. But if they would scatter out over the island they would fare better. The most prosperous ones are doing so gradually and others would follow if the store and school sought out better quarters. The village is just large enough to allow the old adage to come true − "to him that hath". The rich grow richer off the misfortunes of the poor and the poor grow richer.

Camp Kiyeechluk

This is the next camp over the mountain from Gambell. Only two families live here.

Ungottananowin. Lumber house. Fairly clean. One handsome wife and one son in school when they move to Gambell for the whaling. This son, Ochkagami, is the handsomest child here. The family is decently clean, lazy, shiftless, superstitious, unprogressive. Completely of the old regime of things. One young man cousin a little ahead of the rest of them lives here also, Oseuk. He speaks English and attended the men's night class when he came here. You would not expect them to be prosperous with such characteristics. But they are not beggars or miserably poor either.

Konooku. Lumber house. Fairly clean. Two stupid children in school when he moves to Gambell. One larger daughter living with Otiyohok, his brother. When one brother has no children another divides with him. One small child. No wife. Brother to Booshu.

Good hunter.   Industrious.   Good hunter.   Little English.
Progressive. Wealthy. Pays his bills at the store but does not make
many. With the exception of the poor people, most of these people
trade mostly with Pedersen. He brings good quality stuff, exactly
what they want, they can see what they are getting, and they love
more than anything the trading on shipboard. One cannot blame
them. They care absolutely nothing about what things cost. They
want what they want and they will get it. I think the store would be
smarter to copy his methods – charge a hundred percent profit and
pay twice as much for their produce. The store this year paid for fox
skins exactly what Pedersen paid.   But he bought them for
seventeen-fifty and sold them things for twice what the store sold
the same thing for. The store sold cheaper and paid only ten for
skins. They can not see that it is the same thing besides their
advantage of getting something back if the market outside is still
higher. It would be better to sell very high and very fine things and
buy very high likewise. It is the only way to put the store on its feet
with the richer ones.

Kozata's Camp

Kozata. Wife and baby. This is Apata's oldest daughter. She is an
idiot and her baby look to be also. I have not thot of any way to deal
with this.   Certainly an idiotic branch should not be allowed to
intermingle with the other people, but I do not know how to help it.
Skin house.   Dirty.   Industrious.   English.   Montowkoli and
Soonogorok are his half brothers. Wealthy, tho he looks stupidly
poor.   His lone house stands on the mountain on the way to
everywhere. But fortunately for him, it is so near to Gambell that
few people stop for "tea" on the way to and from places. [8]

Taphok

Athelingok. Log house but exactly like a skin house. Cleanest
family on the island. Two wives. three grown daughters married,
tho his youngest Kingonga and her husband Apiti live with him now
most of the time. One small son. Industrious. Wealthy. brother to
Timaroo. Little English. Independent. Friendly. Trades almost
entirely with Pedersen. Wears and uses and eats the very best of

everything.   His wives select the quiet patterns in goods and they know what is goof when they see it.   Best sewers on the island, perhaps.   If you insist, they will make your skins as soft as fawnskin, but they know the art of putting off cheap things on the teacher just as everybody else knows it.

Soonogagrook.   Log house.   Clean.   One wife.   No children. Wealthy. Industrious. English. Fair carver. Progressive. Bought about five hundred dollars worth of things from Pederaen this year and bought the very best of everything nor once asked the price.   I was present.   I mention Pedersen now because he has just been here and it is fresh in my mind.   When I wrote the Gambell people [section] he had not come.

Camp Collier

Nemiyak.   Two room log house.   Seven in one room.   Nemiyak has two wives one adopted daughter school age.   Tatoowi, youngest brother to Booshu, his wife and baby live with him.   He is Nemiyak's   son-in-law.   Very   superstitious.   Oldfashioned. Nonprogressive. No English. Fair carver. Wealthy. This man has the reputation of being the only henpecked man on the island. Farrar met his old wife who is said to boss both him and his younger wife. She is garrulous, cheerful, and he thinks perhaps smarter than most of the women.   We were quite pleased to hear that one woman here had spirit.   Tatoowi is wealthy and speaks English and is not so superstitious   as   his   father-in-law.   In   the   other   room   live Assoonaghak, brother to Nemiyak, his wife, one grown son, Nunraelu and his wife.   He also has one grown son Noongonuk, apprentice in Peniu's camp.   Whole outfit wealthy.   Dirty.   Stingy. They have a bad name because they do not invite every passing team to stop and have tea.   This is the custom here and since nobody every carries lunch, one who does not follow the custom is hated. Nunraelu speaks English.

Sevonga, Sepillu's Camp

Sepillu.   Two room log house.   Only house where one family uses two rooms.   Tho of course it is several families in one.   12 occupants. Clean house. One wife, three sons, two school age and exceedingly bright. One baby and one idiot daughter living with her grandmother in Noongwook's house. Wealthy. Industrious. An iconoclast, intelligent and independent man on the island. We like him very much because he is not cringing nor timid about expressing his own views. He has disagreed with Mr Burn several times about reindeer matters for which we regard him highly since he has been right each time. He is looked up to, a little feared and a little disliked by most of the people because he has cast off all superstition nor will not respect the do's and don't's out of fear of offending others. He is just the sort of man who could and would do big things. His half mother – one of his father's three wives – lives with him, also his foster brother, Tumbloo and wife and his youngest foster brother Atata. These are sons to the man whom his mother married. He was a real father to Sepillu and he is trying to be such a father to his young brothers as he calls them. They all seem to share equally. I expect Sepillu is worth in deer and other things many thousands. [9]

Noongwook: Skin house. Eight occupants. Wife, mother-in-law, two bright sons school age, baby, apprentice Ifgachlak, Brother-in-law to Sepillu, Son of Shulook in Gambell. Wealthy. Industrious. Good hunter. English. Good herder according to Sepillu. By the way, all these people at Sepillu's camp are so wealthy and progressive because Sepillu has organized them into a body of cooperation that exceeds anything we ever saw. They hunt together all under Sepillu's leadership. Sepillu appoints the watchers for the deer and looks after the welfare of the whole camp as if he were the grandfather of everybody. This Noongwook is next to Sepillu in intelligence and willingness to cooperate, They work together like brothers.

Oonmoohook. Skin house. 15 occupants. Very dirt. Wife, one bright little girl school age. Three-small children. Brother Mugayok with wife and baby, apprentice Tungitoo his wife and two children school age and one bachelor Stegurook working for Tungitoo's little daughter, Oonmoohook and Stesurook are herders. Tungitoo will be a herder next year and will move into his own house. Mugayok is not even an apprentice. He merely lives with his brother because he has nowhere else to live. He will become an apprentice as soon as he legally can. Stegurook is wealthy but a whining sort of wheedler whom nobody much likes. Mugayok is nobody. He married Silook's sister. Tungitoo is a no good apprentice. He is a thief. Nobody likes him nor his brother Oitillan in Gambell and I do not know why. He is lazy. Superstitious, or would be if Sepillu would allow it and selfish and dishonest, but so are many others who are not disliked. Oonmoohook is for all the world like a petted child with his cherubic expression and friendly manner, but he is as shrewd as J P [Morgan] himself. He is one of the wealthiest of the herders and nobody ever sees how he gets it. They call him the rich man, because he does not hoard like everybody else. When he has white man's food, he eats it with all his family until it is gone when he immediately gets more. He is careless of his money and will pay the most wonderful prices for the most worthless articles and still he never seems to grow poorer. He is lucky, I suppose. I wish some of his unearned good fortune might be turned over to Ozeerooseuk. This man is a fair herder. A little irresponsible.

Annogiyak. Skin house. Eleven occupants. Wife, daughter school age. Immingan his former apprentice lately made herder with his wife four and four children and Annogiyak's grandmother oldest woman on island living with him. Wealthy. Industrious. English, as all the other reindeer boys. Good herder and good hunter. A sweet sort of man with a lisp. His father is Tutmatolik living over at Cape Chitnak. Immingan is poor and irresponsible, but he is one of the most interesting characters here. He made a splendid apprentice because he is so industrious, but he just has not the make up to take responsibility. He must be looked after. He lives with the man to whom he was apprentice yet and does not seem to want to live in his own house. Indeed, he would starve soon if he tried it. He can do anything but he must be told. But that is not strange. He is a genius. He is the beat singer and dancer and story teller. He is a funny mimic and a lovable person.

Sepillu's whole camp is alive, cheerful, pleasant to be around. There is no sullenness except from Tungitoo. There is always laughter and singing and drums going in some house. They hunt every minute of all good weather. They have killed more meat at this camp than in Gambell. It is a group that might be excited to do almost anything that seemed to Sepillu practical. Sepillu is the ruling spirit. [10]

Peniu's Camp

Peniu. Log house. 10 occupants. Very very dirty. Wife, baby, Apprentice, Gologorongen, his wife and baby. Apprentice Akeyu, herder Kundlook and two old women. Wealthy, lazy in some things, charming, good English, good hunter, only fair herder. Chief of his camp but no authority. No initiative, no force, fearful to correct. Has not the ability to order affairs as has his distant cousin Sepillu. His house is rotten with venereal disease. It is the only family on the inland which suffers so terribly from this foul disease. His whole camp is affected also but not so bad as he is. There is not so much superstition in this camp as in Gambell, tho more at Sepillu's camp. Peniu is fairly free from its trammels. Peniu's father was a Siberian Eskimo, tho he was born here with a St Lawrence Island mother. It is his Siberian blood that make him so behind his friends in independence. Peniu is one of the cringers. No matter what is suggested to him, he agrees thinking to ingratiate himself with the teachers so. But that sort of cavilling does not please us. We want to know what he thinks. He thinks nothing. He seeks to please and in truth, he in one of the most pleasing persons on the inland. He has an attractive bearing and voice. He is unfitted to bear the responsibility of chief of his camp.

Pungowiyi. Log house. 13 occupants. Wife, three small children, brother Wongottollin, with his wife and five children, his apprentice Kiyuchluk. Both brothers Siberians. Born there. It is said that they killed two of their brothers to get their property. Very wealthy. Industrious. Selfish. Does not enter into life here. Lives to himself. Is the largest man on the island and consequently feared and disliked. A herder and good hunter. If he were liked, he would be better than Peniu as chief of the camp, but he would turn all the activities of the camp to enriching himself and unlike Sepillu have no friendly cooperation [by] all sharing equally. They say of him here that he is "everything for Pungowiyi". A little incident that happened the first of the year will show you what he is. Peniu had lost a sack of flour in the changing the freight from the *Bear* to another boat. He was looking for it with the store things and had talked a good deal about it for a sack of flour is a sack of gold to them. Farrar and Sepillu were there in the Fall, they found Peniu's sack with Pungowiyi's things quite by accident and supposed that neither Peniu nor Pungowiyi knew it was there. They told Peniu of it right away and would have told Pungewiyi if he had been there. Peniu was alarmed and begged them not to mention it at all. He said that if he got out of flour Pungowiyi would let him have all he wanted anyhow and that it did not matter. Farrar wanted to straighten out the matter since it to appear that a theft had been committed, but he saw that it would make it harder than easier for Peniu so he let it go. Pungewiyi is not stingy. Only selfish.

Metuchluk. Log house. 11 occupants. Wife, baby, mother-in-law, Apprentice Noongonuk with his wife and two small children. His wife's three younger brothers and sisters large enough for schools. Not very wealthy. Fairly industrious. Poor herder. Little English. Superstitious. This man never heard of or seen often. He lives quietly and lazily.

Waghyi. A tiny log addition to Metuchlu's house. 4 occupants. Wife two small children. Poor. Lazy. Very superstitious. Poor herder, Poor hunter. Very little English. People say everything is poor about this man. Poor fellow! Farrar says he is absolutely no good and should never have been made a herder, but what is a teacher to do? There is Tungitoo who ought not to be made a herder yet whom Farrar himself [11] will make out a contract for [him] very likely. The teacher is the only one who knows about the situations that arise, yet he does the thing everybody else does because he despairs of making them plain to those whose authority he must secure to change them. I suppose it is just as well, tho, for the reindeer do not know the difference.

Rakok. Log house 10 occupants. Wife, small child, one grown soon, Awetuk, his apprentice, Alowa, and his wife and three children, one of which is school age. His mother. Fairly poor. He is brother to the unfortunate Ozeevooseuk, fair hunter, fair herder, fairly superstitious. fair English. As a matter of fact he is little good. All the men of this camp are either no good or they need some energetic forceful leader with a little public spirit. But what community does not need such a miracle? Sepillu is the only one we have found on this island who is able to combine the qualities of leader with sufficient humility to be tolerable. Pungowiyi would rouse up the camp, but he would have an old Russian tyranny, I expect before many years. There is no leadership there. This Fall when Farrar was visiting the camp, the men were attempting to lasso and mark the apprentices' deer. Nobody in camp save Pungowiyi could use the rope. Farrar was indignant. He told the men who had no ropes and who stood around with their hands drawn in out of their sleeves and warming against their bellies that they must all have ropes next day and must learn how to use them between that night and next morning. That if they had no other rope they must bring a fishing line – any thing. This Rakok, who is a solemn fellow, took him at his word and appeared with a little fish line and what was more remarkable actually caught one deer with it! Farrar told me to tell this incident, but for my part, I don't see why they mightn't catch deer with fish line as well as any other sort.

Tumnik

Kitluchkon. Log house, 7 occupants. Wife, step father, Ekmalowa, his two wives and one grown son, Toosuk and one grown daughter. Wealthy, industrious, good hunter, English. Owes the store about a hundred and fifty dollars. By the way, this Toosuk, son to Ekmalowa, has a Portuguese father who married his mother, one of the wives to Ekmalowa, one time when he was wrecked here. When he left, he gave her many presents and continues to send her "whole trunks of fine dresses" according to the natives. Toosuk, named Booker by Dr Campbell, is black with thick lips and close curls! He is intelligent and charming however and superior to most of these people in his ability to appreciate niceties. He is working for Aningayu's daughter.

Otiyohok's Camp

Otiyohok. Log house. 8 occupants. Wife, very bright son in school when they move to Gambell. His brother Aginaloo, and his two

150

children and Meleeutkuk, a grown bachelor working for Aginaloo's daughter. And Kokasowin, a deaf man from Siberia lives with him also as a sort of servant. Wealthy. Brother to Booshu. Industrious. Shrewd. A wheedler. Very funny. Always laughing. Good English. Independent.

Echuk's Camp

Echuk. Log house. 5 occupants. Wife, two small children, mother. He is cousin to Aningayu. Fairly wealthy. Is dependent on Aningayu for his initiative. Fair hunter. Little lazy. English. He moves to Gambell for whaling in common with the rest of the world, but he becomes upon his arrival Aningayu's "man". He is a nice sort of fellow with a pleasant voice. [12]

Ataka's Camp

Ataka. 16 x 24 tent. 12 occupants. This is larger than most of the houses. Ataka has an old wife and no children. He has adopted two, one of school age. Kingeekuk and his wife, cousins, and Komowiyi and his wife live with him. Kanuchtugayuk, his wife and two children all live together in this tent on the extreme east side of the island. Ataka, and I suppose those who live with him, are wealthy. Ataka speaks good English in the most musical voice I remember to have heard anywhere. He is industrious and usually catches more foxes than any other man. He caught thirty eight this year while the largest number caught by any other man was thirteen. He is friendly, progressive, not objectionably superstitious. A heavy trader with Pedersen but he pays his store bills.

Cape Chirnak

Tutmatolik. Half underground log house with split whale bone roof. Sepillu built it for himself when the deer were over there. It still belongs to Sepillu. 5 occupants. Wife, three children school age. One of his daughters, Mahkanak, is the prettiest girl on the island. She has no tattooed marks, her lips are not too thick, nor her nose too flat nor her face too large for actual beauty. Sepillu's youngest brother Atata wants to marry her, but Sepillu says they are too young yet, and he wants to be sure they love each other. Strange talk for this island! Tutmatolik is wealthy, a good hunter tho he is getting old, always has plenty of white man's food. Herder Annogiyak is his son and boss. No English. His children are bright.

SW Cape

Oktokiyuk. Iwurrigan, and Irrogoo live together, sometimes all three families in the skin house, sometime one family in the lumber house, sometimes two of the families in Grambell where they have also two houses. Oktokiyuk is the boss of the outfit by reason of his shrewdness, extreme cleveness. The skin house in which he lives belongs to old man Anowgatuk, who is dependent on him now for support. 15 occupants when they are all there. Oktokiyuk has a wife and two adopted sons. Old man Anowgatuk belongs to his family. Iwurrigan has a wife, one crippled son, one adopted daughter, and one real baby whom he will give to Oktokiyuk when it is weaned. Irrogoo has a wife and two children. This outfit is wealthy, good hunters, industrious, progressive in the taking on of new customs that will enrich them, superstitious, thoroly dishonest, talebearers and thieves. Oktokiyuk is the shrewdest philosopher and observer of the characteristics of his neighbors of any man we have seen here. He is effusive, flattering; gossiping, cringing and wholly charming – until you find him out. It is nice while it lasts. I have many entries in my diary which humiliate me a little to read now, about his being such a loyal man. He is the one who tells so many tales of teachers and his own people. He is extremely jealous of others. One time I paid a man a dollar and a half for some mittens which his wife had knit for me. Richard told us it was too much and that his wife could do much better. Farrar had her do some for him and just to see what he would do offered him one seventy five for them which Richard accepted with a shamed look at me. We said nothing to him. One year he stole a fox from another man's trap. He was reported by the teacher, but not punished. This year he has committed a forgery on a government slip which belonged to another man. I do not know what Farrar will do about it, but what is there to do? It is a serious offence but unless the officers knew all the past history of the case, they are not likely to regard it as very serious and the influence of any teacher to come would be weakened

report camps

if nothing were done. One can only let reproof which a man who would do that [13] would not much mind, stand for punishment, I tell you about it so that you may let it warn you in time to watch him nor to trust him as we did. He stole many of our personal supplies bout we have only the fact that they disappeared to prove it. We have not reproached him with that. Richard is so lovable – like all scapegoats! – that it is hard to remain stern with him. When we are absent from him we can be sure that we will punish him for his wickedness, but when we are with him again we forget all about it. He cast a spell with his effusiveness which it is hard to break. We have spoken to him about his talebearing and his lying to us and we had a talk with him before we left telling him all these things, but that is not punishment.

Ugulowuk. Skin house with lumber house adjoining, which the store rented this year, 11 occupants. Father Agak, old mother, and their two grown unmarried children. His (Ugulowuk's) wife, three children, brother Umiworri with his young wife. Umworri has heart disease. Ugulowuk is the boss of the family. He is a little like Richard Oktokiyuk, who is his brother-in-law. He is wealthy, not much English. Industrious. Good hunter. Superstitious. Fairly progressive. Indifferent to teachers. He and the Oktokiyuk family trade largely with Petersen but considerably with the store also. Ugulowuk pays his bills, but Richard does not. The SW Cape bunch live to themselves. Nobody like them much because of their tale-bearing and stealing. I do not think Ugulowuk, Harry, steals, but he knows of Richard's lapses or course. They belong to the old regime.

By the way, Irrogoo, Richard's youngest brother was a member of the men's night class when he was in Gambell. He is something of a smart alec, a bit impertinent, but we like that better than meek and false submission. He is shrewd and intelligent and as dishonest as Richard.

Sclkwako's Camp

Sclkwako. Skin house. 5 occupants. Wife, three children, and mother. He is moving his lumber house from Gambell to SW Cape now where he will live most of the year. He whales with that crew. Wealthy. Industrious. English. Good hunter, killed the only polar bear this winter which has been killed. This is the last camp on the island. We are back around to Gambell again. It is about three hundred miles around the island this way and I am tired and I know you must be worn out. I hope it has been worth this work to you. I do not want our likes and dislikes to color the picture for you. One is sure to think his period of activity a momentous one. The natives truly do not remember even the names of any of the teachers save the Campbells and the most recent ones, and most of them have forgotten back to Dooley. I can not think in view of that that anything matters such a terrible lot, still they have grown to their state of superiority over their near of kin the Siberian Eskimos just by the efforts of the teachers. Not much progress is made in any particular year, but certainly some progress has been made in the quarter of a century during which the government has been working. I wish you every success and a pleasant year. I wouldn't take a million for my year up here but I wouldn't give a dime for another one. That is why I am trying so hard to give you the complete story of our year – to ease my conscience for leaving so soon. Mr Burns may remain. He actually likes the country and the climate and feels a wothwhileness in the work that he has not found elsewhere. Take good care of him if he is with you next year.

Best Wishes, June Burn

REINDEER

I [Farrar Burn 1] was enthusiastic over the reindeer from the beginning. It has proved to be not only my most interesting work during the year, but it promises to hold my interest. The reindeer is the greatest blessing the Eskimo has had bestowed upon him and I believe that the most effective work of the Bureau of Education is being done thru this animal.

The reindeer on St Lawrence island are divided into two herds which are overseen by two camps of herders with their apprentices. Both camps are on the north side of the island. The first is about forty miles east of Gambell and is known as Sepillu's camp as Sepillu is its chief herder. The other is about fifteen miles further east and is known as Peniu's camp. Peniu is its chief herder.

There are three times in particular during the fiscal year when the local Superintendent should not be absent from the

report reindeer

reindeer herd. These are the times of marking for the apprentices, the time of fawning, and the time of counting.

Marking for the Apprentices

Marking is done in the Fall of the year as soon after the arrival of the local Superintendent as possible. It should not be delayed until cold weather comes for there is danger of the ears being frozen. I was late in arriving on the island and we did not get to this until the .first week in November. Cold weather, however, delayed its coming until after the ears had time to heal. We were over a week in marking this year because of the inclement weather. We were unable to mark all the deer for one apprentice because there was no room left on the ears. We resorted to a canvass strip about the neck until I could devise some other means for marking them. The apprentices' marks being an addition to the herders', the latest marks are becoming very complicated. We have no aluminum marking buttons. I designed some to be made of walrus teeth which we are trying out as an experiment. A copy of these designs is attached herewith.

This was my first visit to the reindeer camps and I was greatly impressed with the spirit shown at Sepillu's camp and the lack of it at the other. Sepillu is a natural leader. He is business like and uncommunicative. He orders his camp with no seeming effort. Peniu, on the other hand, while charming personally and just as intelligent as Sepillu, has not the natural qualities which make him able to lead men. His father was a Siberian Eskimo and most of the men at his camp are themselves Siberians or of Siberian parentage. They do not seem to have made the progress of the St Lawrence Island Eskimos. They are selfish and indolent and do not cooperate with Sepillu in his attempt to make the reindeer industry a big thing for this island. I would like some suggestions from the Seattle office about how to deal with them. The men of Peniu's camp are too submissive, too apt to take the word of the Superintendent no matter how little [2] he may know of the matter about which he may be enquiring. They will not make intelligent suggestions nor dare to contradict any suggestion of the Superintendent, no matter how foolish it might be. I would have made one serious mistake this year if I had had no other adviser than Peniu. I have not fauna out whether it is that Peniu actually has poor man material to work with or whether the whole difference lies in the qualities of the two men. I could give many examples of this difference, but the one that impressed me most at first was the fact that all the herders and apprentices at Sepillu's camp had lariat ropes and knew how to use them while at Peniu's camp we were able to scrape up only three ropes and with the exception of Pungowiyi not one man knew how to use then. This as well as the weather delayed the marking

Fawning Time

Fawning season here begins usually the last week in April or the first in May. I was determined to spend this time among the herders. School in Gambell closed the last of April and on the following day Mrs Burn and I moved to Sepillu's fawning camp. Sepillu and all his camp had moved the week previous when the very first of the fawns were arriving. Characteristically, Periu's camp did not more until two weeks later after two hundred fawns had been born. It is extremely important that the fawns and does have constant watching during this time as you of course know. Sepillu's camp was pitched at a point a little west of North Cape where the topography of the land is such that the deer may be readily driven to the lee side of the mountain for protection from most any wind. Peniu pitched camp adjacent to Stolbi rocks.

I borrowed a tent, a camp stove and materials for a camp cot from the natives and Sepillu had everything ready for our comfort upon our arrival at his camp. A camping outfit for the use of the reindeer superintendent here is very desirable and I hope you will feel the same way about it when you receive my order for the coming [sic] for the coming year.

The second week of May we had a severe snow storm. The heaviest loss of fawns occurred during this time. Men were kept constantly with the herd watching in relays. With this exception, there were very few losses in the two camps. Sepillu pronounces it a successful year. The bucks and weathers are kept separated from the does until the fawns are strong.

There has been no new blood introduced into this herd for several years. We would like to exchange at least two bucks with the Teller station. I heard while in Home that these deer average larger than those of the mainland, but I have not verified it.

I visited Peniu's camp in May after he had moved. Things were going well there also. By the first of June the fawning was practically over. We returned to Gambell for two weeks before going again to the reindeer camp after the deer had been gathered into the corral for the counting.

Counting the Deer

When I brot up the subject of counting the deer here, I was informed by the herders that these deer have not been counted since Mr Bigger counted them in 1907. It is hardly necessary to make a positive count each year, but one should be made every five years. The herders agree heartily. We decided to consolidate the two herds at the corral as soon after the middle of June as the weather and the strength of the young fawns would permit. This was done without [3] [harm.]

This report was written at Gambell just before leaving for Reindeer Harbor where the corral is located. I am sure we shall have no difficulty. We are planning to assemble all the deer into the corral and drive them into a small pen one by one where they will be counted and inspected as to ownership, sex, age, color and physical condition. Results of this count will be attached on a separate form.

Pasturage

I do not think there is anything that grows on this island that the deer will not eat, including several varieties of moss, grass and its roots, and another variety of small roots which it digs from the ground. There is also a variety of dry moss, black and scaly in appearance in appearance [sic] that grows on the rocks here. Sepillu said that his knowledge of this had saved the deer a few years ago when ice glitters prevented the regular feeding. He drove them to the rocky places uncovered by the snow and they subsisted on this scant food until the thaw. There has not been this difficulty of this sort this year.

Since the reindeer first came, they have been gradually moved toward the east end of the island as the pasturage gave out and in a few years the herds will probably be established near NE

Cape. The location of a reindeer camp here depends on pasturage, hunting, and drift wood deposits. The ground which was grazed bare several years ago will soon be ready for the deer again. Sepillu says it faces ten years for the moss to acquire its normal growth again. There is sufficient food on this island for a herd of the present size, but I do not think it advisable to allow much of an increase. It may be necessary to market a few old does each year along with the weathers.

Marketing the Reindeer

We have never eaten meat so good as reindeer. It is a fancy meat and should demand fancy prices on the market. Last year lambs were selling on foot in Puget Sound at eleven dollars each. When we arrived in Nome the St Lawrence Island reindeer men were disposing of six hundred reindeer under contract to Nome merchants at the same price. The carcasses were sold with skins on and the boys had to purchase Siberian reindeer skins in Nome at a cost of from two seventy five to four twenty five each, delivered thru the native store. This may have been the best that could have been done under present conditions, but we may be able to improve the conditions. We might build a small cold storage house here or cooperate with the mainland natives in building a larger one in Home. I am under the impression that a cold storage has been or may be installed, on the *Boxer* for the purpose of transporting the meat outside. A small canning outfit might be made use of. Or any other means of preserving the meat for shipment so that we may be able to place it where the chances of securing a fair price are greater. If we could retain the skins, it would be far better. These deer are free from any contagious diseases and the importation of deer skins is dangerous.

Sled Deer

There are now about twenty sled deer on the inland. On December 2nd a caravan on ten deer sleds hauled coal from SW Cape to Gambell. Two sacks were hauled on each sled drawn by one deer. With one exception this is the only time that sled deer were used during the year. I was told by the herders that they were too poor to work. I had expected to use deer exclusively for the freighting if possible, but every camp is full of hungry dogs and it is impossible to [4] keep sled deer in their vicinity. The number of dogs is increasing, while the deer is being used less and less. This is because the dog are more convenient. They hang around the houses with in reach when needed, exist on the filth and garbage of the camps and travel at a greater speed. The deer must either be staked a mile or two from camp generally three or four, where moss is plentiful or food must be gathered and stored for them. Neither is done here. They are with the herd unused. Most of the deer are old ones. Few have been tamed in the last few years. I believe the deer is superior even here to the dog for freight transportation if he can be given proper care. His use should be revived and encouraged. It is impossible for the local superintendent to set an example himself while residing in Gambell. There is no moss within several miles of here and the village is full of starved dogs. The same objection can be made to both reindeer camps. If I remain next year and succeed in getting a cabin built at the Reindeer Harbor away from any camp, I shall use deer exclusively for all travel. I shall be able to learn just how much trouble they are and how far they might be made useful here.

Herders and Apprentices

A detailed account of each herder will be found in "People of St Lawrence Island" by June Burn {above}.

Chief Herder

A division of deer between two chief herders is unsatisfactory. Two heads are better than one only when one of them has charge. More could be accomplished by working thru one chief herder. I suggest replacing Sepillu in charge of all the deer on this island, with Peniu, or some other herder with more backbone as assistant, in charge of the second camp. Sepillu was chief herder of all the deer here a few years ago, and I believe received a salary of 25.00 a year from the Government. When the heard was divided this expenditure was stopped. There was some difficulty, perhaps, then which I do not know about. I have had to rely exclusively on

Sepillu for everything connected with the work, for meat, and for transportation. He has responded promptly ad cheerfully every time and has made many suggestions that have meant more work for himself. He is the only native on the island who is giving any thot toward the future of the reindeer. He receives suggestions eagerly, considers them carefully, and accepts those which we both agree are practical.

Enthusiasm

The reindeer men know nothing whatever about the reindeer business anywhere else. They have one circular letter which you sent out years ago and which they still show proudly and read often. They love nothing in the world better than to read in magazines and to find something pertaining even remotely to their lives up here delights them beyond measure. I have been thinking how to arouse some lasting enthusiasm among them without adding to the already overburdened Seattle office. A bulletin published yearly including interesting articles on the reindeer business all over the world would be helpful, for they take as law and gospel what they read in books and would immediately put to trial new suggestions found there, but this "bulletin would be a burden at the wrong end of the line. But I still think some literature of some kind must be sent to them. If you will send magazines old and new containing articles on the deer no matter how far from practical the articles may be, and a few books on the world outlook of the deer, together with some notes on what is being done in Canada, Russia, Alaska Mainland, etc, the local Superintendent could certainly make himself popular getting up a bulletin for them. [5]

I know how effervescent is enthusiasm aroused from outside-in. Still, I think that aroused by a sort of club organization might not be so short lived as we are used to seeing it outside. I have talked to the boys about a club among the herders and apprentices with competitive offices such as, after Chief Herder, Roper, Butcher and Writer, the offices to be won by trial yearly at a little "big time" among themselves. They would love the big time of it, and I believe it would bring them closer together. They are two groups now with little in common. They have nothing setting them aside from other men as reindeer men save the deer themselves. Do you think such an organization of these men would effect this desired unity among them? I want them to know more about deer. Dream more about them. I believe the local Superintendent could do a great deal thru this club yearly to broaden their understanding of their own business. It is little or nothing the Superintendent can do in his ignorance in the line of helping them perform already long familiar duties. He can bring outside information to them, however, and that would be the most welcome service he could render. This is a threadbare idea which usually falls to nothing after the first year. Something steadier, more fundamental, more grown-up is needed but I can not think of it now. Of course I realize that the enthusiasm shown by the reindeer men will be only an image of that possessed by each local Superintendent. I know you have tried out almost everything possible to lift the men into enthusiasm but ideas which have grown old to men long in the work are new and full of possibilities to new men who have not been thru the failures and disappointments. Perhaps if you could give the new man an idea of what has and is being already done, he could build well on that. Certainly, I am puzzled. There is a remarkable group of man up here to work with, Sepillu alone catching so readily to new ideas and trying out so willingly each suggestion, that one wants to leave something permanent with them.

Respectfully,

Farrar Burn Local Superintendent
St Lawrence Island, Alaska

RITES[31]

KAMALERU

One of the St Lawrence Island race worship called *Kamaleru*. If a man has a worship of *kamaleu*, he is the best runner. And so he has a running stick with a piece of reden [reddened] seal skin tied in the end of the stick. And that is his idol. And so when he has a worship, he takes out the stick out side the house and every body come to join the race. And so if the man that had the worship if he has a fox skin, he would take it out for the best runner, and let him have the fox skin for the race. And the next man gets tobacco, tea, or bread. And after the race, the old men and old women eat deer fat with deer meat outside of the house.

The worship last only one day.

And it is over.

HUGHKOWAK

Hughkowak is the name of one of St Lawrence Island Boat worship.

In summer the Eskimo's boat captains' wives fill one poke each of Eskimo vinager [vinegar, fermented greens]. And also the [they] hung some meat to dry. And if they had killed a whale they also fill one poke of whale skin. Only the man that killed a whale fills the poke of whale skin. And all these are ready for the boat worship.

Then in winter when they kill mukluk they take a piece of meat and blubber. And also put them away for the worship. That's all the things. The boat worship begins from February ~ March to April. Some of them worship in February, some in March, and some in April. Worship starts when the new moon comes.

In the day they get ready for the worship and get the vinegar,

---

[31] Koneak ~ Silook lists rites of *atrruk, kamuxtak, akomoleik, kazua, magraluk, iveik, terregrsek,* with vital regard of *Moon* (Leightons 1983:147-8). Ideal men had rites to become either strong or fast.

dry meat, and piece of mukluk meat and blubber. And open them up. And put them in the middle post of the house. And also get the pokes and irons for the whale and also put them in the house. And in the night the boat [2] captain sings half the night only about the whale. Then tomorrow the men that belong to the boat takes down the boat and then the boat captain and his wife brings the pan full of vinager and another pan of dry meat and mukluk meat and put them into the boat. And the boat captain's wife goes home. So then the men pull the boat down to the ice where they find [open] water. And stay there till the sun comes up. Then they threw tiny pieces of vineger, dry meat, mukluk meat and tobacco into the water and pray at the same time. Then after praying, all the boat men eat. After eating they pull the boat home and put the back in its place. And they all go to the boat captain's house. Only the boat men or the crew. Then they give to every house that is on the island a little pieces of dry meat, vinegar, and tobacco. The rest the boat crew divides them up to them selves. And the worship is over. They believe that it will help them to catch whales and walrus, etc.

END

MUGALUK

Mugaluk is the name of one of the St Lawrence Islander's worship. Treading to each other at singing and dancing is call in Eskimos *Mugaluk*. The Eskimos believe that if some one gets sick, and if they call the *Mugaluk* they will cure the sick person by this worship. The worship starts stats all ways when winter comes, don't care if the man that has the worship call the worship at summer time. He have to use it in winter. Six families have this worship of *Mugaluk* not many years ago. They have to use this worship every year for five years. If they call the *Mugaluk* some of them use wooden carved foxes and some wooden carved seals and walrus heads for an idol. And two idols a man and woman about five inches high. And they have it at day and night time. It lasts about six days. If a family has a worship their relations come to take part if they wanted to go. Any body can go to see them sing and dance any time at day or night time. [2]

HOW MUGALUK BEGINS AND ENDS

If a man had a worship of *Mugaluk*, first, he would make lots of little wooden idols in day time. Then after noon he fastened the idols to the rope that he had tied in the house. Then his wife gets a lamp and puts the lamp in the middle of the house and lights it. And allso [also] they hang little pieces of seal skin. And after their work is all gone [done] the family goes out and goes to their relations and say, Tomorrow^ will be *Mugaluk*. And they would sing in that house in the outer room. And go to another house. And do the same way. Then they come home and sing in the dark for a while. Then to morrow the relations come to join the worship. And so when they come the man that is the head of the worship goes out to the outer room and some of their best friends come. While the people are going around the middle post of the house, head man of the worship goes in front of them and sing while they are going around the post. And then every body goes in the sleeping room and tells stories. Then the third day [3] they just come to tell stories all day and talk about the worship. Then the fourth day, they all come to go around the post once more. And go in and tell stories. Fifth day every body comes to join the singing and dancing and treading. And so man and women put their things on the floor and dance for once song. And the dance is over. Night comes. Every doctor man comes to sing at night time if they want to come. And so they do all kinds of wonderful things. And anybody can go to see them things. They want to come. When they are finished singing, the head man of the worship goes to the outer room and puts away the idols and lamps. Then at sixth [day] head man and his family gets up very early in the morning and take the wooden idols out side of the house and light a fire and burns them idols. When they burn, the worship they think the worship goes where the man saw him. And they think that the worship when he goes of the house. That the worship tells stories to the devil that gave it to the man.

And the Mugaluk is over tell [til] next year.

KILLING A WHALE OF [BY] ESKIMOS

If any boat kills a whale, they would go around the dead whale tow times in thier [their] whale boat. And also put

Aghunghowak on the body of the dead whale. Then after they had done those things, they take of [off] the whale's fluke. And when they take them off, they take of the fins. And they take of the nose of the whale. And they take the eyes off. And a little piece of whale's chin. And also a little piece of whale skin from the belly. And after those things, they also take off one side of the whale bone. And on the other side, they take off nearly half of the bone. And so the other boats join in when they are taking off the bone. And also the man that had killed the whale fills one poke of whale skin. And the other boats get all they want of the whale skin [2 / 32] and so these things are the holy parts of the whale

     { The eye
     { nose
     { fins
     { fluke
     { and a little piece of whale chin and piece of black skin from the billy [belly] of the whale and one poke full of whale skin
            That's all the holy things

ABOUT KILLING WHITE BEAR

If the people of St Lawrence Island see a bear, the man that saw the bear would have the bear skin and the head. Don't matter if the other people kills the bear. He belongs [gets] the bear head and the skin after they kill the beer.

Of it they are out hunting in their canoe and see a bear and kill it, the bear head and skin belong to the captain of the canoe.

After they kill the bear on the ice they go around the bear two times with their canoe and say like this while they are going around the dead bear: *Gho gho gho.*

Then they get to the bear's head and stop to say gho gho gho. They go around to the right side of the bear and say the same words. After that they cut up the bear.

They cut off the bear's head with the skin attached on the head. That is the holy part of the bear. And they take off the skin of the bear and some meat and come home.

When they get home many old men and women goes to get some meat. And so the captain of the canoe cuts up the bear skin and gives some to the old men and some meat.

And the rest of boat crew divides the meat up that is left. Then the captain takes the head and puts it under the door outside of the house. And he lights a fire close by the bear's head. He tells his wife to bring a piece of deer fat. And so the boat captain and his crew eat the fat before the head of the bear.

After that the captain takes the head in the sleeping room. And they put on the necklace on the bear's head. Then tomorrow some old or young people come to tell stories to the bear's head. They tell stories to the head of the bear for five days. [2]

After those five days, they cook the head and eat the meat of the bear's head. And when they have eat the meat off, they take the bear skull outside of the house and tie the skull behind their house. When they tie the skull of the bear, they always point the mouth to the north.

When they tell stories to the head of the bear, they think that the spirit of the bear tells to other living bears that the two legged people were very good to him. The Eskimos believe that the bears change to men at their home place somewhere.

END

ECLIPSE OF THE MOON

There is a reason when the moon eclipses. They believed when it is in eclipse, it is the moon fainting and they believe there happens something [happens there] to another place and so they believe the moon is telling a story about the country that has trouble.

When it could not be seen, the old woman or old man would sing some kind of song with a scapula for a drum in the out doors. They believe by doing this, it will come to life or show its light again.

STORIES

ANIMALS

ABOUT THE FOX AND THE CROW

Once there lived Mr Fox and his wife Noo-tang-owin. And Mr Crow lived with them and his wife Me-dea-ka in the same house. So they had many children. Mr Fox and Mr Crow had to hunt all the time.

But Noo-tang-owin and Me-dea-ka had to stay home with there [their] children. Mr Fox had brought food every time he went hunting. But Mr Crow had not bring anything at all sometimes. So they had no more food. They had a hard time, so they had a famine. But Mr Fox and Mr Crow didn't stop going hunting. At last Mr Fox said to Mr Crow tomorrow I am going to King Salmon's house and I am going to take my sled with me.

So he went. And got to King Salmon's house and went in to see him. All the other salmons told him not to talk to [too] much so the King Salmon wouldn't get mad at him. So King Salmon saw him and said to Mr Fox, sit down here and wait till I come in, and I will let you eat when I come in. And King Salmon went out, and he saw Mr Fox's coat and he put the coat on, and went in and said to Mr Fox, How do I look like. Mr Fox said, Why did you put my coat on? You look so big [2] and strong that I think you will tear my coat. Please King Salmon, Take my coat off. The Mr Fox fooled him, just to make him think he was a big strong salmon. So King Salmon went out smiling, and took off Mr Fox's coat and came in, and said to the other salmons to get food for Mr Fox. So the salmons got food quick because they were afraid of their King. Then the Fox was ready to go home. So King Salmon told the other salmons to load his sled meat of all kinds.

Then Mr Fox had a big load of meat. He was very glad. So he went home and got home at night time. And he called his wife Noo-tang-owin, Come out, I have a big load of meat. So she came out and helped her husband. Then they went in and had a big dinner. While they were eating, Mr Crow called Mr Fox and said to him, Where did you get them load of meat? Mr Fox said to him, I will not tell you. I will go again if we have no more food. But Mr Crow said, I will go tomorrow and see if I can't get a load too. So Me-dea-ka said to her husband, Don't go, you will do something wrong where Mr Fox [3] gets food for us. But Mr Crow said to her, I will go and bring a bigger load of meat for my children. So Mr Crow went on his way to visit the King. And he got there all right, and he went in. And the salmons said to Mr Crow, Don't talk to [too] much. King Salmon will get mad at you. Oh never mind, Don't be afraid of him, he is to [too] small to be afraid of. And he is no good at all. Will give me food, I am very hungry, five me some thing, to eat quick. So the salmons said to him, but we have to obey our King, and do what ever he tells us to do. Then the King came and told Mr Crow to sit down and wait for him.

So King Salmon went out and he saw the Crow's coat and put it on, and went in, and called Mr Crow, How do I look like? Mr Crow said, Well you look like nothing! Why did you put my coat on? Take it off quick and give me food! I am very hungry and want to go home as soon as I can!

Then the King was mad and told his servants to open the water, so they did, and the salmons house to [into] a river, and nearly drowned Mr Crow. So Mr Crow got nothing but [4] nearly drowned. So Mr Crow went home and got home when it got dark, and called his wife Me-dea-ka, I am almost dead. I have no food King Salmon did not give me food.

Then Mr Fox said to Mr Crow, Now we are going to have famine again because you made the King mad. So they had a famine once more. Then Mr Fox went hunting again. He was gone for two days, he went out on the ice and found a dead walrus and carried it home and got home when it was night. So they had food once more. When Mr Fox came in Mr Crow said to him, I will bring walrus tomorrow just like you did. Fox said all right, You can bring a big walrus. So tomorrow the Crow went. And he found many walrus sleeping on the ice, and so he fastened one of the walrus and was ready to carry him home. But the walrus got up and went into the water. And Mr Crow went with him because he was fastened to him. So Mr Crow drowned.

END

Stories animals

THE RACE BETWEEN THE REINDEER AND THE FISH

Once there was a reindeer buck who could outrun any other reindeer on the island. Why, he could run faster than any other animal at all. One day he ran a race with a white fox and the fox was so slow that the reindeer ran around and around the fox who was running straight ahead as fast as he could.

This made the reindeer very proud and he made fun of every other animal. One day he was prancing up and down the beach with his head high in the air, showing off before all the young does when a fish stuck his heed out of the sea. The fish said "What's all this noise about?"

But the big buck was too proud even to notice the little old fish. One of the younger bucks answered the fish. "Don't you know who this is?" he asked. "He's the fastest runner on this island". He told the fish about the race with the fox.

The fish laughed. "He may be the fastest runner on land", he said. "But that doesn't prove that he is the fastest animal in the world.

The big buck was listening now. If I'm not the fastest runner in the world" he said, "Who is?"

The fish replied "I don't know but I'm the fastest runner in the water and you haven't beat me yet".

At this, all the animals on the shore laughed, and the big buck said "When do you want to start?" And the fish said "In the morning at sunrise".

So it was planned.

During the night the fish called together all his fish friends and told them of the coming race and they all agreed [2] to help him. So he placed them all around the island near the shore.

Before sunrise the big buck was down on the beach with all his friends. The fox and many other animals were there to see the race.

Just at sunrise the fish stuck his head up out of the water and said "Are you ready?" And the reindeer said "Ready!" And the fish said "Go!" and plunged under the water again. The reindeer stuck out along the beach and when he had run just a little way a fish jumped up out of the water ahead of him and shouted "Come on!"

The reindeer ran faster. He was sure, now, that no little old fish could swim that fast. But just then another fish jumped up out of the water and called out "Come on!"

The reindeer ran faster still trying to get ahead of the fish for, of course, he thought it was the same fish all the time. But the faster he ran, the oftener some fish poked his head up out of the water and shouted to him to come on!

At last the reindeer got back to the starting point. He was panting hard. But his friends and the fox and all the other animals were laughing. For the fish had been back for a long time. Just then he jumped up out of the water again and said "It certainly took you a long time". Then the reindeer fell down dead. He had run his last race.

END

We could of course add a moral as per Aesop's fables and we ...

Maskin's version

A RACE BY A REINDEER AND A FISH

One day a reindeer bade a fish to run a race with him. But the fish told him to begin next morning. So the reindeer went home.

The fish sent messages to all the fishes near him to appear along the shore next morning. So all the fishes did.

Next morning the reindeer came and called the fish that they should begin and they did begin.

After running about a mile he asked the fish if he is going alone. So the fish answered that he is waling in front of him. But the real one was way back.

So the reindeer ran all his speed and asked again. And the fish always answered in front of him.

Then the reindeer fell down dead because of running so hard.

END

Stories animals

SNIPE

One time little snipe eating little worms near lake. Then raven come sit down and sing:

Iyong Iyong Iyong Iyong Iyong Iyong (six times)
Nievam sanani ani iyong
Naskoqune acholachloko
Iyong Iyong Iyong Iyong Iyong Iyong

Making fun because snipe always bobbings his head eating.

Then little snipe begin also to sing:

Iyong Iyong Iyong Iyong Iyong Iyong
Autatkokatne iyong matucktigani Ka!
Poowatachokuk
Iyong Iyong Iyong Iyong Iyong Iyong

Snipe retorts with "You eat dog manure between Eskimo houses. Maybe I always move my head [bob] but you move your body."
Then raven fly off caw! caw! caw!

QUAIL SONG

I ya ya ya ya yunga
I ya ya ya ya yunga
Iyunga yayunga
Iyunga ayunga
A yang A
I ya ya ya ya yunga
Iyunga yayunga
Iyunga yayunga
A yung A
Ang ang a yung
A yung A!

Sokitlpi ya ya ya yunga
Sokitlpi ya ya ya yunga
Samaginka tagilakok
Kawakak
Iyunga ayunga
A yang A
I ya ya ya ya yunga
Iyunga yayunga
Iyunga yayunga
A yunga A
Ang ang a yung
A yung A

Stories animals

PUFFINS

There lived many women on the top of a cliff. In that day the people thought it was not good for them to cook late at night in the out doors. But one of the women cooked some food outdoors very late at night.

The neighbors told her to quit, but she keep on cooking. While she was cooking they saw a great fire coming from the horizon.

When the flame of the fire came near, the woman who was cooking dive into her stove and came up in the water, becoming a puffin. And so one by one they dived. And came up in the water changed to puffins.

So the people believe that the puffins were once women.

PUFFINS

There lived many women on the top of a cliff overlooking the sea. In that day the people thought it was not good for them to cook late at night in the out doors. They did not know just what would happen to them if they did it. They believed it would be something terrible. One night, a woman said that she was not afraid, so she built a fire outside her igloo and put a pot of seal meat to boil. The neighbors told her to put out the fire, but she only laughed at them and kept on cooking. After a while hey saw a great fire coming from below the horizon in the east and they became very frightened. All but the woman who was doing the cooking. And the big fire came closer and closer and the women dived from the cliff into the sea. All but the woman who was doing the cooking. She only laughed, and ran to the edge of the cliff and looked over. And what do you think she saw? She saw every woman go down, down, down, in the water, and when they came up, they were all turned into puffins. All but the old woman who was doing the cooking.

And if you ever paddle by in your kayak at night you can hear the old woman who was doing the cooking laughing on top of the cliff.

END

Stories animals

ORPHANS

OONŌSŎSŎKĀNGŬ

Once upon a time there lived a boy with his grandma in the igloo. And they had no neighbors with them. But it was storming for days and days, and so Oonōsŏsŏkāngŭ had to shovel every day, so that the snow wouldn't cover the igloo. Then Oonōsŏsŏkāngŭ got tired shoveling every day. And he said to himself, I wonder what makes it storm so much. And he did not shovel any more, because he was wondering what he should do to stop the storm. So he found a thing that he should try and see if he could find something that makes storms. And he started off walking toward the storm. When he got a long ways from his igloo, there he saw an old man shoveling the snow toward his igloo, which he had cut out with his adz. And when he shovels the snow that he had cut out with his adz [it] would make such a storm that Oonōsŏsŏkāngŭ couldn't even see his feet. And the old man saw him and asked him if his name was Oonōsŏsŏkāngŭ. And the boy told him that his name was different, and told him that [2] he never saw or heard about Oonōsŏsŏkāngŭ. And his name was very different. But he was Oonōsŏsŏkāngŭ. So the old man told him that he was making Oonōsŏsŏkāngŭ work hard shoveling his igloo. So Oonōsŏsŏkāngŭ said to him make more storm for him. "I am going to watch you shoveling". But the boy did not watch him shovel, but he was thinking how he could stop him for making such storm for him, so he thought if he should run away and take his shovel, but he thought if he sun away with the shovel that the old man would use his big feet for shovel. So Oonōsŏsŏkāngŭ thought if would be better to take his adz. And while the old man was shoveling Oonōsŏsŏkāngŭ stole the adz and ran home as fast as he could run in the storm while the old man was shoveling. So that old man didn't see him at all so he got home safe from the old man, and hid behind his grandma. His grandma saw that he had an adz in his hand, and she asked him where he got [3] that adz. But Oonōsŏsŏkāngŭ didn't say a word to his grandma. The old grandma was so afraid about Oonōsŏsŏkāngŭ which he stole some-body's adz. And while grandma was crying, she heard some body coming upon the igloo. It was the old man which made the storm for Oonōsŏsŏkāngŭ. The old man walked so hard that the dust fell down from the igloo. The old man called, "Oonōsŏsŏkāngŭ give me my adz. I want it very much". So Oonōsŏsŏkāngŭ said, I will not give your adz because you will make storm for me again if I give it to you. The old grandma was so afraid of the old man she told the boy to give his adz quick. But Oonōsŏsŏkāngŭ said I will not give it to him because I am tired shoveling. And again the old man called the boy, "Please my boy give me my adz. Tomorrow it will change to summer, and the flies buzzing will wake you up and the birds singing merrily above your igloo, and you will have a river close by your igloo, and it [4] will be full of fish. So please Oonŏsôsôkängû give me my adz." "But I will not give your adz to you because you will fool me". The old man said to him again "I will not fool you my boy, it will came true". So Oonōsŏsŏkāngŭ let him have his adz once more. And then the old man was very glad to have his adz again that he laughed all the way to his home. When the old man had gone, Oonōsŏsŏkāngŭ and his grandma went to bed.

But Oonōsŏsŏkāngŭ could not sleep at all because the ole man promises him good things that he should see if he got up in the morning, and thinking of the promises of river full of fish. But he slept for a little while. But he got up very early in the morning and went out to see all the things that the old man promises them and it was so. He saw birds and all kinds of things. And he went to see the river that was promise to him [5] and he found the river, and it was full of fish. So Oonōsŏsŏkāngŭ went to tell all the things that he saw and the river full of fish, to his grandma. And he said to his grandma, "What will we use for a met, we have no net at all?" But the old grandma said to Oonōsŏsŏkāngŭ "Don't weary [worry] about the fish net. I have a good fish net". So they went to the river but the old grandma went naked into the river to catch fish. And so they caught enough fish to eat for years and years. Now they had plenty to eat.   END   1921

A BOY THAT IS AN ORPHAN

There lived a boy in the village who was an orphan. So he sleeps out doors. But the people wanted him to sleep in their house, but the boy wouldn't sleep [inside]. He likes to sleep out doors. When it is day, he goes to some house to have his dinner. And one rich man lived in the same village where the boy lived. And so the rich man gave the boy clothes when the boy's clothes need to be changed. So the boy didn't have to work for his living at all. He eats when ever his [he's] hungry and sleeps when ever his sleepy out doors by him self alone. And it was winter. So he had a bed where the ground wasn't covered with snow. So one night when he was at his bed, a boy came out from under the ground where this orphaned was. And the boy that was an orphan asked the boy that just came our from the ground if he had perants [parents]. So the boy said to him, I am an orphaned. And the other boy jumped and said to him, I am an orpahaned, too. So the two orphaneds hug each other and kissed each other. They were very glad to be togather [together] all the time. So it was day now. And the [2] two orphaneds went to eat at the rich man's house. When the rich man saw the two boys, he asked the first orphaned where he found that other boy. So he said to the rich man, He came out from the ground. And then the rich man gave them some thing to eat. And the two orphans went out from the rich man's house. And the two boys was that way all the time: eat and sleep and get clothes from the rich man.

One day the two boys went to the rich man's house again. So the man told them two orphans that in the village the people had no more food. And told them that his food was getting very short. So he said to the boys, This place is going to have a famine. So the rich man told them to go to his friend. And his friend was far away from his home. So he told the two orphans to go over to his friend's village and live with him. And he told them that he had lots of deer. So the rich man gave them each of them, clothes and some meat for them to eat on their way to the rich man's friend. And so the two orphans started. And while they were on their way an awful storm [3] came. So them two boys dug the snow and build a snow house and went in. So night came and the second orphan asked the first orphaned to tell a story. But the first told him to tell a story first. So the second orphaned told a story. The second boy or the second orphaned was a devil that came out from under the ground. So he told a story and this is his story.

> Once upon a time there lived two orphans and they were walking to a place where they could eat. And the storm came so the [they] dug the snow and went in. and a big

devil came to eat them up. End

And so the two boys couldn't sleep all night. So the earth shoke [shook] and the first orphaned went out to see what was comeing. Sure enough a big devil was comeing to eat them up. So he went in and told the devil orphan that the devil was comeing. And the first orphan had a tiny shovel in his mittens. So he took of [out] the tiny shovel and throw [it] at the devil. So he killed the devil that was comeing to eat them up. And so the devil orphaned told the first orphaned to tell a story. So he told a story to the devil orphan. And this is his story.

Once upon a time there lived two orphans and they were walking to a place where they could eat. And the storm came. So they dug the snow and went in. and two big loons came to kill them. The End.

And so the devil orphan went out to see what was comeing. And he saw two big loons comeing to kill them two boys. So he went in and told the first orphaned that the loons were comeing.

And so the first orphan changed into a bird and flew away. So the loon at the devil orphan.

END

THE STORY OF AN ORPHAN [and walrus name]

Once upon a time there lived an orphan and he was going to the shore to get somthing [something] that the waves had brought to the shore. And so as he was going on his way, he saw a walrus in the sea. And so the orphan asked the walrus, What is your name? What is your name, walrus? Then the walrus said to him, My name is Iyu-hoyu, Iyu-hoyu. As soon as the walrus told him his name, the boy run home as fast as he can, and saying Iyu-hoyu, Iyu-hoyu as he ran home to tell his grandmother. But he fell down and forgot the walrus name. And he stand up and said all kinds of names, but couldn't think of Iyu-hoyu. So he went back to the shore. And as he was going, he saw the walrus again. And so he asked the name of the walrus again. And the walrus said to him, My name is Iyu-hoyu, Iyu-hoyu. And the boy ran home as fast as he can. And [2 / 37] he got to his home all right. But he fell down when he went inside the house and he forgot the walrus name. And he said to this grandmother, I forgot the name off. I couldn't find the name. And while the orphan was thinking about the name of the walrus, he [his] grandmother said to him, I know what you are thinking about, you are thinking the name of the walrus, He name is Iyu-hoyu, Iyu-hoyu. And the boy said to her, Oh, yes, I forgot all about Iyu-hoyu, Iyu-hoyu. So the orphan learned the name of the walrus.

END

THE STRONGMAN AND THE ORPHAN

There was a strongman whom every body in the village was afraid of. When his neighbors killed anything, a walrus or a seal he would take it away from them.

In the same village there was an orphan who lived with his uncle.   One morning the orphan borrowed his uncle's hunting weapons: harpoon with walrus kin rope, seal hook, gun, and knife. And walked a bit on the young ice to hunt. After a while he heard a pounding, pounding, pounding, pounding from the shore and he knew it was a walrus breaking up through the ice with his tusks. Coming up for air. So he ran to where the noise was and when he got near the noise he stopped running and stepped on tip toes to the spot where he could see the big white tusks just breaking threw [through]. And he crouched near by an waited. Pretty soon the walrus forced both tusks through the ice hole and then his head and breast. The orphan jabbed [2] the harpoon head into the tick skinned neck of the walrus and the walrus snorted water into the air and ducked down under the ice and away at full speed. But the harpoon head held fast and slipped from the pole and the orphan played at the skin rope, reversed [toggled] the harpoon and jabbed the back end into the ice and looped the end of the rope around it. ...

*The original story from which this one was adapted, for "outside" readers. It is typical of all the St Lawrence island Eskimo folk tales. The only way you can tell when the story is ended is when the teller of the story blows on his little finger. Then everybody laughs shrilly and someone else tells one equally unemphatic and with the most

stories orphans

blunt realism! The originals have a strong Oriental feeling not unlike modernistic art – some of them are pure Picasso or even Klee!

Farrar paid Maskin 25¢ for every tale he would bring in. He went round St Lawrence Island that year (1920-21) gathering up the stories, wrote them into a big ledger which is now almost full, and then came back to us for his flock of quarters. He was "plenty rich".

A BLIND ORPHAN
in Maskin's own version

There was an old woman and her grandson. This boy was born blind. They had many neighbors [neighbors]. The neighbors hate them and never give them any meat.

One day they had no more food. The boy asked his grandma to go and see some bones in the cellar if they had little meat so that he could quench his hunger.

But his grandma told him that she was sure there is no meat in the cellar. Then the boy went by himself to see. When he went in, he felt some bones and tried to take out.

While he was trying, some one called him from the corner of the cellar telling him that these bones were belong to him. But the boy told the speaker that it was his.

Then the voice told him if he would not take these bones home, she would lick his eyes. The voice was the rat of the cellar. Then the rat licked his eyes until he could see anything that lives under the sea.

Then the boy went home leaving the bones. Next morning the neighbor went hunting in their canoes. The boy asked all the boat captains to go in their boat but no one liked him.

Then he saw a man preparing to go hunt with his two daughters. He had no crew. The boy went there and asked the man to go in his boat. The man told him that he could.

The man told the boy to be the header. So the boy was the header.

Then they went out farther and saw a big whale and caught it. They killed the whale first time. So he gave one of his daughters to the boy and after that he was successful hunter in the village.

END

stories orphans

THE BLIND ORPHAN OF ESKIMO LAND

Away up north in an Eskimo village there lived a blind boy
He was born blind
He was an orphan,
His father and mother died when he was a baby
He lived all alone with his grandmother
She was a very old woman
She was too old to go hunting
The boy could not hunt
He could not see to shoot or use the harpoon
They had a hard time
Often they were very hungry
They had to beg food from their neighbors
The other people in the village did not like them
They thought they were too much trouble
They would not give them any meat
They gave them only their old bones
There was not much meat left on the bones they gave them.
That is why they gave them to the poor

One time there was a big snow storm
It snowed and snowed for many days
The wind blew hard
The snow flew by with the wind
It was so thick that one could not see very far
It was hard to stand up in the wind
The Eskimos had to crawl on their hands and knees from house to
      house
Nobody went hunting for walrus or seal
It was not safe to venture out on the ice
There was danger in being blown out to sea
Everybody ate up all their fresh meat
They dug into their cellars and ate all their rotten meat
They would not even give away their bones
The orphan and his grandmother were starving
They did not know what to do

stories orphans

The grandmother was crying
She was sorry for her grandson
She told him that they were going to starve to death
The grandson said, "I am going to look in our cellar for some old
    bones
She said, "It will do you no good
There is no meat on those bones."
He said, "I will look any way"
He meant that he would feel, of course
He couldn't look because he was blind

The cellar was away from the house as all Eskimo cellars are
It was just a hole in the ground
It had some pieces of old whale ribs over the top
That is how they kept the dogs out
Sometimes they got in any way

The grandmother said, "You will get lost in the storm"
He said, "No I will be careful
He tied a long rope about his waist
The rope was made of walrus skin
That is the only kind of rope they have up there
It was a very long rope
He tied the other end to a pole in the house
He went outside
The wind blew him down
He crawled on his hands and knees
He crawled about for a long time
At last, he found the cellar
The wind had blown the snow off the whale bones
He pulled on aside
He slid down into the cellar
It was dark down there
He did not mind that
It was all the same to him
He was blind anyway [2]

He felt about among the old bones
He gathered an arm load of them

He started to climb out with them

He heard a small voice
It came from the other side of the cellar
"Blind boy those bones belong to me"
The boy was startled
He did not know what to think at first
After a while he spoke to the voice
"Who are you who claims our bones?"
He heard the voice again
"I am the rat who lives in this cellar
Please do not take my bones away
If you will not, I will lick your eyes
I will make you see!"
The boy believed the rat
He put the bones down
He lay down among the bones
So that the rat could reach his eyes
The rat came to him and licked his eyes
Sure enough! He saw a little light
It was the light at the top of the cellar
He had to close his eyes at first
He had never seen the light before
It hurt his eyes
After a while he got used to it
He jumped out of the cellar
He ran to his grandmother
They forgot all about being hungry
They were very happy and excited

After a while the wind stopped blowing
They could no longer hear the roar outside
They went to the little door and looked out
The storm was over
They ran out of the house to the neighbors
They told them all about their good fortune
The neighbors laughed at them
They did not believe what they said about the rat

The ocean is frozen up there most of the year
The wind and the current keeps the ice broken up in some places
The shore ice does not drift away
It stays all winter
The Eskimos keep their boats on the shore ice
There were many boats back from the waters edge
The storm had drifted some of the ice away
There was open water for several miles off shore

The men were all going hunting
The boy and his grandmother went down to the beach
Some of the men were pushing their boats into the water
They were going out to hunt for whale
The boy wanted to go with them
They only laughed at him
They thought he was still blind
He went from one boat captain to another
They would not take him along
The orphan then saw a man and his two daughters
They were trying to push their boat into the water
No one would help them
The man was too old to hunt they thought
His daughters had to go with him
The women used to laugh at the daughters
They called them "he women"
They did not seem to mind [3]

He ran over to them
He helped them push the boat in
The man asked the boy if he wanted to go with them
The boy jumped into the boat
He was very happy now
When they got out from shore
The boy looked down into the water
He was surprised
He could see fish and everything swimming about
He told the man about it
They were all surprised
No one else could do that

stories orphans

He could see better than any body

The man told the boy that he could be the "header"
The boy went up forward to look out for whale
That is what the "header" does
He stood up in the bow of the boat
After a while he saw a whale under the water
He directed the old man and the two girls where to row
They rowed over just above the whale
The whale came up for air
He came up right close to the boat and spouted
The boy shot the whale with the whale-gun
The harpoon struck the whale and held fast
In the harpoon head there was a small bomb
It exploded inside the whale
There was a long rope attached to the harpoon head
On the end of the rope were tied a lot of seal-skin pokes
The seal skin pokes were blown up with air
The whale dived to the bottom of the ocean
He had a hard time doing it
The seal-skin pokes were hard to pull under
The whale could not go very far
He became very tired
He was bleeding to death
He was growing weaker and weaker
Finally he died
He came to the surface of the water
not far from the boat
His belly was turned up
It had barnacles on it like on a bottom of a ship
The men tied more ropes onto the whale
They towed him to shore
The tide went out and left the whale on the beach
They worked for many days cutting it up
They cut off all the blubber for food
They also melted some of the blubber into oil
They heat their houses with whale oil lamps
They also saved a lot of the lean meat
They cut the whalebone from its mouth

stories orphans

They saved this for the traders that go up there in the summer
They were very rich now
They gave a lot of meat to the others

The man asked the boy if he wanted to marry
The boy looked teased and hung his head
He made marks in the snow with the toe of his muckluck boot
After a while he said "ah"
That means yes in their language
Then the man told him to take his choice of the two daughters
Poor girls they both loved him
He chose the prettiest one
They were married
They loved each other very much
The orphan was the best hunter among the Eskimos now
He built a new house of walrus skin
It was the biggest house there
His old grandmother lived with them
She loved her great great grandchildren very much
They were all very happy
They were always kin to rats
So they had more rats than anybody
                                                END

A BOY THAT IS AN ORPHAN

There lived a boy in the village who was an orphan. So he sleeps out doors. But the people wanted him to sleep in their house, but the boy wouldn't sleep [inside]. He likes to sleep out doors. When it is day, he goes to some house to have his dinner. And one rich man lived in the same village where the boy lived. And so the rich man gave the boy clothes when the boy's clothes need to be changed. So the boy didn't have to work for his living at all. He eats when ever his [he's] hungry and sleeps when ever his sleepy out doors by him self alone. And it was winter. So he had a bed where the ground wasn't covered with snow. So one night when he was at his bed, a boy came out from under the ground where this orphaned was. And the boy that was an orphan asked the boy that just came our from the ground if he had perants [parents]. So the boy said to him, I am an orphaned. And the other boy jumped and said to him, I am an orpahaned, too. So the two orphaneds hug each other and kissed each other. They were very glad to be togather [together] all the time. So it was day now. And the [2] two orphaneds went to eat at the rich man's house. When the rich man saw the two boys, he asked the first orphaned where he found that other boy. So he said to the rich man, He came out from the ground. And then the rich man gave them some thing to eat. And the two orphans went out from the rich man's house. And the two boys was that way all the time: eat and sleep and get clothes from the rich man.

One day the two boys went to the rich man's house again. So the man told them two orphans that in the village the people had no more food. And told them that his food was getting very short. So he said to the boys, This place is going to have a famine. So the rich man told them to go to his friend. And his friend was far away from his home. So he told the two orphans to go over to his friend's village and live with him. And he told them that he had lots of deer. So the rich man gave them each of them, clothes and some meat for them to eat on their way to the rich man's friend. And so the two orphans started. And while they were on their way an awful storm [3] came. So them two boys dug the snow and build a snow house and went in. So night came and the second orphan asked the first orphaned to tell a story. But the first told him to tell a story first. So the second orphaned told a story. The second boy or the second orphaned was a devil that came out from under the ground. So he told a story and this is his story.

> Once upon a time there lived two orphans and they were walking to a place where they could eat. And the storm came so the [they] dug the snow and went in. and a big devil came to eat them up. The End.

And so the two boys couldn't sleep all night. So the earth shoke [shook] and the first orphaned went out to see what was comeing. Sure enough a big devil was comeing to eat them up. So he went in and told the devil orphan that the devil was comeing. And the first orphan had a tiny shovel in his mittens. So he took of [out] the tiny shovel and throw [it] at the devil. So he killed the

devil that was comeing to eat them up. And so the devil orphaned
told the first orphaned to tell a story. So he told a story to the devil
orphan. And this is his story.

Once upon a time there lived two orphans and they were
walking to a place where they could eat. And the storm
came. So they dug the snow and went in. and tow big
loons came to kill them. The End.

And so the devil orphan went out to see what was comeing.
And he saw two big loons comeing to kill them two boys. So he
went in and told the first orphaned that the loons were comeing.
And so the first orphan changed into a bird and flew away.
So the loon at the devil orphan.

END

THE BLIND ORPHAN
OF ST LAWRENCE ISLAND

By Farrar Burn, adapted from an Eskimo folk tale
as told by Maskin
who had been "outside" and learned English

Away up North in an Eskimo Village there lived a blind boy.
He was born blind. He was an orphan. His father and mother died
when he was a baby. He lived all alone with his grandmother. She
was a very old woman. She was too old to go hunting for seal and
walrus and whale. Not often does an Eskimo woman go hunting.
The boy could not hunt. He could not see to shoot or use the
harpoon. They had a hard time.

Often they were very hungry. They had to beg food from
their neighbors. The other people in the village did not like them.
They thought they were too much trouble. They would not give
them any meat. They gave them only their old bones. There was
not much meat left on the bones. That is why they gave them to the
poor orphan and his grandmother.

One time there was a big snow storm. It snowed and snowed
for many days. The wind blew hard. The snow flew by with the

stories orphans

wind. It was so thick that one could not see very far. It was hard to stand up in the wind. The Eskimos had to crawl on their hands and knees from house to house. Nobody went hunting for walrus or seal. It was not safe to go out on the ice. There was danger of being blown out to sea. Everybody ate up all their fresh meat. They dug into their cellars and ate all their stored, rotten meat. They would not even give away their bones.

The orphan and his grandmother were starving. They did not know what to do. The grandmother was crying. She was sorry for her grandson. She told him that they were going to starve [2] to death. The grand son said "I am going to look in our cellar for some old bones." The grandmother said "It will do you no good. There is no meat on those old bones." The grandson said "I will look anyway." He meant that he would feel. He couldn't look because he was blind.

The cellar was away from the house as all Eskimo cellars are. It was just a hole in the ground. It had some old whale ribs over the top. That is how they kept the dogs out. Sometimes the dogs got in anyway.

The grandmother said "You will get lost in the storm". The boy said "I will be careful". He tied a long rope around his waist. The rope was made of walrus skin. That is the only kind of rope they had up there. It was very long. The boy tied the other end to a pole in the house. He went outside through the small square door in the big walrus skin house.

The wind blew him down. He crawled on his hands and knees. He crawled about for a long time. At last he found their cellar. The wind had blown the snow off the whale bones. He pulled one aside. He slid down into the cellar. It was dark down there. He did not mind that. It was all the same to him. He was blind anyway. He felt about among the old bones. He gathered an armload of them. He started to climb out with them.

Then he heard a small voice. It came from the other side of the cellar. "Blind boy, those bones belong to me!" The boy was afraid. He did not know what to think. After awhile he spoke to the voice, "Who are you who claims our bones?" [3]

He heard the voice again. "I am the rat who lives in this cellar. Please do not take my bones away. If you will not, I will lick your eyes. I will make you see better than anybody. You can see things down under the sea."

The boy put down the bones and lay down among them so that the rat could reach his eyes. The rat came to aim and licked his eyes. Sure enough! He saw a little light. It was the light at the top of the cellar. He had never seen light before. It hurt his eyes. He jumped out of the cellar. He ran to his grandmother. They forgot all about being hungry. They were very happy.

After awhile the wind stopped blowing. They could no longer hear the roar outside. They went to the little door and looked out. The storm was over. They ran out of the house to the neighbors. They told them all about their good fortune. The neighbors laughed at them. They did not believe what they said about the rat.

The ocean is frozen up there when it is very cold. That is more than half the year. But the wind and the currents keep the ice broken up out from shore. The shore ice is broken and piled up in big blocks but it does not drift away. It stays all winter. The Eskimos keep their boats on the shore ice.

Many walrus skin boats were there, back from the watery edge. The storm had drifted some of the ice away. There was open water for a long way off shore.

The men were all going hunting. Everybody was laughing. Soon there would be meat again. The boy and his grandmother went down to the beach. Some of the men were pushing their boats into the water. They were going to hunt for whale. [4]

The boy wanted to go with them. The men laughed at him. They thought he was still blind. He went from one boat captain to another. They would not take him along.

Then the orphan saw a man and his two daughters. They were trying to push their boat over the rough ice into the water. No one would help them. The man was too old to hunt they thought. His daughters had to go with him. The women laughed at the daughters. They called them Man-woman. The daughters did not seem to mind. The boy ran over to them. He helped them push the boat in. The man asked the boy if he wanted to go with them. The boy jumped into the boat. He was very happy now.

When they got out from shore, the boy looked down into the water. He was surprised. He could see fish and everything swimming about. He told the man about it. They were all surprised.

No one else could do that. He could see better than anybody.

The man told the boy that he could be the Header. The boy went up forward to look out for whale. That is what the Header does. He stood up in the bow of the boat. After awhile he saw a whale under the water. He told the old men and the two girls where to row. They paddled over just above the whale. The whale came up for air. He came up right close to the boat and spouted. The boy shot the whale with the whale gun. The harpoon struck the whale and held fast.

There was a long rope fastened to the harpoon head. On the end of the rope were tied a lot of seal-skin pokes. They were blown up with air. The whale dived to the bottom of the ocean. He had a hard time for the seal-skin pokes were hard to pull under. The whale could not go so far again. [5]

He became very tired. He was bleeding to death. He was getting weaker and weaker. Finally he died. He came to the surface not far from the boat. His belly was turned up. It had barnacles on it like the bottom of a ship. The man and the boy tied more ropes to the whale. They towed him to shore. The tide went out and left the whale on the beach. They worked for many days cutting it up.

They cut off all the blubber for food. They would melt some for oil. They heat their houses with whale oil lamps. They also saved a lot of the meat. They cut the whalebone from the whaler mouth. They saved this for the traders that go up there in the summertime. Now they were very rich. They gave much meat to other Eskimos.

The man asked the boy if he wanted to marry. The boy hung down his head. He made marks in the snow with the toe of his mukluk boot. But he quickly said "Ah". That means "yes" in their language. Then the man told him to take his choice of the two daughters. Poor girls, they both loved him.

He close the prettier one. They were married. They loved each other very much. The orphan was the best hunter among the Eskimos now. He built a new house of walrus skin. It was the biggest house in the village. All the big dances were held at his house. His old grandmother lived with them. She loved her great grandchildren very much. They were all very happy. They were always kind to the rats so they had more rats than anybody•

END

stories orphans

Eskimo Folk Tales as told to Farrar Burn
by an Eskimo on St Lawrence Island, Alaska

A BLIND ORPHAN

There was an old woman and her grandson. This boy was born blind. They had many neighbors. The neighbors hate them and never gave them any meat.

One day they had no more food. The boy asked his grandma to let him go and see some bones in the cellar if they had little meat, so that he could quench his hunger.

But his grandma told him that she was sure there is no meat in the cellar. Then the boy went to see anyhow. When he went in he felt some bones and tried to take them out.

While he was trying some one called him from the corner of the cellar telling him that these bones were [to] belong to him. But the boy too told the speaker that the bones were belong to him.

Then the voice told him if he would not take the bones home she would lick his eyes. The voice was the rat of the cellar. Then the rat licked his eyes until he could see anything that lives under the sea.

Then the boy went home leaving the bones. Next morning the neighbors went hunting in their canoes. The boy asked all the boat captains to go in their boats but no one liked him. When he saw a man preparing to go in hunt with his two daughters he knew of course that man had no crew. He went there and asked the man to go in his boat. The man told him he could go. The man told the boy to be a 'header'. So the boy was the 'header'.

Then they went out farther and saw a big whale and they caught it and killed it the first time. So the man gave one of his daughters to the boy and after that he was successful hunter in the village.   END

A BOY AND HIS [BAD] GRANDMOTHER

Once upon a time, there was a blind boy who lived with his Grandmother. And they had not much food. They lived on rats and squirrels because they had no one to hunt for them. And the boy was blind so he couldn't hunt for his Grandmother . but he kills rats and squirrels with his bow and arrows. His Grandmother tells him where to shoot at. So one day his Grandmother saw three white bears coming toward their igloo. And she told the blind boy to get ready to shoot the white bears. And she told him where to shoot at. So the boy shot at the bears and killed every one of them. But his Grandmother said to him, You [2] missed them all. Why didn't you shoot good. The Grandmother folled [fooled] the blind boy because he couldn't see any thing at all. So the boy went to sleep. And while the boy slept, the Grandmother skinned the three bears and hung the meat up to dry. And she was cooking some meat for dinner. And she went and had her dinner of bear meat. And the blind boy woke up and said to his Grandmother, What did you cook for dinner? I smell something good. I am very hungry. Grandmother said to him, I have cooked rats for dinner. We have only rats and squirrals [squirrels]to eat. So his Grandmother gived him rats to eat. She did not give him bear meat.

So the blind boy went out. When he got out of his igloo he heard a loon singing a far off. So he went on creeping where the loon was singing. The loon was singing in the lake. So the blind boy got to the lake and stopped. And the loon came to him and cured his eyes. So the boy saw the loon and the lake and every things to see. Now he had eyes to see his grandmother[32]. And the [3] loon told him that he had killed three white bears. But your grandmother didn't let you eat bear meat because you was blind and could not see her eat bear meat. So the boy went home to his grandmother and went in. And she did not know that he can see now. So the boy said to his grandmother, I smell something good. I am very hungry. So his grandmother gave him rats to eat instead of bear meat. When the boy saw the rats that he had to eat and said to his grandmother I see that you have lots of bear meat. And his grandmother said, Oh, How did you open your eyes that you can see? The boy was mad at his grandmother. So he caught his grandmother and rolled her in walrus skin and throw his grandmother in the sea. And the grandmother sank and she came up

---

[32]   While the boy remains blind, the word Grandmother begins with a capital letter, but once he is sighted, grandmother is all lower case.

and was changed into beluga [whale]. And she told the boy to bring all her things and throw them into the sea. And she was gone. And she had beluga husband so the boy had lots of bear meat for himself.

END

THE ORPHAN WHO WAS A SINGER

There lived an orphan that sang all the time at night. And he had no house at all. He had to sleep in some of the houses in the village. It was a big village.

But in that village, the people did not like him because he had done something wrong. At last not even one of them would let him into their house. So he walked away from that place.

He was walking for days and nights. He had nothing to eat all those days.

At last he found a dead seal. So he had food now. He ate that day. And he slept that night the first sleep since he had left the village.

Before he started walking again, he ate all the seal. He walked for a long time again. At last he saw an igloo far off. He was glad.

A man and his wife lived in that igloo. They had no child. But the woman's husband was not at home. But she gave him something to eat. She asked him: "Do you live in some village nearby? This is the first time I have seen you".

So the orphan said "I have no parents. I am an orphan. I came from Gambell. I am looking for somebody. I am glad I am here".

And the woman said to him "Can you be our son? My husband went hunting. He will be here very soon".

They saw the kayak coming and the woman and the orphan went to help him. And the orphan worked at the kayak while the man and his wife were talking about him. And they all went home at once. So they had the orphan for their son.

At that place they had mukluk to eat. So the orphan had a good home. And he was a better hunter than that man.

stories orphans

*Gambell is the English name of the main village on St Lawrence Island where we got the tales. The Eskimos of course call it something else but we were too green then to check on that and ask Maskin to use Eskimo names where he could. Gambell was the name of the first really good missionary who lived and taught on St Lawrence. His name occurs over and over in these stories. *?*
*Oddly, the village is sometimes ....

ORPHANS BROTHER AND SISTER

There lived a boy and a girl. They were sister [and brother]. They were orphans. They had many neighbors.

One stormy day in winter, they had a famine. They could not go out to hunt because of the storm. One day the orphan boy made an ice pick, its length was as long as his first finger, and a stick of the same length. Putting them into his mittens, he went to the shore.

Then he got on the ice, he pulled the pick out from his mitten. It was a big ice pick. He then began to make a hole. When he made a hole, he put the pick back into his mitten. He pulled out the stick and it was a long pole. Then he let the pole down through the hole, and began to twist. (As we do when we are getting kelps.)

Then he pulled it out with the kepts and a hair seal with it. He went home. When he entered, his sister cut the seal up. When she cut it all, she sent out and came in with lots of willow leaves. Then she divided some part of the seal for their neighbors.

She put some kelp and leaves to every dividend and went out and took them to their neighbors. When they had eaten all the seal, the boy went and did the same way and brought mukluk. When he came in, his sister did the same way. When they had eaten all the mukluk he went and bought a walrus. One day a young man whom they did not know came to marry his sister. Telling him that he had a sister whom he would give to the orphan boy. So the boy contented [consented]. The young man took them both to his house. When they got there, the boy did marry the young man's sister.

One day the father of the young man grew restless. The boy asked his wife about the worrying father. The girl told him that some day many men came and sing song and danced. When they were beaten they would take half of their deer.

The boy just laughed. So one day it happened. There came a number of men and the sang. Their dancer was a white fox, who danced differently. When they [were] done, the boy sang and his dancer was an owl, who dances more better than fox. So they beat [them]. The men were killed by the owl.

END

FAMILIES

MAN

At one time the creator was journeying to some certain country and as he was traveling, he dropped his mittens, which fell on the island.

These two mittens changed to human men. One day these two men made out a plan to ask the creator to have some one with them so they might not be lonesome. So they sent a squirrel to the creator.

When the creator received the message, he wondered. He thought and thought about these two men on the island and at last it came to his mind that they were his own mittens which he had lost some time ago.

So he made two images and called them women and sent them to these men.

THE FIVE MEN CHANGED INTO SEA GULL

Five men always hunt. And every time they kill a whale. When ever they kill a whale they would call thier [their] worship *mungnesook*. And so they were out hunting again. They didn't got any thing that day. And so the youngest of the five brothers call to his oldest brother if we should call our worship *mungnesook*? Don't matter, we don't get any thing. Will it be alright? And his oldest brother said to him, it is not right for us to call our worship without killing a whale. The youngest brother said to brothers, I am going to call that worship anyhow. And his oldest brother said, Well you can call the worship. And the youngest called the worship/ and then an awful storm came at once. And the wind blew them away. They stayed about one month. After those days, the wind came down [abated] and they saw the land. And went to the land and so they [saw] an ugly house at that place. Then tomorrow they look for village, only they [2] found one house. When the man that was in the house saw them five men, he was very glad. And so he gave them food to eat. After they had finished eating, the man and his wife ate. And the man said to them, Why do you call me so much? And the five men whispered to them selves and said to one another, I think this is the man that we call when we kill whales, our worship *mungnesook.* The man told them, You five brothers must try to go back to your place. But the five brothers answered him, We have no boat and nothing to make a boat. And so the man gave them a big log to make the frame of the boat. And the man said to them, You can get whale skin to cover your canoe [*umiak*]. And so they went but the man said to these not to take the biggest whale but to take the little whale. The man told them that the big whale was holy and if they would go to it, they wouldn't come back. They would stay there all the [3 / 64] time. Then they went over and they saw lots dead whale, and one of them was very big so the youngest brother said to them, Let's get the skin from the biggest whale. So the younger boy went to the whale and he went close and he couldn't move any more. The oldest brother told him not to go. But he wanted to go him self. So he went and couldn't move any more. And then the next boy said to his brothers, I am going to my brother. And so he went and he couldn't move. And then the three brothers came back. And left two at the whale. And so the man said to the three brothers, they will go home. But they will [be] changed to sea gull first. And so the man changed them into sea gull. So they went. But they did not reach home. But was [were] always sea gull [from] that time to now.   END   Paid at 1 May 1921

THE STORY OF FIVE LITTLE CORMORANTS

Once there live a man and his wife. But they had no child. They wanted a child very much, but couldn't get one. And they were no very young too. It was winter, so her husband went fishing every day. But he was thinking about how they could get a child, like the other people. So one day he went fishing again. He couldn't

stories families

catch fish for a long time. At last some thing was biting his fish line, so he pulled up the fish. And it wasn't a fish at all. But it was a water fairy. They man was very much frightened about the water fairy. So the fairy told the man not to be afraid of her. She was a lady fairy and she told the man that she had come to tell him good news. And she said, Your wife will have a baby in her belly right now before you go home. So the fairy went down in the hole where the man caught her [ice fishing?].

The man came home quick to see if the fairly told him truth. So he went home and saw that his wife had her belly full. They were glad. And the man told every things that the water fairy told him. So the man [2] went fishing again. While her husband was gone, she had a birth. But it wasn't a real baby, but they were five little cormorants that the women had in her belly. When she saw them five cormorants, she did not know what to do with them. She was ashamed of them. So she put them in an old rain coat and hid them some where. At last her husband came home from fishing. And he saw that his wife belly was gone. So he asked her about her belly. And she told him that she had five little cormorants. So they kept them just like real babys.

And the man went fishing every day. So when he comes, he would feed them fish. And so the five cormorants were full grown now. Then the man made a big tub and filed it with salt water for them to swim and dive in. Also he put every fish that he caught in the tub for them to eat when ever they wished to eat. There perants [Their parents] loved to watch them eat. It was lots of fun for them to watch them cormorants do all kinds of things. So one day the perants went out, and [3] they were thinking How they could change them cormorants into real persons. And while they were thinking about them. They heard them singing just like we sing. So the mother went in to see if they had changed into real persons. But they were just as they are. So the mother went out very unhappy.

Every day the perants went out to listen [to] them sing. When the perants went out, the cormorants would change into real men. So one day the mother saw them while they were singing in the crack of the house. And their [there] she saw four good looking young men and one good looking young girl. And the girl was dancing for them boys. When five cormorants had changed into four young men and one of them was a girl. Then the to perants went in as fast as they can and tore all them five cormorants skins. And they were changed. They were no more cormorants now but five beautiful childrens. So their perants were happier then ever. Then the father made a big kayak for them. And they brought lots [4] of food for their perants. And they were the best hunters of all the world [at] that time.

END

LOST BROTHERS

There was a very strong man who had five brothers. These brothers were hunters, but the eldest one do not go [to] hunt.

One day when hey were out hunting in a canoe, the wind rose and carried them away.

They drifted on an unknown town. In that town lived a strong man also. He let them lodge in his house.

One fine day the eldest brother took his kayak and went searching [for] them to every town. At last he came to the town where they are.

He landed at night. He went to a very small cottage and went in. There he saw an old woman alone. So he asked her if she hasn't hear [heard] anything about them. But the old woman told him that she did not know about them.

Then the man told her if she would tell him about them, he would give her his sword [club] which was made of bone. Then she told him that they had a cheif [chief] who brought his brothers to him. She told him, next morning the chief would have a fun with them.

The man asked her if they would invite her. She told him that they [always] invite her whenever if they do some thing.

After talking to her, he cut her face skin and hands [skin off] and paste them on his face and hands. Also he put on her clothes. He then waited.

Next morning an invitation was brought. He then went to the meeting.

He was looked like that old woman which [who] he killed. Then the chief took a piece of rope whose end was knotted. He took the oldest of these five brothers and whipped him. The chief was very cruel.

So once he whipped them one by one. At last he took the youngest and before he was whippen, he cried out saying that if he would be seen [saved] by his oldest brother. The old woman stood angrily but not the real old [2] woman: the strong man. He tore off the old woman's clothes and took the mask off and he grubbed the cruel chief, killed him. Then he closed the door, and asking his brothers, pointed to every one who was kind to them. After letting the kindest men out, he killed all those who was unkind. Next morning they returned home in four large canoes.

END

LOST BROTHERS

There was a very strong man who had five brothers. He was the oldest one of the sic and was therefore the boss. The brothers were hunters, but the eldest one did not hunt. He remained at home to look after things and repair the kayaks, harpoons, and to make woven skin ropes and things. One day when the brothers were out hunting in a big skin canoe [umiak], the wind arose and carried them away. They drifted for days and days and finally landed on a beach near an unknown village. In that village there lived a strong man who was the chief. He was very overbearing and seemed to get a lot of pleasure out of bullying the others, especially all new comers. So he went down to the beach with his followers and they took the five brothers to his igloo and made them prisoners there.

One fine day the eldest brother took his kayak and went in search of his five brothers. He paddled for miles and miles, stopping at many villages that he had never seen before, inquiring for [2] his brothers. At last he stopped at the village where they were. He landed there at night and went in to the first igloo he came to. It was a very small igloo and there was no one living in it but a very old woman. She looked at him with surprise s though she recognized him and he noticed it, but when he asked her if his five brothers were in the village, she told him no. He thought she was lying to him and told her if she would tell him about them, he would give her his sword [club] which was made of bone. She then told him where his brothers were and that the chief had invited the people of the village to gather at his house the following morning where he was going to make fun with the prisoners. The eldest brother then asked her if she was invited and she told him Yes. Then he took off his sword and said, Well here is my sword and when the old woman reached out her hand for it, he cut her head off. He then took [off] the skin from her face and put it on his own face, and took the skin from her hands and put them on like a pair of gloves. He next removed her clothing and dressed him self to look just like the old woman her self. When morning came he went out and followed the native to the chief's igloo where his brothers were and everyone thought that he was the old woman. When he got there, he saw his five brothers all bound with seal skin rope and they looked very sad and homesick. After every one had come into the room, the chief came in with a whip in his hand. The whip was made of several pieces [strands] of wolf's skin rope with knots tied in the ends. He went up to whip them one at a time. He began whipping the oldest ones first until he cried for mercy and every body but the old woman laughed. The chief [was] very cruel. When at last before he began whipping him, the youngest brother cried out saying that if his oldest brother could see him now, he would not whip him. At this the old woman stood up, and walked over to the chief, and jerked the whip from his hand [3], and took from under 'her' clothes the sword made of bone and cut off the chief's head so quickly that every body was frightened. They thought that the old woman had turned into a very strong devil and they ran out of the igloo and hid in the mountains. Then the old woman removed her mask and gloves and there stood the eldest brother. He cut his five brothers loose and they all went down to the beach. Together and very happily they paddled home in their big canoe, towing the little kayak behind it.   END

THE GIRL ROBBED BY A GIANT

One day many girls went out to the mountains to get some reeds. While they were gathering some reeds, a giant came and put them into his big coat and hung them to a post. He left them there and went home. After a while a bird passed by, they called to her to come and free them. But the bird would not. Soon a snipe came, they called to her again but he [she] would not.

At last a fox came and freed them, except one who was sleeping. So they left her there. Later a giant came with his knife.

When he came, he cut one of the slaves [staves] and found that it was empty. Then he cut the other side, and the girl cried out that she would be a slave for him. So he did not killed her. He took her home. He let her put on his big clothes.

One day while she was playing near the big house, wearing the giant's clothes, her father came and asked her to go home. But she told him that she [was] going to put on her [own] clothes first. So she entered and told the giant that the neighbor teased her that she had big clothes. Then the giant told her to put on her clothes. So she did. She went out and her father took her home. Before they walked farther, the giant went out and saw them. So he ran after them.

When he came near the girl stooped down and drew a line on the ground and walked. When she looked back, she saw a big river that the giant could not pass. So she watched there. Then the giant asked her the way to pass, the girl told him to take a mussel shell and pass. So he found a mussel shell and tried, but the shell sunk. At last the girl told him to drink it.

Then the giant began to drinking [up] the river. When he got up his belly [2] was filled full. Then the girl told him to jump up. The giant tried to jump. His belly broke. So the girl killed him.

END

THE GIRL AND THE GIANT

One day some girls went over the mountains to gather willow roots for food. When they were about to return home, a giant came along and caught them and tied them up in his parki and left them there intending to get them on his way back to his home cave. After he had gone, a little snow bird flew by and heard the girls crying. He looked for them a long time before he found that they were inside the big parki and when the girls heard him chirp outside, they begged him to let them out. So the little snow bird pecked and pecked on the big parki but he couldn't make a hole in it because it was so tough and the poor girls continued to cry, which made the little snow bird very sad to think that he could not help them so he began to sing to them thinking to make them happy and so he sang and sang until they became quiet and he could hear them sleeping inside the parki and he flew away. [2]

After a while a white fox came along and when he saw the parki all bundled up on the snow he became very curious and very cautiously went up to it and sniffed all around it and scratched on it with his foot until some of the girls awoke and begged him to let them out. So the fox began to gnaw and gnaw on the skin and because he had such sharp teeth he soon tore a hole in the parki big enough for the girls to crawl out one at a time. As soon as a girl would get out, she would run home as fast as she could she was so scared. So all of them escaped but one girl. She was still sleeping and was left all alone in the parki [parka] until the giant returned. Then the giant found that she was the only one left, he was angry and took his hunting knife out of his belt and said he was going to kill her. So the girl was very frightened and begged him not to kill her and promised to be his slave and work for him if he would spare her life. So the giant changed his mind and took her to his heart and dressed her some of his old clothes because they would be too heavy for her to run away in and he made a slave of her and she worked for him a long time. [3]

The girl was very sad and homesick for she thought of her father and mother and playmates all the time and wanted very much to run away. But the giant's clothes were so heavy that she could hardly walk with them and could not run at all. Over night she had a dream. She dreamed that she was awoke and a little snow bird flew into the big skin house and through the little round ventilation hole into the sleeping room and down into the pillow log near her face! The little snow bird whispered in her ear that he was the bird that sang her to sleep and he was sorry that she didn't wake up in time to get away with the other girls. Then he whispered a lot of secrets in her ear and flew away.

The next morning before big daylight the little girl slipped out from under the sleeping room curtain into the big room and climbed on top of the sleeping room where there were a lot of things stored away in seal skin pokes. After a while she found the one tied with reindeer sinew, [4] and when she opened it, sure enough there was her [own] clothes, and she put them on. oh my, she felt as light as a feather. They were so light compared to the giant's big clothes that she could almost fly. She forgot all about the giant and began jumping up and down on top of the sleeping room. She made so much noise that the giant woke up and she heard him shambling around for his clothes and she jumped off of the sleeping room and ran out of the house. The giant ran behind her and yelled at her and said, "How did you find those clothes?" And the girl said, "A little bird told me." And the giant said, "Give them back to me!" And the girl ran like the wind, with the giant after her because she felt so light she could beat the giant for a while, but pretty soon she began to grow tied and before the giant caught up with her, she drew a line in the snow with a stick and jumped over it and ran on. The snow began to melt and the water ran along the line. And it grew wider and widen until it became [5] river. And when the giant came o the river and saw the girl on the other side, he didn't know what to do and he said "How did you get over there?" And the girl said, "I came over in a mussel shell." And the giant picked up a mussel shell and tried to swim across with it, but sunk to the bottom. When he came up, he cried to the girl, "What must I do now?" And the girl said, "Drink the river dry!" And he drank and drank until the water was all in his belly. And he was a big gas balloon. But when he tried to walk, he was too heavy to move and the girl said, "Why don't you jump out?" And he jumped so hard that he burst open and the water washed him into the ocean. Then the girl ran home to her parents and playmates and they were all very happy again. Away from the giant, she said "A little bird told me!" but her mother didn't understand, but we do, don't we.

END

THE STORY OF A MAN THAT ALWAYS
LOST HIS SONS WHEN THEY ARE
GOWN UP TO BE A MAN

Once upon a time there lived a man and his wife. And so they had lots of sons. But when they are full grown, when ever they go, they never come back. And so the perants had only one youngest son left. And so the perants didn't let him go anywhere. Because they were afraid that he might be lost as his brothers did.

stories families

So one day the boy ran away without asking his perants. And so the boy went on his way. When he got far from his house and while he was walking, the earth came high and so he rolled down and was caught by a big net. And so he had a hard time to take of [off] himself from the net. And he was at the net one day. Then the next day he hears some body walking. And he saw that it was a big giant coming to see his net. And when the giant saw that his net caught something, [2] he said I am very glad. I caught a seal. My children will have something to eat when I get home. And so he took off the man or the boy and tied him and carried him home on his back. And when the giant was walking, the boy said something. And scared the giant and the giant took him down and tickled him. And when the boy almost laughed, he didn't tickle him any more, and so carried him again. The boy was palying [playing] that he was dead. And the giant reached his home. So he called his wife. And said to her, I caught one seal and so we will have a good dinner. And so the giant took him in, and his wife put him on the plate. And so the giant and the children and his wife eat. After dinner his wife took a big knife, and was going to cut him up. And so the boy made his belly move up and down. And scared the woman. And so she was afraid [3] to get close to the boy again. And so she said to his [her] husband, I will cut this seal up tomorrow. When the seal gets cold. And so she put the seal and the plate to the big room. And they slept. And when they slept, the boy got up and he saw a big ax and took the ax and killed the giant and his wife. And after he had killed them perants then he killed their children with a knife. And so he went out and came back to this home. And he told his perants that he killed the divel [devil] giant which killed your sons. And his perants said to their son, We thought you was lost as your brothers. And so the boy was not afraid to go any where now. There were nothing to be afraid now. And his perants got many children again. And they didn't die no more.

END

THE STORY ABOUT A BOY HERDER

There lived a man and his wife, and they had a son that looked after his father's deer [reindeer]. So they had lots of deer.

But the boy had to stay in the herd all day and night. But he would take food to eat when is watching the herd of deer. And so fawning came. And so many fawns came that year. So one day he went around the herd to see if the fawns came. And what did you think he saw? He saw a big sled deer having a birth. And a child came out from the sled deer. And the child cried when he came of from the belly of the sled deer. When the boy saw that the sled deer had a real child, he went home and told his perant [parent] that the sled deer had a child. And so his father told him to bring the child home. And he told his son that he had a brother now. And when he [was] big [2] he would help him watch the herd. And so the child grow very fast. He was growing every day. And soon he was big enough to watch the heard. And so he watched the herd all the time. And the other boy didn't watch the herd any more. Because the deer son wanted to watch the heard only him self. So one day the boy went to see his herd which the deer son was watching for him. And when he got close, he was that the deer son was eating the deer up. And so he watched him. And the deer son did not see him at all. He was eating one third of the boy's deer. And so he was thinking that if the deer son eat all the herd up that he would eat him and his perants. So he ran home as fast as he could. And he got home and didn't ever tell his perants about the deer son that was eating up the deer. But he ran off and ran away [3 / 46] from his perants. And so he was far away from his home now. And on his way he saw an igloo, so he went to the igloo and he saw only one women [woman] in their [there]. And the woman told him to come in. so he went in. And the woman give him something to eat. And the woman asked him where he was going. And the boy say to him [her] that he was looking for a girl for a wife. And so the woman said to him, You are not looking for a wife. You are running away from your deer brother. And then the woman told him that his brother eat all the herd and his perants. And now he is calling you to come to him because he want to eat you too. You better go home to your brother. And the boy said to him, I will not go home. I am afried he will eat me too just like my perants. And the woman said to him, I will eat you my self. I like to eat man too. If you don't go home to your brother I will eat you for my dinner. But the boy said to her again, I am afried he might eat me just like my perants. And so the woman said to him, If you go to your brother you can use my sled deer and my sled. And if you get to your home, ask him like this Where is your perants and your herd. If he want to eat you, try to come as fast as your deer can run. And so the boy did as the woman told him to do. He went to the woman's sled deer. And the deer had lots f legs in his body. May be it had 20 legs altogether. And so the boy went on his way to his brother. So he went to the house. And the deer son saw his brother and they kissed together because they were glad to see each other. And the boy asked the deer son, Where are you perants and your herd? And the [3] boy said to him, I don't know where they went. I am very lonesome here by my self. And I want to eat you for my dinner. And the boy ran out as fast as he can to his deer sled. And made his deer go very fast back to the woman's igloo. And while he was going he saw the deer son was doming after him to eat him up. And he was getting very close. And the boy cut off one leg from his sled deer and threw it to the deer son. And the deer son eat the leg and come after him again. And the boy cut of [off] another leg and threw it to the deer son. Now the deer had only 4 legs. And so he heard a voice saying to him, Shut your eyes. So he closed his eyes. And so he heard something behind him and he opened his eyes and saw the woman that give him the sled deer. She came to help this [4] boy. And the woman eat the deer son up. And the boy was safe from his brother. And the woman said to him, There is a mountains way over there and the other side of that mountains there is a village. And there is an old woman at that place who made the child come to kill every one of you and your herd of deer. She did that because your father was her husband before. I will give you power. And if you want to kill her, you can kill her, or if you don't want to kill her, all right. And so the boy went. And he got there and the boy went to her igloo. And the boy killed her. And all the people was afraid of that old woman. But the boy killed her. And so the boy was king over that village. And he had a wife there and he was happy all his life.

END

THE STORY ABOUT AN ORPHAN WHO GOT
THE RICH MAN'S DAUGHTER FOR WIFE

Once upon a time there lived an orphan who had married the

rich man's daughter. So one day his Father-in-law told him to get some wood. When night came the boy was ready to go. And so the orphan's wife wanted to go with him. So he said, You may go. So they went, him and his wife to get wood. Then they got where there were [was] lots of wood. And they had a stone ax with them. So the orphan found a big log. Then the orphan start to cut the log with the ax. And his wife sat right before him. So he told her not to sit in front of him. So the ax would kill he [her] if the ax should break. But his wife didn't care what he was talking to her. At last the ax broke and went right to the head of his wife and killed her. Then the orphan was very afried because he killed his wife. And the girl had many brothers. So he put her on his sled with some wood he got and came home. When he got home, he heard that his wife's brothers were singing. Then the Father-in-law [2] came out and asked his son-in-law, Where is your wife? And the orphan said, She is coming. Then the orphan told his Father-in-law to take off the rope from the sled. And the orphan went in the igloo. When he got in the youngest brother was dancing. So he said, Let me dance too. While the orphan and his brother-in-law was dancing, he hear his father-in-law crying. So the orphan killed the youngest brother that was dancing with him and ran out and ran away as fast as he could. He was running all day and all night, day after day, never stop. Then he found a little igloo. In that igloo was an orphan and his grandmother. Then he told them two to watch if any body comes, to wake him up. Then he went to sleep. He slept for days and nights, only they wake him up to let him eat. And the other orphan was watching for him, he went out all the time to see if some one was [3] coming. So one day he went out again and he saw some thing coming. So he went in and wake the orphan. So he went out. And he said to the other orphan, Can I have you kayak? The other orphan said to him, I need that kayak my self. So the orphan asked for the kayak again. So he said, You may have it. Then he said to him, Can I have your dog too? I want to put the skin on and kill the dog. Then the orphan that killed his wife said to the other orphan, If I change [in] to a dog. If my enemies get here, I will howl all the time. So you can take me to the kayak and say [near] to them people, What [Why] do you howl so much. I am afraid of them people. So you take me to the kayak. So the orphan's enemies get to the little igloo. And the orphan change into a dog. So the asked

stories families

the orphan, Where is out brother-in-law? If you don't tell us, we will kill you. But the orphan didn't tell [4] them that he had changed into a dog. And so some of them said, If this dog was our brother-in-law we would kill him. Some of them point spear at the dog. So the dog howls very loud. So the orphan said to them men, I am going to take my dog and tie him in my kayak. He howls too much. So he took the dog and tied him to the kayak. So the dog changed to be an orphan and was on his kayak. And his enemies went back. And he was safe.   END

THE BOY THAT WENT FISHING

Once there lived a boy and his sister in an igloo by them selves alone. They lived just on Tom Cod. And so the boy had to fish all the time. But the boy was a very good fisher. And so one day he went to fish for tomcod and made a hole in the ice and let his fish line down the hole. And so he caught something very heavy and heard a baby crying. So he caught a water baby. And he pulled the baby on [to] the ice. And the baby was crying. So the boy saw that the babies [baby's] belly was full and the boy stepped on the billy [belly] of the baby. And lots of tom cod came of [off] from the babies mouth. And the boy was very happy because he had now a water baby that bring him lots of fish then ever. And so he when [went] home with lots of tom cod. And when he came home, his sister asked him how he caught so many tom [2 / 51] cod. But the boy did not tell her that he caught a water baby. And so the two had dinner. Then the girl got up very early in the morning. And looked for his [her] brother's fish line. And she found the line. And on she went to fish. While his brother was sleeping. So he found the hole that his brother made and she let her line down. And she caught something very heavy and she pulled it up. While she was pulling her line, she heard some one crying. So she dropped her fish line and ran home. Because she was scared. So she got home and his brother was sleeping yet. And his brother woke. But the sister didn't tell him that she lost his fish line. And the boy said to her, Where is my fish line? The boy couldn't find them. So he told his sister that they were going to starve. Then one day the boy walked [3] one day into the field. And he saw an igloo. And so he went to see what was in there. And he saw lots of reindeer in the igloo. And he saw a woman that belong [owned] the deer. And so he spit on one of them deer. And the deer died. When the woman saw that one of her deer was dead, she threw the deer out from the igloo. So the boy took the dead deer home. And when he came home, his sister asked him where he got the deer. But the boy didn't tell his sister. So the girl got up very early n the morning and went to the igloo to get some deer. So she saw lots of deer inside the igloo. So she spit on one of them. And the deer was dead. So the woman threw the deer out. And the girl tried to carry the deer but it was too much for her. And so the girl called to the woman to help her. But the woman didn't help [4] her. But the woman whipped her because she was killing her deer. So the girl went home, and told her brother that the woman whipped her. And the boy said to her, Now you broke all the placed where I get food. Now we are going to have very hard time. So you and I will starve. After that the boy couldn't get food any more. So they had a famine.

END

THE STORY OF TWO BROTHERS

Once there lived two brothers. But they didn't live together in the same village. One of them lived at Ekalowrrak and the other lived at Sacktook. And the one that lived at Sacktook had six sons. But [the other] that lived at Ekalowrrak only had two sons. And both of them were singing men. And had lots of devils [spirits].* And Ekalowrrak-me lived on fish. And he fished all the time. And Sacktook-me lived on seals and walrus and whale. So one day Ekalowrrak-me sons went out to fish. And while they were fishing a black bear came and tried to kill them two boys. But they didn't let the bear kill them. But they nearly killed the bear. The man that lived at Sacktook had sent his devil to kill them two boys that lived at Ekalowrrak. I don't know why. And so when them two boys came home from fishing, they told their Father about the bear that tried to kill them. And the Father said to his sons, I don't know why he sent his devil to us. And he is my brother, and he has six sons. And he lives at Sacktook [2] And he said to his wife, Wash the igloo from Top to the floor. And so she did wash. And then the

stories families

husband went out and called his devil: the big white bear. And he went in. After a while, the big white bear came in and said to his master, What do [you] call me for? And the man said to him, I have a brother and he lives at Sacktook and he has six sons. Now they are out hunting. So if you want to kill them all, you can kill every one of them. And if you kill them all, take their hearts our and bring them to me. When the man finished talking to his devil big white bear, the Bear growled one time and went on his way to Sacktook. So the bear got to Sacktook and saw them six men. They were just comeing^ home from hunting. So the [bear] killed them all, not one left. And after the bear killed them, he took out all the six hearts from them. And the bear went home to his master at Ekalowrrak . and the devil bear told him that he had killed them all. Then Sacktook-me was wondering about his six sons. So he went to look for them. And he found one of them dead. So he called his devil wolf. And the wolf came. But the wolf couldn't make him alive.

So the wolf went away. So Sacktook-me called his devil whale. So the whale came. And made the boy alive. When the boy alived again, he told his Father that all of his brothers were all dead. And every one of them had no hearts. After the boy finished talking to his father, he was dead again because he had no heart. If they all had hearts their Father would make them alive again. The Father went home very sorry over his dead sons. So Sacktook-me call his devil wolf again and told him to kill Ekalowrrak-me two sons. But the wolf didn't kill them at all, only they killed the wolf. So Ekalowrrak-me had stronger devils than his brother that lived at Sacktook. So now Ekalowrrak-me's sons could go any where they wish to go. Not being afraid of Sacktook-me devils.

END

A STORY ABOUT A STRONG MAN

Many years ago, there was a very strong man on St Lawrence Island who bossed over all the people at that place. And every body was afried of him, because he was so strong. And so in those days, the people of St Lawrence Island found a dead whale other side [of] the mountain. And the whale had very large bones. But the strong man had all the whale bone. And so there lived other side [at] the Tophuk, a very strong man. But the people at St Lawrence Island didn't know he was a very strong man. And so he came to St Lawrence or to Gambell to get some whale bone. And they got where they found the whale. But the Gambell strong man wasn't over there. And so he took ten pieces of whale bone. And hid them under the ground. And came to Gambell. And so the men that was cutting up the whale come home to tell the strong man that lived at Gambell that the man came from other side. Tophuk took ten pieces of bone. And the strong man at Gambell was very mad. And so he went to Tophuk strong man and said to him, Why did you take my whale bone without asking me? But the man didn't say not one word to him. And the strong man said to him again, Why did you take my whale bone from me? I will fight you. May be you think that I am not strong. And so the strong man at Gambell caught him but the man tat lived at Tophuk killed the strong man that lived at Gambell because the man that lived at Tophuk was more stronger than him. So he had the whale bone for himself.

END ~ True Story

THE STORY ABOUT THE OLD MAN

Many, many years ago there lived an old man and his wife in the igloo. And they had no children at all. And so they had no more R— tobacco. And so he said to his wife that he was going to another place to try to get some tobacco. And so he went on his way. And he got some tobacco and came home. And while he was coming home it got dark [as] night came. And on his way home he saw an igloo. And he thought he would go over to that igloo to drink some water. And so he went and he went in the igloo and the igloo was dark. The old man was very afried [afraid] of something he did not know what to do. No body [alive] was in the igloo. Everyone in the igloo was dead. He didn't know what to do. He walked back and forth inside of the igloo because he was thinking that the divel [devil] would catch him if he ran out. So he talked to him self, I am going out side [2 / 41] to get my tobacco that I left out side of the igloo. And he hears some one in the igloo talking to him and said to him, I will go out and bring your tobacco in for you. And the old man said to him, You don't know where I put the tobacco. I will go out myself and get the tobacco myself. The divel was talking to the old man. And so the old man went out of the igloo and ran home as fast as he could. And while he was going home, he saw a big divel coming out from the igloo after the old man. But the old man threw something at the divel that made the divel go away. And so he got home. And give the tobacco to his wife. So they had tobacco once more.

END

A STORY ABOUT A GIRL THAT HAD A SWEAT [SWEET] HEART

There lived a young girl that didn't want to have a husband. Lots of young men tried to marry her but she didn't like that. But she had a sweat heart. And so she had a great love on that young man. Her sweetheart was her uncle. And so the girl's perants heard that she had a great love on his [her] uncle. So the girl's perants killed the girl's uncle, because he ashamed of his daughter. So he killed the man. And when night came, the girl went out and cut the man's head off and brought home her uncle's head because she loved him very much. And she took the head to her room. And she had the head for a long time. So while she had her uncle's head, the head began to smile and talk. And the two would talk to each other all night. And when it was day the girl would go and get wood for her perants because her perants had no sons. So while she was gone the husband said to his wife, [2] go into our daughter's room and see what is in her room. She always take to some one every night. So the woman went and looked all over her room. And she saw the girl's uncle's head. And she told her husband that she saw the head that he killed. And the man said to his wife, Go and tell every one that our daughter had changed to a divel. And tell them to move from this place to another place tomorrow. And so she told all the people at that village. Then tomorrow the perants told thier [their] daughter to go and get lots of wood. And so the girl went to get wood. So the people and their perants went off on thier boats to another place. And when the girl came home, she found that every body had gone and not one [was] left. Only she was left and the head of her uncle. And so she cried all day. And while she was crying, the head said to her, Make a big fire and throw me [3] into the fire. I am going to get my body. And I will come back and change to a man again. And so the girl did as she was told to do. So her uncle was changed to a man. And he took the girl for a wife. And so the man made a house and the two lived thier [there] and was happy. And the man made lots of toy deer. And they were changed into real deer. So they had lots of food that year. And they had a child and it was a boy. And so summer came. One day when they were out they saw a boat coming. And the man said to his wife, If they are your perants, they are your perants. I my self will go up to heaven. And if you want to go with me, you can go. Or if your do not want to go with me all right. And the girl said to her husband, If they were my perants, they wouldn't leave [4] me by my self alone. So I will go with you because I love you very much. So they went up to heaven. And the perants cried at the place where they lived and was dead at the day because they wanted to see their daughter very much.

END

A MAN NOT VERY GOOD HUNTER

Once upon a time in he village the people brings lots of meat and kills lots of seal but that man didn't get anything. He had a bad luck all the time. So one day, the other people killed a polar bear. But he wasn't there. So the storm came and the people that caught the bear just took of [off] the head skin and the skin. But they didn't take any meat because they were afraid from the storm. And when the people came home, the unlucky man went to seek for the bear's carcus [carcass]. While he was walking, he heard some one chattering as though very cold. And he went toward where he heard noise and he saw the bear without his skin standing up. The bear came alife [alive] again without his skin. The bear said to the man, Don't be afraid of me. I will not harm you. Just come to me. And the man went to him. So the bear asked him, Have you anything in your clothes? And the man said, I have a little piece of bear large intestine. [2] And so the bear said to him, Give me that intestine and the man gave it to him. And the bear changed it into bear skin, and he put on the skin which he had changed. And the bear told

stories families

them that he will kill any animals which he sees. And the bear went away. So the man sent him after the bear went away. Then in the morning the people went out hunting. But the unlucky man was the first one to kill a seal. And after that he was the best hunter in that village. And so bear made him the best hunter of all. N R

END

AN UNLUCKY MAN

There was a man who was unsuccessful hunter. When he goes out hunting he sleep on the side of a bloc of ice. At home his wife was begging some meat for him.

When every one of the hunters went home, he would went home, and never killed anything.

One day while the wife was begging some meat for him, the neighbor's wife told her about him.

One fine day he went hunting again. Then about an hour [later] the wife went to search for him. She came to the spot where he was sleeping. She then saw him sleeping. Then she took his weapon and went home.

When the man woke up, he saw that his weapon was not there. He thought about what to say about them. At last he thought a plan about them.

Then he went home and before entering he told that he had caught a seal. While he was holding it [he] saw that his harpoon was almost covered up by the ice. Leaving his line, he run to get his harpoon but it was gone. Then he ran to the line, and it was gone. He told his wife to go and ask [for] some of her brother's weapon. Instead of asking from her brother, she gave him his own.

Next morning he woke up very early and he got ready to go hunt for he was ashamed. Then he went our and walked on to the ice. There was a seal hole and [he] watched. A few minutes [later], a seal came up. He struck it. Then after a while it comes up, it was not a seal, it was a skeleton man. Then the skeleton of a man fought with him. When he finished fighting with him [it] went again into the hole. The man's face was swollen. He thought again to fool his wife about it when he came home. [2] He told his wife that he caught a seal. It was so big that he could hardly hold [it], so he tried

stories families

to hole by biting the end of his rope. While holding it, the seal pulled stronger than before and made him to hit the ice on his face, and it made swelled up.

Next morning he went again to saw a hole again and watch. A few moments [later] a seal came up and he caught it. It was a big seal. After that he was the best hunter in the town.

END

THE MAN THAT SLEEPS
ON THE ICEBERG

Once there lived a man that went hunting but he never hunt but always sleeps when he goes out to hunt. And that's why he never kill an think [thing] at all. But the other people that went hunting with him always kill seal, walrus, and mukluk. So some body told his wife that her husband don't kill seal because he never hunt but only sleeps on the ice. And so the man's wife was a beggar. So one day the man went to sleep on the ice again. So his wife went with her husband. But the husband didn't see her because she hid when the man looked around to see some body. So the woman watched her husband to sleep. And after a while the man slept. And so his wife went to him and took his harpoon and his rope and may be his rifle too. May be he had a rifle or not. And she took them home and hid them.. and so the man came home [2 / 59] and told his wife that he caught some thing very strong. But that animal was to [too] strong for me. So I lost my harpoon and my rope. The man didn't know that his wife took the things home. And the woman said to his [her] husband, Well too bad you didn't catch that animal. And his wife had many brothers. And so the man told his wife to try to get some rope and harpoon from her brothers. And so the woman went out and got the man's things and give them to her husband, but her husband didn't say any thing at all. The man was very ashamed of him self because he told a big lie. Then all the people at that place laughed at him. Then tomorrow the man went hunting again. This time he looked for a seal hole. And so he found a seal hole, and he saw some thing in the hole. And so he strike [3] at the seal. And so the seal went down very fast. The man was very glad that he caught some thing. And up the seal came. And it came out from the

stories families

hole. But it wasn't a seal. But it was a man skeleton. And the skeleton fought the man. And made his face swell up. The man's face was black as ink because the skeleton fight him. When the skeleton got through fighting, he went down the hole. Then the man went home. And the people saw that his face was swelled up. And so they asked him how he did that. And he said to them, I fell down from the ice right on my face. So he told a lie to the people again. When his face got well, he went hunting once more. And he saw a hole again. And so a seal came up. He was afraid that it was a skeleton gain. But he [4] strike it once more. And the man pulled it up. He was afried [afraid] of the thing, but it was a real seal. Now he was very glad that he caught a seal. And he came home right away. The first one to kill a seal that day. After that he did not sleep on the ice any more. But he got to be the best hunter in that place. The skeleton made him the best hunter of all.

END

THE STORY OF A MAN THAT HAD
A WIFE OF DIVEL [DEVIL WIFE]

Once upon a time, there was a man that had a wife. And at where he lived there was a big village. And at that place, they only hunted moose. And so every one of them got many deer. And the man went hunting too but he never hunts. But he all ways goes to a lake and stay there all day. And so a whale would spout and then a fine lady would come out from the whale and go to the man and sleep all day thier [there] and talk and kiss them selves. And when night come, the man would come home without any mooses. So he was that way all the time and he never caught any thing at all. And so some of the men told the man's wife that her husband had another wife and that's why he never get any mosses [mooses] just like we do. And so when her husband came home, she asked him where he was hunting. And his [her] husband said to her, I have been out hunting far away and I didn't see any thing at all. I will go again tomorrow. And so he went the next day. So his wife went with him. But she would hide when the man looked around to see some one. So the man got to the lake and stayed there. Then after a while a big whale came out from the lake and a nice lady came out from the body of the whale and went to the man. So the woman went home. She was very mad at her husband because he had a wife of a divel. And when the man came home, his wife said to him, You never go hunting for moose. And you let me begg [beg] from other people for us to eat. And so the man asked her, Where did you hear that? And she said, I saw you with a lady by the lake. You had done that for a long time. So the man fainted and was dead.

END

THE MAN THAT HAD TWO WIVES

Once a man had a wife. And he loved his wife very much for many years. So one day the man saw a very good looking girl. And he wanted to get her for a wife. So he married her. Now he had two wives. After a while he was mad at his first wife. So he did not love her no more. Because he had a very good looking young girl for a change. And he told his Nooleapick to go out. And told her that she was no good at all. Now he had a good wife. The man's igloo had three rooms. It was a big igloo. So the Nooleapick went out to one of them rooms and lived there. And she had very short of food to eat. But her husband and his Nookaghauk had every thing to eat. And they lived happy. But the Nooleapick was unhappy, and had not much of food. So she got food from some women that lived with them [as neighbors]. There were many houses at that place. Where the man lived. At last Nooleapick couldn't get food. So she got poorer and poorer every day. Because she couldn't get food any more. But her husband and his Nookaghauk had lots to eat. It was winter at that time. And spring was comeing. And the people at that village were getting ready for whaling. So one day the people on their skin canoes. And Nooleapick's husband had a boat. And so [2] he went whaling. When the boats had gone Nooleapick went to her husband's Nookaghauk asked her if she could give her some food while her husband was away. But she said to her, My husband told me not to give you any of the meat that we have. So Nooleapick went away feeling very bad about Nookaghauk that she didn't give her any food. So it went on.

Now it was beganing^ to melt the snow. And all the boats went hunting again. So they caught a whale. And brought the

stories families

whale home. And the man that had two wives had killed the whale. So every man, woman, even children, went to see the whale. And Nookaghauk was going. So Nooleapick said to her, Bring some whale skin for me to eat. And while Nookaghauk was gone, Nooleapick killed a dog and was cooking her dinner. Now they were boiling. And so Nookaghauk came home with out any whale skin. So asked her if she brought any whale skin for her? But Nookaghauk said to her, I will not bring you whale skin. Because our husband told me not to give any food to eat. He told me that he is going to make you starve to deaths. So [3] Nooleapick took the boiling cooked dog meat that she had cooked and poured them into Nookaghauk's ears, and killed her. Now Nooleapick was afraid that her husband would kill her now, because she killed his Nookaghauk. So Nooleapick went and dressed Nookaghauk in her best clothes. Then she went to hid herself so their husband wouldn't see her. At last the husband came and saw that his Nookaghauk was dead. And so he was mad and said to his Nooleapick, I think you killed my Nookaghauk. And so I am going to kill you right now. And he ran to his Nooleapick's room. But she wasn't there. So he looked and looked all over the igloo. But he could not find her at all. So the man went out to work [on] his whale again. So Nooleapick went out and walked a long ways from his [her] husband. So the man had not more wives as he was before. END

A WOMAN THAT HAD A BIRTH IN THE FIELD

Once there was a woman who had a baby in her belly that went out to pick something from the ground. She wanted some willow roots. So she had a birth away from the village by her alone. Then she had a child. And it was a boy. So she covered the child with leaves. And came home. So she leave her baby. And didn't even tell her husband about the child she had covered with leaves.

So the woman forgot about the child that she had far away from home. So the child grew fast and was a big boy now from living just on the things that grow on the ground.

So one day the black bear saw the boy. The black bear changed to a woman and came to the boy. And took the boy to her den. The two lived together. And the bear would hunt deer and ducks and other animals for the boy to eat.

So the boy grew very fast and was a man now. And the bear was getting very old. And the man took the hunting for a change.

The man was a very good hunter and was very strong and fast in running. And he brought many deer for the old bear to eat. And so the man never saw any other man or any village because the old bear always tells him not to go toward the sea because many devils lived over there. And the bear said to him if you go you will not come home. She told the man this because toward the sea there was a big village and the man's parents lived there.

The old bear was going to eat him when he was full grown.

So one day the man went toward the sea. And there he saw a big village. And they had a dead whale. They had caught a whale. And he saw many people that were just like himself. [2]

All of them had two legs and two arms. And one of the old men asked him where he lived.

The man told him that he lived with an old black bear in the den. And he told the old man that he was with the bear when he was a baby. He thought the old bear was his mother.

And then the old man came and said to the young man, "You are my son". And you better come because your mother will soon eat you up.

And so the young man went on his way to the old bear. He reached home. And the old bear said to him "Why did you stay away so long?" I think you went towards the sea and there was no devil. But there was a big village over there and many people that look just like me. And they caught a whale and I am going ever there to stay.

The old bear got mad and tried to kill the young man. But the man killed her because she was old.

And so the young man came back to his real parents. But they were very old parents. And the young man was the strongest and fastest in the village.

END

A WOMAN WENT UP TO HEAVEN

There was a man who had two wives. He was a good hunter. Every spring, he caught a whale. Later he began to hate one of his wives. She had a child, a boy.

One spring while he was out hunting the two wives had a quarrel. Then the one who had a child went to the shore fearing that her husband would fight her. She hid behind the block of ice. While she was hiding, she heard chattering near. Then she heard men talking.

After a few moments, some one called her to step into their boat. She stood up and stepped into their boat. They told her to cover her head.

They paddled and when they had paddled a few miles, they told her to step on land. So she did. When she looked behind, they flew away. They were birds.

When she looked the other way, she saw a man walking back and forth. His belt was on the extreme edge of his coat and his sleeves were not cut. He had his hood on, too. Then he put out his right arm and the wind arose and blew the woman with her child, into a big lake.

She swam to the shore. When she came on land, the man put out his other arm and again she was blown into the lake farther than before. Again she swam.

When she was on land, he took off his hood. She was blown near to the middle. She swam to the shore again. Then he took his belt off. The wind blew her to the far side of the lake. She swam and almost drowned. [2]

The man then came to her with clothes for her and her child. Then he told her that he was washing her. Then he brought her to his house and married her. He was God.

After two or three years, she bore another child. It a boy again. In the house there, she saw a smaller house which God told her not to look in. But one day while the man was away, she stooped down to see into the little house. She saw a small woman who was dressing a deer skin.

This little woman had just one eye, one nostril, one arm, one leg, and half a mouth. She was the moon.

While the first woman was looking at her, the house began to shake. Then she went in quickly, fearing from her husband. Then the husband came scolding her. He asked is she was homesick.

The woman told him that she was homesick but that she did not know the way to go home.

Then he told her to plait three whale sinews. She did. When she had finished, it was a long rope.

Then God, as they called him, let them down to earth with a large house and a boat, too.

When they were on land, they were great hunters.

*Such words as 'heaven' and 'God' in our language are not quite like their words for the same ideas. But since I do not know what would be a good translation for their God concept I cannot do anything about it.

*In these stories there is the same extra regard shown for a boy child as in other literatures. And yet these Eskimos were extremely shy of women so that a man sometimes had to work long years for a prospective father-in-law before he could win a wife for himself. You would think that a girl child would, for once, be held in high regard!

*There was one quite lovely young girl, Amamunga, whose father kept one man after another working for her until she was "shame for think not marry at all" as she told us and Farrar saw to it that old Shulook gave her in marriage to the current man who seemed to us the last man she would ever have wanted! But Amamung was desperate by this time.

THE WOMAN THAT WENT INTO THE SEA

Once a man and his wife quarreled. They had one child, a boy. Then the woman went out with the child to the shore.

The neighbors told the man that his wife was going to the shore but before he go out his wife went right into the sea. Then she walked forward under the sea.

She came to a hollow place where she finds lots of seaweeds. There she ate and the boy ate. Whereon she had done eating she went again on her way. Again she came to a hollow place and there she find other kind of seaweeds.

Then after walking some distance she came to a small house. She entered without saying anything. In the house she found the men of the house had short arms and legs. Their eyes were large like owl's. They were seals.

They gave her some sea-worms and crabs. She ate only the crabs and none of the worms.

Next day she traveled on and she came to a house again. When she entered it, she found the men of the house were the same as the people of the first one she had seen but they were larger. They were Mukluk as we call the big seal that we used for a boat bottom.

She stayed one night there and next morning she went on her journey. Again she came to a house. When she step into it she found many heads with tusks and she saw many skins. They were walrus.

Next morning each of the men of the house took a head and skin, putting them on as their clothes and went out. When the day was gone by they came in but some of them were gone. For they had been killed. Some of them came in with a harpoon-head in them where they had been struck by the men. [2]

So the woman cut around the harpoon head and cook the skin and ate it. The men of the house said that she was eating man flesh but she did not. She stayed there a long time because she ate clams nearly every meal.

Then when she got tired of this house, she went out and traveled the same direction as before. After traveling awhile she came to a house. When she entered she saw some skins of whale. She stayed there longer.

One day the man of the house asked her if she was home-sick? She told them that she was home-sick but that she could not know the way home. Then the young man put a skin of a whale on himself, becoming a whale and took the woman and her child to their home. And so she got home safely.

END

WOMAN WHO TOLD 'HIS' HUSBAND NOT TO KILL FEMALE SEAL

Once there lived a man who had to obey his wife for not killing female animals. But she told him that he could kill all kinds of male animals. And he was a good hunter.

Sometimes he would have a hard time to find male seals. And so he would kill the female seal and would exchange them to other men for male seal. And those other men kills male or female whenever they see them. Only that man could not kill female animals because he was afraid of his wife.

So one day he couldn't kill a male seal so he killed a female seal. But he couldn't exchange the female for a male seal. So he went home, don't matter if it was a female seal. So he paddled home on his kayak.

When he was getting close to the shore his wife ran to meet 'his' husband. Nobody had told her that he had killed a female seal. She was very angry to 'his' husband because he killed female seal. So the woman jumped into the water to eat up 'his' husband. She had changed into devil and was going for him to eat him up. But 'his' husband paddled as fast as he could go for his life nd he was going faster than his wife.

So he paddled and paddled. At last he saw the mountain far away so he kept paddling for that mountain. He reached the mountain but it wasn't a mountain but a very high cliff and it was an island. It was very high all around it. No way to get up on the cliff. He couldn't find a way to climb up. And his wife was getting very close to him. So he closed his eyes and a good fairy[33] [2] took him up the high cliff. So he was safe from his wife now.

When he got up there he saw an igloo and went in and no one was in the igloo. It had two rooms. In the first room he saw a long thread hanging from the roof down to the floor and he touched the thread and went to see the other room and he stayed in there. When he was thinking about his wife he heard someone coming. He thought it was his wife coming to eat him up. But it was two girls that belonged the igloo.

The first girl came in and saw him and said to him, You will be my husband. Then the other girl came in and said the same thing to him. The last girl that came in, she was the one that had the long thread in her room. So she said to him, You will be my husband

---

[33] (I ~JB wonder what this conventional white-man creature actually is in the Eskimo mind. Some animal I imagine. Probably Raven. Maskin often slipped into such white man expressions which ruin his stories, but there is nothing to do but let them stand).

because you touched my thread and you came in to my room first. You better come here or I'll bring your wife here to eat you up.

Then the other girl told him not to go over to her room. But the man wanted to go over to her because he was afraid of the girl that was going to bring his wife. But the other girl told him not to go over, don't matter if she brings your wife.

So the two girls had a quarrel over the man. Both wanted to get him for a husband. And the girl that had the thread called the man again, Come quick, I am going to fish your wife with my thread. The man wanted to go but that other girl won't let him go. Because she wanted him to be her husband.

Again the girl called him, Come quick and she was fishing now for the man's wife. She fished his wife's coat and showed the coat to the man. The man saw the coat and knew it was his wife's coat. So the man wanted to go over. But the other girl wouldn't let him go. So the girl fished for the woman. Sure enough his wife was coming up now. He heard her voice saying to him, Did I [3] tell you to kill female seal?

When the man heard those words, he was afraid. So he asked the girl that wouldn't let him go to that other girl what he would do now. So she told him to go to her father's igloo and stay with him.

So the man went to her father's igloo. And at the door he saw two big black bears. They were very hungry looking bears. So he went in as fast as he could run. He heard the noise of the bear's jaws as he ran over them.

When he got in, he saw an old man sitting down with his head covered up. The old man asked him, What do you want? He told the old man that his daughter had sent him to stay here.

After a while the man's wife [go] up to the igloo and said to the old man, Give me that man. I want to eat him because he killed female seal. But the old man didn't say a word to the woman. But the woman didn't stop talking. At last; the old man said, Get out from here, very loud. And a big fire came out from the mouth of the old man and burnt up the woman that was talking so much. And the old man said to the man, Go out and see if the woman is burnt up. So the man went to see. But he didn't even go out from the igloo because he was afraid from the bears and from his wife.

So he went in and told the old man that she was burnt. But

the old man said to him, You didn't even [go] out from my igloo. If you don't obey me, I will burn you as I burn your wife. The man went out this time because he was afraid from the old man. He saw only the lungs of his wife. Only her lungs were left so he told the old man about the woman that only he found her lungs. The old man told him to go and have his daughter for his wife. So he went.

And the old man burnt the girl that had the thread. So the man had a wife again and was happy once more.

END

A GIRL CHANGES TO A SEALION

There was a man who had only one daughter. This girl was idle. She had stiff sleeves. One day the father took her and fastened a rope on her ankle and hanged her on the side of a cliff.

Not long after he went out camping, traveling in a canoe. Also his neighbors went. They passed by the girl. When they were near she called them to take down herself. But none of them did. They just passed by without seeing her for the father had told the people not to unloosen her.

At last her parents passed by. She kicked backwards and break the rope. She fell into the sea and came up changed to a sea-lion. She swam to her father's boat. She came up near her father.

Then she threw off her hood and she was not a sealion but the man's daughter. Then her father called her to come up into the boat.

Then the girl put on her hood as before and then she overset the boat. And she swam to the other boars and overset them all. And so she changed into a sea-lion. And so the sea-lion was once a girl.

A MAN WHO KILLED A NUMBER OF DEMONS

There was a man who lived alone in an island. His neighbors had gone away to some places. One evening he went to all the igloos and called in that he was going to have a meeting. These igloos were bare. Then when he came to his house, the spirits

stories families

came to the meeting. Some come under the ground, the others on the surface. When they all come in he took a bone pick axe and killed many devils. Some of them went away with a sore.

When he lay down to sleep, they would call to him to go and cure those he had wounded. But he would tell them to get away. When he cold not sleep, he would go and sleep on one of the rocks in the water wearing eye-glasses. The devils came near him and tried to go to him, but they thought he was not sleeping. So nearly every evening he did the same way. I hear only that long.

The eye glass [snow goggles?] of the Eskimo that I have seen is made of wood and had a hole in the middle.

STORY ABOUT SIBERIAN STORY

One man in Siberian place is very strong. He kill everything. When springtime come he go across the river to reindeer place. He come back full of everything: skin, clothes, deer meat. He have one wife and no children. He get home with deer skin and food. He divides half his skin and food, he give them to poor peoples. Next spring he rest, he no go again, never go.

Then wife have little boy. Pretty boy. Fourth year go again to reindeer place for skins. He go very fast. [1b] he take up everything: walrus skin, mukluk skin, walrus meat, whale meat. He give to reindeer herders, men very glad. He say tomorrow he give reindeer. That man he have more than thousand. Tomorrow he kill two reindeer. He say tomorrow I kill 8, 11. He not kill only two

Very soon two all gone. He send again to camp. Herder kill one and say tomorrow kill more. He no kill. Man say he want go home. Maybe soon all food gone. Herder say, "You go?" He say, "I go." Herder say, "I kill for you five." So he kill five and man go to other herder and other herder kill fifty. Bymby [bye and bye] man go. Little head wind. He pull hard, more little [2a] head wind, more little head wind. Bymby he pushed to shore. Build a house. Bymby winter come. He tell his man go with dog sled. Get many dog sleds, his own place come get him.

Bynby little while big sickness come. Every people have sickness. Some die some no die. Little Aganohuk no sick. Mother sick, father sick. Middle night father die, morning mother die. Little boy no die. Dog stay in living room. Female dog. He no eat dead man. Little boy never get hungry. Never die. He sleep then wake up. No die.

That big dog tame. When he go outside, he come home very kind to that little boy. Sometimes go away 3 or 4 days. Come home. Kind to little boy.

Little boy no think. Bymby holes [2b] in his clothes because nobody look out for him. Dog have house outside. He fix nice. He go in house and pull little boy by his sleeve to own house. Little boy get hungry. Mother no good for food getting, rotten. He go to dog's house. He see pups drink milk [suckle] on belly. Dog put him on his [her] belly. He drink milk. Bynby dog go out of house. He bark. Little boy go a little way. Dog go more. He bark. Little boy go a little more. Bynby Little boy see on beach hair seal. Then that dog jump on to seal and catch him by his foot. Bynby that dog kill seal in his neck. Little boy want meat. He see dog eat seal. He [had] no [3a] knife. Little boy eat meat just like dog. He get blood all on face. Dog lick clean [with] his tongue.

Bynby he go from beach. Bynby dog sick. He die. That little boy leave [left] alone again. He cry. His mother died. He stop where that dog die. He think, I'm better die too. Because when go some place, he did. Bynby he see lion. He lie down. He think lion kill him. Bynby lion come, pull his head back. He call him by his name and tell him, "What you living here?" Anagohuk say he have no mother. Lion say "Poor Anagohuk come with me." Little boy afraid. Lion takes off his hood. He have face like ours. He take little boy and throw him on his back. [3b] Then he take little boy home. He make him light. Bynby he hungry. He drink milk same as on our woman from lion woman. Bynby little boy big. Lion woman say to Aganohuk "Me old woman. I stop nearly 100 years I die. Suppose me die? You take me up that little hill. Then you go outside. I have 3 cousins over there." Lion teach little boy how to spear and bow and arrow. He play. Bynby he see that big lion already die. He cry loud. He say, "Lion, lion, why you leave me?" when cry finish, he wash lion, put on his clothes, put out lamps. Fix everything. Then he go outside. He see close a [4a] squirrel home. He think maybe hey the cousins. Little squirrel come and say, "Aganohuk my father say come in eat." Aganohuk try to go in but house too small. Only his foot go inside.

Then oldest brother come out and say, "Why don't you go inside? My father say come inside."

Aganohuk say, "I'm try. House too small for me. Only my foot [fits]!" Then squirrel say, "Come and I show you how." Then he go on top of little hill and look everywhere. Bynby he run and jump on that hole place. Then he go inside that that [sic] hole. Only his tail sticks out. He shake his tail, say "picurookorookorook."

Bynby Aganohuk go look around everywhere like squirrel. Bynby he turn around and run [4b] to hole. When he get to hole, he jump. Then he shake his hips all same squirrel and he say "*picurookorookorook*." He hurt a little bit. Then he inside. He look around. Oh, big room. It have 3 holes. Before he eat, that little old woman squirrel give him milk again. She say, "Aganohuk, what's a matter you come?" He say, "My lion mother die." She say, "All right, you live here." Bynby he go outside to play with little squirrels. ^At first they beat him. All time running. By & by he all time run faster than squirrels.^ He kill everything. He kill caribou. First bow and arrow. Then just spear. Then nothing. He just kill by himself. ^He run & catch caribou with hands.^ He bring to squirrel house. I don't know where he leave him [them].

Bynby that old man squirrel says, "Aganohuk maybe you want [5a] get married sometime. I see there north side one woman. One strong man got daughter very fine. Very, very fine. That man daughter got 3 husbands. But nobody ever see daughter. She stay inside box. Daughter very beautiful. Hair half one side red. Other side black. Sometimes that father want while little ducks to eat. He say, "Son-in-law I want ducks!" Bynby 3 men go kill white ducks. One man kill one; one man two; one man three. He bring them."

Bynby that man want sheepskin for her. The squirrel say to Aganohuk, "Suppose you go tomorrow that way, two days. You stop at big wood sticking in ground. You go other side, you see lots of apples. You eat em. You go little bit other side that hill. You see lots prunes. Lots sleep. Bynby you look [5b] other side that hill you see the river. That river runs looks blue & black & red. You drink. Prunes & apples, water ^sweet^. Bynby you go two days again. 5 days you walk [to] that man's place."

Aganohuk never sleep. He think about that girl with red & black hair. He make him a run [timing] stick. He go. Started after finish run stick. Only one day, not quite middle noon, he see big wood sticking in ground. "Suppose me walk two days, me see big stick. Suppose me go wrong way!" Then he go little other side, he see apples. He say, "Maybe I go right way" because Aganohuk strong, fast man. He eat apple. He go other side. He see lots of prunes too. He eating, eating. He go one. He see river [6a] black & red & blue. He drink. Sweet, sweet. Prunes, apples & water sweet. His drink finish. He look sun. Going down. He start run like fire. Bynby nearly dark, he see there big house. Big house. Big house. Then he go. He stop [at] that big house outside. He no go inside. He sit down to sleep. He not sleep. He think maybe kill him. Bynby man come outside with pan. He empty pan. He go inside. He say, "Some man outside, clothes no like ours." Father put on boots quick "I go look." (Actions [gestures] with everything). He go outside. He say, "What you going?" Aganohuk say, "I'm going to get married. Maybe some man got a daughter?" Man say, "Come in." He go inside. Tell his wife, "You feed him, that my [6b] son-in-law." From son-in-law one daughter! He feed him. That man put a towel on the rack. Aganohuk's towel. 4 towels. That man he go to daughter's box where she sleep, girl sleep there, never see. Father make dirty the box. 3 sons-in-law they quick get a towel & clean em. Aganohuk never clean. He never come to marry the box. I don't care, he never clean. Aganohuk work everything, but he never clean the box. Bynby father said, "Well, that fourth son-in-law maybe he not want a get married. He never clean the box. Better tomorrow morning he get me little ducks to eat myself. I don't like same kind meal all time." [7a]

Bynby Aganohuk go to get little white bird: ptarmigan. He see them that mountain very far. Bynby Aganohuk leave 3 men. He go very fast. He got big lake [with] middle little island. Lots little white ducks over there. Bynby Aganohuk jump [to] that island. He never move, he take ducks & tie to rope. He throw to land. He go home. Bynby he go – nearly sunset. He throw [in], "Here ducks!" Father say to wife, "You get ducks." Woman get [them]. She grunt. She put in. Man say, "*ho ho ho ho* – very fine man. I hear he have dog, squirrel mother. Very fast. Very strong. I think very fine man." Bynby next day other men come. One man one; another man two; another 3. Father [7b] throw them in a corner. He say, "*ho ho ho ho* I have fine son-in-law. I have doughnuts & coffee all time now."

Then he tell again, "More better he get me sheep for skin, my skin no good now!" All men he go. 3 men go creeping with pointed arrow. Aganohuk go straight standing up. Men say, "More better you go like us. Sheep very wild." Aganohuk not afraid then he go. He see them sheep. He run under bluff. Aganohuk to run after them. 3 men shoot & shoot & shoot. He [They] never kill em. Aganohuk go under the bluff. 3 men go back. Aganohuk kill five sheep. He put em on rope. When [8a] 3 men come home, Father he say, "Where other man? Four son-in-laws now only 3?" 3 men say, "He go on bluff, maybe he die." Then Aganohuk come. He throw in the sheep. "Here's your sheep. Now make your bed." Then father say, "Aganohuk fine man. I hear he have dog mother, lion mother, squirrel mother. Strong fine man. There's your wife inside box. You go get a married." Then he go inside [box]. He find Aganohuk very fine lady inside. He puts out his arm, the lady put her head on the arm, they sleep.

The 3 men Aganohuk's servants. When box dirty, they clean box. Aganohuk no work any more. He married.

Tfi! Finish.
Immingau's Dream Story

PEOPLE

KONEHOK

When he was at his house, he heard some one saying the ship was coming. And so he went out and saw the schooner, but it was far away. And so he went to the north shore. And the schooner was sailing toward the mountain and the wind was getting strong from SE wind. But they couldn't get closer because the wind was ahead of the schooner. He saw two men at the stern of the schooner. One of them was a white man and the other was mainland man. And they had a big dog with them in the schooner. And she had lots of load too. When the schooner first came it was a very good day, not much wind. And *Unalga* was at Gambell before the schooner. So *Unalga* went to the schooner and went around her. Maybe they talk to each other. And it was stormy so that he came home before the schooner anchored. So he said maybe the schooner went away or SE wind blew her away.

(That's all he saw)

KESTWEK

The ship came from the north of the Siberian mountains. Then they got here. Then *Unalga* went to the schooner and pass the schooner. May be they talk to each other. And after *Unalga* came back and anchored again. And the schooner came and anchored too. And he saw a big red dog in the schooner. And they had plenty of load on the schooner. One of them was a white man. And he was at the stern of the ship. And they had the foremast sail up. And he saw one of the mainland man on board the schooner. And they help up their arms. Maybe they were glad to get to St Lawrence Island. But the wind was very strong from SE wind and it was stormy that day. And the paint of the schooner was white. But the storm blew them away.

(That's all he saw)

APATA

He saw the schooner coming from Siberia. And she got to Gambell and he said to the other men that was with him that the schooner could unload some of their things if they threw a rope to the shore to some of the men that was at shore. Don't matter the wind was strong. The man at the stern of the schooner never look at the men that talks to him from the shore. He thinks they could unload some of their things if the other Eskimo men didn't tell them to go to the little harbor. But the wind was very strong from SE. And so they anchored right at the point of this place. And so the storm grew more stronger. If they had anchored at the west beach they would be safe. And they had a dog in their ship and it was a very big one. And so the schooner went off toward the North and she was gone.

(That's all he saw)

stories people

PELOWOK

He saw *Unalga* first anchored at St Lawrence Island a far off from the shore. The wind was from SE. Then the schooner came. And so I went to see the schooner coming. So she anchored at the north side. And so the SE wind got stronger all the time. And it was snowing very badly. But the schooner had lots of load. And the schooner had white paint. And they had a big dog with them. There was a man on the schooner that had an Eskimo rain coat on. And so he thinks the man belongs to the mainland people. More SE wind came and snowed lots. So the schooner went sailing with just one sail. So they were far out now. After a while he couldn't see them no more because it stormed to [too] much. And after they had gone, he came home right away.

(That's all he knew)

ANDREW

The ship came toward from Siberian mountains. When the ship got close to Gambell, *Unalga* went to the ship and went around her. And may be they talk to each other. And when they were sailing back and forth by the wind. And while they were sailing, SE wind came. They had only the foremast sail up, and they using their engine too. And so she got closer to the shore. And some of the Eskimo men told them to go to the harbor. But the wind was to [too] much for the schooner to go ahead. There were lots of men who went to see the schooner. And so he went too. And the storm got worse, and so she didn't go ahead any point and so she anchored not very far from the shore. And some of the Eskimos got where the schooner was anchored. But I was slow running so I got there last. And I saw she had lots of load of things and they had a dog. While the ship was there anchored. The wind got worse and so the ship pulled its anchor and went [2] away toward the north. We couldn't even see the houses close by because it stormed so much. And after the schooner had gone away, I went home and I try to see *Unalga*, but I couldn't see her because SE wind was very bad that time.

(That's all he saw)

stories people

JAMES

The ship came in October 1920. *Unalga* was here at the same time. In the morning the schooner came from towards Siberian mountain. They thought they were belong to Siberian ship. When the schooner got close, then *Unalga* went off and went toward the north and she came back to see the other ship and so she went close by and may be they talk to each other. And then *Unalga* anchored again. That day was NE wind and so the wind changed to SE wind and it was storming and so I took my whale boat to the north shore. When he was taking his boat to the north shore, he saw the schooner coming. But it as snowing that day. And so he couldn't see the *Unalga* at all because it stormed so much. And when they were sailing back and forth because [of] head wind. So they got closer. The men that was helping him with his boat ran off to see the schooner [2] because she was almost to anchor. Then after he him self went to see the schooner. So she had only the foremast sail pulled up. As they were sailing by the winds, they were using their engine too. They would turn off their engine when they turn off shore. And she had eight horse power engine. And so the name of the schooner was *Ukevak*. He saw that schooner at Nome, Alaska. But they were sailing by the wind just the same. If they had a strong engine they would be safe. But they were geting [getting] closer and closer. And I thought they were bringing things for the CB and LA Store. And the wind got stronger and stronger. So some men said it would [be] good for the schooner to go to the little harbor. And so the Eskimos went walking before the schooner to the little harbor. But the schooner [3] didn't go ahead any more because the wind was very strong from the SE. When the schooner turned off shore they couldn't see them any more because it stormed very bad. And so the men thought that the schooner couldn't get in the harbor. So they come and when they came, they saw the ship coming toward the land very fast. And so she anchored about 50 feet off the shore. And they pulled down their sail. But they didn't stop their engine. Se wind blew very hard. So the men of the schooner came out and pulled their anchor up. There were four men working. And so they pulled up their foremast sail up. And off she went. The wind got more stronger than ever. So we couldn't see her no more. And I think she was lost or got lost. If they had

stories people

anchored at the west side they would be safe from great SE wind.
(That's All)

CAPTAIN JACK

He was born at Indian Point. He learned to talk English on the Whalers because he went with them all the time. That is how he learned to talk. He came the same time that Mr and Mrs Gambell came to St Lawrence Island.

CAPTAIN JACK

He was born at Indian Point. His father's name was Angoolook, and his father was very rich. Angoolook was an Indian Point man but he lived at St Lawrence Island. He went to Indian Point when they had a war between Siberia and St Lawrence Island. Captain Jack learned to talk English by being a sailer [sailor] on the whaling ships and goes out side with them whalers. He came before Mr Gambell came here to Gambell. He interpreted for Mr and Mrs Gamble, Mr Doody, Norega, and other teachers to Dr Edgar Omar Campbell. Captain Jack interpreted. They pay him every time for interpreting. When he interpret to the traders, he fools them so he gets more things than the other men on the island that had something to trade. His kins now on this island are Eddie's father Lincoln and his brothers and Booker and his father. He was a very good fox hunter. Don't matter there was no fox on this island. [2]
So he was drunk all the time. He brought the whiskey from the traders and all the traders like him because he talks English. He never fight, only when he drink, he like to drink more and more. He was punished by the [US Coast Guard] Cutter by [for] drinking too much whiskey and was caught by the officers and they took him out side and was brought [back] the next year. His wife died at Gambell in the school room. When Dr Campbell was here. And Dr Campbell adopted Captain Jack's daughter. So Jack went to his home to Indian Point. And he died at Indian Point. He never hunt for other game only he hunts fox.

stories people

CAPTAIN JACK

Captain Jack was born at Indian Point. His father's name was Angoolook, and Angoolook was an Indian Point man too. Angoolook was very rich man because his father was very rich when he lived at Indian Point. But they came to St Lawrence Island. Captain Jack learned to talk English on the whalers because he went on ships to work and he went outside. That's why he learned to talk so well. Jack interpreted first for Mr Gambell and all the other teachers to Dr EO Campbell. All the teachers pay him for interpreting and they pay him good because he talk very good English.

When he interpret for the Eskimos, when they had plenty [of] money, he would steal money from them. And he told them that he was over all the people here.

Kin kins now are on this Island, Andrew and his mother, Jmmier and his brothers, Eddie and his father, Booker and his father.

Jack was a very good fox hunter. He caught the most fox all the time. Don't matter there [2] were no fox on the Island. And so he was drunk all the time because he bought the drink all the time. And so he was very good for hunts. He bought the whiskey from the traders and from the people of Gambell. He bought 2 bottles for one fox skin all the time when he trade to the Eskimos at Gambell.

Jack never fight, only trouble he had when he was at Indian Point. One man almost killed him. And he was punished by the Cutter by drinking too much whiskey and he was caught by the officers and they took him out side and was brought [back] the next year. So Jack had a wife. But his wife had one eye. Dr Campbell took her eye off. And after that maybe be two years after, she died at Gambell.

And so Dr Campbell adopted Jack's daughter. So Jack went to his home and he was dead at Indian Point. He was a very good hunter in every thing he went for.

THE GRIPPE

I am confined to my bed with the grippe. At any note that's what June and I think it is. I ache in all my muscles. I am useless. Every time I roll or twist to a new position a series of dull muscular pains shoot through me. I never had the grippe before and always considered it a common every day ailment of no particular importance. During my childhood, my father was a county surveyor. Besides the transit with its awkward three legs called a tripod, he carried a little a little hand bag which contained survey chain and pin for marking the measurement, [1b] his notebooks and pencils, and very often a cold lunch for his noon day meal. The little hand bag he called his grip. I can see him plainly in my mind now. As he disappears up the hill with the transit on his shoulder and the little leather grip dangling at his side by the leather strap about his neck. Such a little insignificant thing it was that little grip of Dad's. And when my brother would read aloud the evening from our little daily paper to the effect that Mrs Ward of East Elm Street was confined to her bed with the grippe, [2a] or that Mr Poliver is unable to be at his office the week owing to an attack of the grippe, I always thought of that little old grip of Dad's and the illness of the afflicted stirred not the least bit of sympathy within me. But now it's my turn. I haven't seen my name in the paper. It may be there and it may not. There's one thing certain, however, and that is that hereafter when I hear that someone has the grippe, I may think of Dad's leather hand bag but I won't stop there. I'll go a little farther in my mind. And think of a trunk, a huge shoe drummers? trunk.

June 15

Dear Friends,

   We had a fine trip and landed safe at Plover Bay.   If everything goes the way I expect then this will be the greatest adventure the world has ever known.   You may have gathered as much from what you know of me, but, of course, I could not tell you much before reaching my goal.   I have now the rim of it with every confidence though you also [2] know the rocky road I have come and the length of the one before me.   Yet I can assure you that take supreme pleasure in it inspite of impatience with the difficulties. When the face of the world changes then you will know that I have succeeded and you may rest assured that Joe and I will always remember you.

Your Friend,
H Bruning[34] OK

---

[34] See p60 for his stranding and later fate.

In Maskin's Ledger
Eskimo Stories [inside cover]

No 1 ~ The Story of the Women who told 'his' husband
not to kill female seal or any other kind of animal Copies to ?Aun
5pp AB > CD pencil

About the Fox and the Crow 6-9 CD > GH pencil

The story of five little cormorants 10-13 2 lines   GH > KL pencil

A boy and his Grandmother 13-15 KL > MN pencil
       Blind Boy typed pages

The man that had two wives 16-[18] ink MN > OP   Nooleapick
Nookaghauk
       Typed pages, handwritten
       Purple typed a woman that went up to heaven

The story of two brothers [19-21] ink QR > ST

A boy that is an orphan [22-25] ink ST > WX

Nugaluk [26-28] ink XW > YZ {pages cut out}

Hughkowak [29-30] 7-8 ink Hughkowak is the name of one of the
       St Lwrence Eskimos Boat worship

Kamaleru [31] 9 ink One of the race worship called Kamaleru and
       it is over

Konehok [32] 10 ink that's all he saw

Kestevek [33] 15 ink that's all he saw

Apata [34] 16 ink that's all he saw

Pelowok [35] 17 ink that's all he knew

Andrew [36] 18 , [37] 23 ink that's all he saw

James [38] 24 ink that's all he saw
 Ukevak schooner [39-40] 27 -28 ink That's all 1 page cut out
        Race between reindeer & fish handwritten, typed

Killing a whale of Eskimos [41-42] 31-32
32 and so these things are the holy parts of the whale
        {The eye
        {nose
        {fins
        {fluke
and a little piece of whale chin and pice of black skin from the billy
of the whale
and one poke full of whale skin
that's all the holy things

about killing white bear [43-45] 33-35 ink copied to all?

Story of an orphan [46-47] 36-37 ink so the orphan learned the
        name of the walrus

The story about the old man [48-49] 38, 41 ink {39-40 cut out} the
        end

Story about a strong man [50-51] 42-43 ink the end true story
        paid

        Strongman & orphan handwritten

Story about a boy herder [52-57] 44-49 ink the end

The boy that went fishing [58-61] 50-53 ink

        Typed Long sheets Children's Department page 3 Eskimo
Legends don't kill females

A man not very good hunger [61-62]   54-55 ink N.R> ~ unlucky hunter

The strong man and his wife [63-64] 56-57 ink

The man that sleeps on the ice-berg [65-58] 58-61 ink the end
    Purple Typed an unlucky man

The five young men changed into sea gulls [59-61] 62-64 ink Paid
    at May 1 1921 paid

The story of a man that always losts [lost] his sons
when they are grown up to be a man [61-64] 67-69

the story of a man that had a wife of divel [devil] [65-66] 70-71
pencil end

A story about a girl that had a sweat [sweet] heart [67-70] 72-75 ½
    page pencil

A woman that had a birth in the field [71-74] 75-78 copied the end
    Typed p75 in the book

The story about Rich man and his brothers [75-79] 79-82 pencil
    Typed lost brothers

The story about an orphan pencil
who got the rich man's daughter for wife [80-83] 83-86 2/3 page

The story about an orphan who was a singer [84-86] 86-88 pencil
    typed an unlucky man / orphan who was a singer 2 sided pale
    blue long sheet

blank 91

Captain Jack [87] 92 pencil

Captain Jack [88-89] 93-94 pencil

Blank 95

Captain Jack [90-91] 96-97 pencil

Blank 98-118

Thrift [Musings]

Before I sleep, I'm carving all the time. You see me no carving. I making star. Something when Xmas come I don't know. You see sometimes I visit Gambell. Only sit down, no do something. I'm hunting, come home

Today I find a new think. Next time I think I don't care. I go look at my trap. I take sandpaper. Only sit down on sled. Polish. I been to other trap I put a [in] my pocket things. I'm look at trap. Cover up. When go away. I'm take out my things. Polish again.

I don't care. Try all time bymby. Before sleep I came. Waiting for daylight. Me no like [1b] rest. I'm come all time.

Suppose Xmas moonlight. I visit Gambell. I don't care! Suppose me no sleep. I'm coming back.

We love somebody. I make 'em present.

Last winter I'm give present my father-in-law, 2 lbs smoking tobacco. That old woman his wife 5 yds that striped – what you call 'im. ticking?

We Xmas her last winter. Mrs Sashner here, we fill up you know dat ol tube – oh full. Something. [2]

The Dr [Bruning] is backed by the US govm't. Everything he has was explained. Lenin was educated in the temple of Jerusalem. He is backed by Wall Street. They're going to get all the gold in Russia for Guggenheim. Lenin more jokey? than Kerensky. Stupid Russians easy to rule. Dr wanted to tell me everything. I said no, I knew all I wanted to know. It's all known outside. [3]

I don't care. Not very good. I'm trying all time thing. I don't care. No very good. I'm try 'im. Skin canoe. Everything. Some men don't know everything. He speak "maks" in sled, please! Because I'm poor. I don' care. I'm tryin. I like a make 'im soft all time, my sleeve.

Amworri everyday looks like a sick. I don't care. No sick.

Looks like sick. "What did Amworri do when he worked for his wife?" I do no!

I don't care. Not very good. I like polish good, no good carver, me. Make 'im good polish, anyhow. [4a]

Seal Skin Rope

Young mukluk. We make warm up first a little. No cold. We put a something pan – put a first under grass – a box. Anykind. A pan. We put a warm place. We leave a 3 days. Oh some from days, because feel all time. Easy to take off. 'im we take out. After take out but wipe. 'im easy to come off. Then we make 'im rope.

We cut rope round & round. After cut, put stick middle rope. Twist 'im. Make 'em clean. Bymby put something stick on, we make 'em – like that [4b] Bymby hang up dry. We very careful. Sometimes dog eat. Make 'im higher. Bymby dry. Suppose shining t[h]ree days. We roll up, take in house.

We got enough rope. You no see. Oh, plenty rope on that rack.

We make 'im for Siberia. Young mukluk. Young walrus for us. Because strong. We trade for one skin, one rope. We no sell young walrus. Oh strong.

Walrus rope all same. In a fall we hang up outside. Shining. He can make fur come off. Sun [5a]

White Leather Spotted Seal

We make 'im like a rope. Easy to take off fur. We soak it in water. Twist it twice. Dis a way and other way. Oh plenty work. Changing water. Maybe six times. Some woman make rotten because he don't know.

When wash twist oh tree four times. We tie up sleeves. This neck sewing. We fill up wind blowing. We make 'im fat. We try blow. Rest, try again. Make fill. Before take outside, we take out snow behind house. We waiting sun go down. Suppose cold. We polish quick. Snow make 'im freeze. We got a [5b] stick on head. Stand 'im up anyplace. On rack. He froze. He stand up. Next month. Everybody he make 'im white leather. Because today not much cold.

Ten days. We feel. Soft. We cut him open middle. Cold

weather, maybe five days.

Bymby we hang up rope. Outside north side. We very careful because kind easy to getting dirty. Because soft. We very careful. You know sometimes rain. Little bit. I take in inside quick. We hide all time – you know [6] cold place. Because before dry.

Sometimes make from young mukluk for reindeer harness. Sometimes make white leather seal throat. Because thin. Edna speak "best kind, this". Few woman make this throat. Most woman no make this kind. [7a]

Rain Coat (walrus guts)

You know they got something on. Scrape 'em first. Easy. Be careful break. Outside first. Inside marble. He fill up. Today he use 'im marble. Everywoman. Before: stone anything walrus tooth we make 'im round like marble. Only lazy man wife, he use it stone. Marble fill up hole. Put little water. Make 'im slippery. Easy to turn round. Inside. We make 'im turn round. ~~Push marble~~. Tied knot in a end. Push marble in with thumb. Make 'im turn round (inside out)

When turn round, soak it in a water. He fill up guts, about this much, – a long – how long? [7b] arm. Sometimes short arm. He bring water out with thumb and finger. Bymby no more – he bring back other way. Tree four time. Changing clean water everytime. Bymby he shaking everything in big pan, making clean. Bymby looks like a clean, he take out water. Empty. Put a stick about this much a high (8 ft). hang up this way an' that a way(loop over & over stick) fast other end. He fill up wind. Bymby he make 'im little more bigger everything. (stretching) go little bit farther. He watch 'im what place smaller. He make 'im [8a] bigger. Take out wind. And put him in a water. And take out a water. Squeeze him. Everything (all of them). He take a dry place. I mean clean place. No dust. On gravel sometimes. He put a straight, like a line on a ground. He fill up wind again. Dry 'im all day. He waiting for shining. He dry one day. You know little bit tight one side the guts? Other side little bit loose? He cut a loose side. No making right now. Put a cloth, twist 'im, put a guts under foot. Hold end with rag. Suppose no rag easy to slip off hand. Pull [8b] hard. Make 'im hard. Oh like wood sometime. About keep one month –

ten days – sometimes ten days one month – he making raincoat – that's all. Guts from one walrus make two coats sometime. [9]

On going outside

Suppose I got enough in my pocket – full – I got out. Only I'm afraid. Supposed I got a-nough, I can go very quick. [10]

I watch first Edna – I visit two times. I watch. Because working woman. Before ask a father. I ask Edna. Nobody listen [hear]. I ask. He [she] speak 'yes'. After I tell father.

He [she] look a nice. Good for me. Before – little. He play all time on me. Sometimes on top. I think he lover me.

Before marry I sleep he house. He make a something fancy my belt. I no see.

Bymby I marry. Could't think all day. Getting dark. I feel like a lay down. Because father in law maybe think lazy. I like a lay down [11a] after sleep, he not take way my wife. I'm hurry for night to come.

(Edna sitting here making reindeer tendon thread. Richard telling about when he first married. She tears off thread from tendon, separate until same thickness all way, runs it thru her lips, holds one end in left hand, rolls the thread over back of left hand to twist it. Twists every end together so. Makes separate needlefuls. Looks as easy as breathing.)

Some woman he [she] don't know making things. Only asking about old boots. Every thing ask, food.

Sometimes I speak I'm visit tomorrow somewhere, Gambell, other [11b] camp. Edna he speak 'You got a old coat'. No old. Maybe little old. He speak 'You sleep alone more better!' Bymby, I'm sleep. Next morning new coat. New boots sometime. Before rheumatism he make a fast. Now little, more slow all time. Me too, sometime make thread. I can boots, too. Edna father can sew. My family, everyman, can sew. Understand boots, parki – everything.

Eskimo man like a father. Suppose father work all time, he teach son. He work too. Father lazy, son lazy. Mother lazy, daughter all same. [12a]

[Talking to us about Farrar's being sick] I make 'em change, you. No think about Xmas. Only get well. Maybe gone, never come back. Xmas every year."

ōōwạngạlō ōōngō – ō
Koyangavōōng ē yạ
ạgạnē pŭnạngāngāugā
Kāmōksāgavanināng aug ay a –ham–
ōsēạmạ aạngạ
Kīyōktōnăăăăngạ
Malagohona a a na a k
Eyayanga nge ya
Koyaso
Wakouguva ay ay a
Kiyungnalougwa
Eyang a a anga a aug aug aug a
Eyauganga
E ya
E yi ya Iyanga
A a eyang a
Eya yang a Eyang a Eyanga
E ya ya   [12b]
I ya E yaa haug aug aug a

ạ–ạ–ạng ạ I ya ya ya
yạ ạngạ
yī yē yā yo yạ anga
I yī yē yā yạ
A yhạ hanga
Yī ha
E ya ya yang ang ang a
E yā yhạ
ạ–ạ–ạng ạ
I ye ya ya ya anga
I ye ya ya ya anga
I ye yayayanga
I ya ya ya yang ang ang a
E ya ha
Em hi
Yam hi
A eng go le go tak

Ang an a yang [2]

A a ōōnŭ
ạtōōclăgōōng ōngạ
nīyạngạrōwạạngạ
ōōtạnạkōtạ ạngạ
e yhạ hạ ạngạ
yī hạ
ē yā yā yạ ạng ạng ạng ạ
ē yā hạ
ē ā āngōm
ạtōōclēgōōng ōng ō
awōlărōwạạnga
nīyạngạrōwạạngạng a
ōōkwŭchkĕn
em hī
yam hī
ạ ēngōlēkōtạ
āng āng ā yang!

INCREASING OF ESKIMO VOCABULARY

Along with the changes which are taking place in the life of the Eskimo with the advent of civilization and its products there is a corresponding ^increase^ in his ^vocabulary^. Many articles formerly unknown to the Eskimo have come into his possession, and are now a permanent part of his life; these have to be designated by special names. The process of naming new articles is a natural one and shows how the vocabulary of a people is enlarged to meet the demands of enlightenment and progress. The vocabulary of any people is never greater than the demands of its development, neither does it lag behind progress, but is always abreast with it.

Many of the articles retain the same name, with the pronunciation changed to suit the language; in other words, they are "Innuitized". Flour becomes *avlawak*; store, *stowak*; ink, *ingik*; pliers, *playak*, etc.

Some articles derive their name from their similarity to other articles suoh as, bread = very light sea foam; cooked beans = ear wax; dried apples = ears; dried prunes = stones; dried peaches =

tongues; flour = very line snow; glass = thin ice; gun powder = ashes; paper = a dried eye; tin can = iron intestine; tea = meat juice; sugar = coarse snow, as it appears in spring when thawing; shot = the same word as for reindeer manure; scissors = crab's pincers; syrup = the same word as for a black oil which overflows from native oil lamps.

Other articles derive their names from the use to which they are put. Pencil = that which makes marks. Marks such as a pencil [-2-] makes always relate to tattoo marks. Pen = to dip with; typewriter = the plural of the word for pencil; bottle has two name, one is dipper, the other means = that which contains whisky; baking powder = to make rise.

Still others derive their names from particular characteristics. The word for saw means = motion back and forth; pepper = that which bites the tongue; the word for primus stove is the same as = that which indicates the noise it makes; watch = heart beat; the word for cube sugar means = something that goes in one side of the mouth. This comes from the habit the Eskimo has of putting a piece of cube sugar in his cheek when drinking tea instead of putting the sugar into the tea. Mirror = with to look at the spirit; letter = sent words. The word which means scales is derived from their soothsaying, and comes in a round about way. A person who is a spiritual medium ties a string around his head and passes a short stick under it. When in a reclined position the spirit, called a helper, enters the head and the medium is ready for consultation. Anyone then may come and ask questions which are to be answered by yes or no. When a person has asked a question he grasps the stick with both hands, holding it in a horizontal position, and tries to lift the head of the medium; if the head is light the answer is 'no', if it is heavy the answer is 'yes'. The word by which this performance is designated means scales.

It is interesting to note that Eskimos from widely separated sections who have never intermingled ^in many cases, use a word of the same meaning to^ designate the same article.

VOCABULARY OF SIMPLE WORDS

ā as in play
ă as in hat
ą as in what

ach, ich, uch, etc pronounced as in the German

tạtclēma pronounced with tip of tongue on upper teach and air
    forced out the side of the tongue & lips to make the tcl

′ main accent

' secondary accent

wạlĕnkạkōn = thank you

ītạgǐnạchtŭk = that's all right

yōōk = man

ạgạnạk = woman

ạgạnŭk = day

bānǐchtŭk = good ~ that is good

bānābǐstạk = very nice, beautiful, superlatively fine

kōyạngạ = I am glad ~ happy

bĕyōkạtŭmpkǐn = I like you (singular)

    ″ tumpsǐ = I like you (plural)

bĕnĕkạbǐchtŭmpsǐ = I love you very much (plural)

kākmǐk = dog

nŭksŭk = seal

īēvak = walrus

ạnạkōngwạ = leave taking "I am going home now"

ạkōmǐ = have a seat ~ sit down

ạhạmŭngạ = that's enough

tạkōkŭt = that's all

lạlūrŭmkạ = white man ~ woman

    ″ kǐt = white men ~ women

tclspōōk = yow ~ they use it on many occasions meaning 'you
    before me ~ instead of me ~ with me'

akevik = a woman's water proof boots

nlucktak = ″   ″   ″   ″

abeyaka = man's   ″   ″   ″

kingaura = man's snow boots

bohon = woman's parka with white fancy snow parka

moowak = runner's shoes

sevoowook = red leather fancy winter shoes

asapenak = fancy shoes (of hair seal)

Iknakanik = fancy deerleg shoes

Pirit = summer shoes, deerskin parka

ahnami = deerleg shoes
koonvga = fancy fawn leg skin vest
Ahnaugarak = a slipper
Panga = fancy slipper
Okwala = fancy glove
Numalahak = fancy cartridge bag
Panganonak = "   "   "
Tokoya =   "   "   "
Aga =   "   "   "
Inki = tobacco pouch
Ango = fancy telescope case
Anaraclkoyak = a slipper, snow parka
Angeeko =   "   "   "
Akayaka = wrestler's pants [2]
Arayangi = fancy snow parka
Owawan = a white leather
Nimiyok = fancy child's sled
Tootmatik = a white fox skin, a set of dog harness
Tatowi = a white fox skin
Sepilu = a reindeer sled, fancy deer harness
Tamblo = a reindeer sled, plain deer harness
Anarayak = a dog sled
Peniu =   "   "
Onmookhak = "   "
Pangowiyi =   "   ", deer harness
Atiyohak =   "   "
Khyachlook = a deer harness
Womkon = a set of ivory carvings, domino
Irrogo = a belt buckle
Noongwook = a pepper shaker
Apata = an ivory picture frame
Ongwaluk = a napkin ring
Unotingauwan = an ivory toy sled
Nimiyok = a paper knife
Akolki = a belt bunkle and two watch weights
Maskin = a harpoon head
Bolowon =   "   "
Tangyan = a fork, a knife, a spoon, and two chains
Ooitellin = ivory chain

Atiyokak = two old ivory buckles
Wapahotak = a sinke with ivory fish hooks
Farrar Burns = an ivory carved cross and a pendent [3]
Okwala = fancy rain coat
Agayagok = fancy belt
Upakok = cartridge case
Seegahok =   "   "
Koronochtika = gloves
Oningayu = cribbage board, scissors
Ozeevosook = cigar holder
Okwahani = fancy slippers

223 forks	3 922 enamel plates
8 5 teaspoons	1 enamel platters
6 12 tablespoons	3 2 china plates large
2 6 enamel cups	1 potato masher
2 7 enamel saucers	4 193 knives

April 3, 1929 The Burn Ballad Bungalow on G Street in Washington, DC. http://www.shorpy.com/farrar-and-june-burn?size=_original-captionhttp://www.shorpy.com/farrar-and-june-burn?size=_original- caption

[outline]

1. Victoria
2. Nome
3. *Bear*
4. King Island
5. Storms
6. St Lawrence Island
7. Landing
8. selling store supplies to Natives
9. old man Anoguatuk who came to look
10. Describe Eskimo house + family life + drinking tea
11. Hunting seal
12. Hunting walrus – describe our hunt with boat
13. Hunting whale – Hunting fox
14. Hunting polar bear (Tell about worship)
15. Skinning seal & walrus & making rope & walrus leather
16. [blank]
17. Fox hunting
18. Reindeer herds & herders
19. Reindeer skin clothing
20. Language

> 1 – atasic
> 2 – malagok (MALAGOK)
> 3 – pingiyut (PINGIYUT)
> 4 – Stamat
> 5 – tatclema
> 6 – agavanluk
> 7 – magaragavenluk
> 8 – pin gi yuning ing loo luk
> 9 – sta ma ming gnng loo luk
> 10 – kola
> 11 – kola atasic - saphuklokuk
> 20 – yuwanuk (2 men)
> 21 – yuwanuk atasic

dog = kakmik
boy = magilagrek
girl = aganaghak
man = yook
woman = aganak
sit down = akomi
stand up = nikovi
morning = oona
I am very happy = kovabichtonga
I am going = anakongwa
I love you very much = be ne ka bich tump kin
I like you = be yo katumpkin [2]

I love you (plural) = be ne katumpsi
Beautiful = benabistak
Good = banelchra
Now ~ today = matin
Seal = nuksuk
Walrus = ievak
Polar bear = nanook
Flower = patsarook

Table of Contents
Eskimo Recollections Leightons 1983

SILOOKS

Paul Silook was the son of Ugwitelen and Wamiiyaq of Gambell, on St Lawrence Island. He loved to read and write, and worked as translator for the Presbyterian church, substitute teacher, and assistant to the early archeologists that excavated on the island in the early 30s and 40s. He left behind a wealth of literature about the island and culture, and his works are housed in the Natural History Museum of the Smithsonian Institution, the University of Alaska Museum in Fairbanks, and the Alaska State Museum.

Paul Silook, also known as Koneak, was born at Gambell, St. Lawrence Island, Alaska, sometime in September 1892. Largely taught by watching others, Paul Silook grew up trading for supplies, fishing for auklets, and hunting for seal, walrus, and other local wildlife. As an adult he apprenticed to a reindeer herder for less than a year, worked as assistant teacher (to June Burns among others) and later as translator, transcriber, boat captain, and general handyman. He married Miriam shortly before 1919. They had 7 living children, a miscarriage, and a still-born. At age 73 he managed to kill his first whale.

Paul Silook gathered data on the Bering Strait and northern Alaska from 1912 to around 1945. After he became a man by shooting his first polar bear, Paul began assisting Otto Geist in his archaeological field-work on St Lawrence Island, then assisting other researchers and scientists such as Henry Collins, and Froelich Rainey (who suggested these islanders to the Leightons for comparison with Navahos). Paul Silook was an avid recorder of the stories, traditions, and life and times of his village as well as those around him. His granddaughter, Suzie Silook, daughter of Roger, reported that he wrote "over 1,000 pages. All the rituals, how they were conducted, how animal spirits were treated ..."

He wrote a 200 page autobiography for Alex Leighton at Cornell, did most of the ethnographic detail work for Otto Geist at the University of Alaska. During the Great Depression he wrote to Henry Collins at the Smithsonian expressing his desire to keep the St Lawrence Island excavations going without the expense of continued charter flights to Alaska, stating, "If I am satisfactory to you ... you would not have to send a white man". The offer was not considered. His collections can be found at the Natural History

Museum of the Smithsonian Institution, the University of Alaska Fairbanks's Alaska and Polar Regions Collections, and the Alaska State Historical Library.

Son Roger Silook and family, Yupiks from "Bush" Alaska, were encouraged to relocate to Chicago, invited to give up their subsistence life style – a harsh and demanding existence – in order to take their place in a great American city with a government promise for a good, new life, trading in the past and its old traditional ways for the convenience and opportunity of living in the modern world. Over his wife's objections, he decided to accept the relocation offer. When they arrived in Chicago, the family was placed in Chinatown, where, because of their Asian appearance, it was thought that they would "blend" right in. (http://www. litsite.org/index.cfm?section=History-and-Culture&page=Life-in-Alaska&viewpost=2&contentid=872&pg=294&crt=3 \ http:// library.alaska.gov/hist/hist_docs/finding_aids/ MS276.pdf)

Roger Silook, *Seevookuk*: Stories the Old People Told
on St Lawrence Island 1974.

Siberian visitors 1 building skin boats troubles with Siberians 4 friendly victory 6 Eskimo magicians 7 more magic 9 trading & waring with Siberians 10 visiting in Siberia 13 reindeer herders 14 ready for home island villages coming of the whales 16 catching whales 17 whaling ceremony 18 main whaling ceremony 20 summer camps 21 return to village 22 exercise & games winter comes 25 time of starvation 27 living is easier in Siberia 28 coming of spring 30 hunting bull walrus 34 seal & oogruck hunting 35 netting fish 36 getting birds 37 more fishing & hunting 38 eskimo clothing 41 kokoluk & ivetuk Eskimo pottery 43 making tools 45 using sinew Eskimo calendar 46 birds 48 trading with whalers 52 more about island birds 53 animals 54 using sled doges 55 seevookuk 57 fishing at Ivektuk 59 advenurous times 60 Punuk islands 61 other villages 62 mysterious death learning from whalers 63

References

Ackerman, Robert E 1976 The Eskimo People of Savoonga. Phoenix: Indian Tribal Series.

Alaskan Sportsman

Apassingok, Anders, Willis Walunga, and Edward Tennant, eds. 1985 Lore of St. Lawrence Island: Echoes of Our Eskimo Elders, Vol. 1: Gambell. Bering Strait School District, Unalakleet, Alaska.
    1987 Lore of St. Lawrence Island. Echoes of Our Eskimo Elders. Volume 2: Savoonga. Jan 1.
    1989 Sivuqam Nangaghnegha: Siivanllemta Ungipaqellghat - Lore of St. Lawrence Island : Echoes of Our Eskimo Elders, Volume 3: Southwest Cape.

Bandi, Hans-Georg 1969 Eskimo Prehistory. Ann E Keep, translator. University of Alaska Press: Studies in Northern Peoples 2. [German 1965]

Boeri, David 1983 *People of the Ice Whale* ~ Eskimos, White Men, and the Whale. NY: Harvest / HBJ Books.

Bogoras, Waldemar 1904-1909 Chuckchee. NY: American Museum of Natural History 11.

Burgess, Stephen 1974 The St Lawrence Islanders of Northwest Cape: Patterns of Resource Utilization. University of Alaska: Anthropology PhD.

Burn, June 1941 *Living High* ~ An Unconventional Autobiography. New York: Duell, Sloan and Pearce.

Byard, Pamela 1980 Population, History, Demography, and Genetics of St Lawrence Island Eskimos. University of Kansas: Anthropology PhD.

Campbell, Dr Edgar Omar 1901-11 Notes Juneau BIA

Collins, Henry B, jr 1937 Archaeology of St Lawrence Island, Alaska. DC: *Smithsonian Miscellaneous Collections* 96 (1).

Doty, William F 1900 The Eskimos of St Lawrence Island, Alaska. Sheldon Jackson, compiler. DC: 9th Annual Report on Introduction of Domestic Reindeer into Alaska 1899: 186-223.

Ellana, Linda 1980 Bering-Norton Petroleum Development Scenarios and Sociocultural Impacts Analysis #1. Fairbanks: Alaska OCS Socioeconomic Studies Program, Final Technical Report 54.

Elliott, Henry W   1898   The Seal Islands of Alaska. DC: Seal & Salmon Fisheries and General Resources of Alaska #3: 3-288. 4 volumes.

Fienup-Riordan, Ann 1990 *Eskimo Essays* ~ Yupik Lives and How We see Them. The Real People and the Children of Thunder: 71-93. Rutgers University Press.
    1991 *The Real People and the Children of Thunder* ~ The Yup'ik Eskimo Encounter with Moravian Missionaries John and Edith Kilbuck. Norman: University of Oklahoma Press.
    1994 *Boundaries and Passages* ~ Rule and Ritual in Yup'ik Eskimo Oral Tradition.   Norman: University of Oklahoma Press.

Gambell, Vene C   1898   Notes with Regard to the St Lawrence Island Eskimos. Sheldon Jackson, compiler. DC: 8th Annual Report on Introduction of Domestic Reindeer into Alaska, 1898: 141-144.

Geist, Otto, and Froelich G Rainey   1936   Archaeological Excavation at Kukulik, St Lawrence Island, Alaska: Preliminary Report. DC & University of Alaska.

Heathcote, Gary 1982 Exploratory Craniometry on Western Arctic Skeletal Groups. University of Toronto: Anthropology PhD.

Hippler, Arthur 1970 Islands: 39-45. From Village to Towns" An Intermedidate Step in the Acculturation of Alaska Eskimos. Richard Woods & Arthur Harkins, eds. Minneapolis: Training Center for Community Programs, University of Minnesota.

Hooper, Calvin 1881 DC: Report of the Cruise of the US Revenue Steamer Corwin in the Arctic Ocean, 1 November 1880.

Hughes, Charles C 1960 *An Eskimo Village in the Modern World.* Ithaca: Cornell University Press.
    1984 Saint Lawrence Island Eskimo.   Handbook of North American Indians. David Damas, ed. Arctic 5: 262-277.

Hughes, Jane Murphy   1960   An Epidemiological Study of Psychopathology in an Eskimo Village.   Cornell University: Anthropology PhD.

Jacobson, Steven A 1977 A Grammatical Sketch of Siberian Yupik Eskimo, as spoken on St Lawrence Island.   Fairbanks: University of Alaska, Native Language Center.

Jolles, Carol 2002 *Faith, Food, & Family in a Yupik Whaling Community.* Seattle: University of Washington Press.

Keim, Charles 1969 *Aghvook, White Eskimo*: Otto Geist and Alaskan Archaeology. College: University of Alaska Press.

Leighton, Alexander H, and Dorothea C Leighton 1940 Fieldnotes, St Lawrence Island. June – August.

1983 Eskimo Recollections of their Life Experiences. *Northwest Anthropological Research Notes* 17 (1/2): 1-437 Fall/Spring.

Little, Ronald, and Lynn A Robbins 1982 Draft Final Ethnographic Baseline: St Lawrence Island. Napa: John Muir Institute & Anchorage: Alaska Outer Shelf Office, Socioeconomic Studies Program, Minerals Management Service.

Maynard, Washburn 1898 The Fur-Seal Fisheries. DC: Seal & Salmon Fisheries and General Resources of Alaska #3: 289-309. 4 volumes.

Miller, Jay 2014 *Rescues, Rants, and Researches*: A Re-View of Jay Miller's Writings on Northwest Indien Cultures. Darby Stapp and Kara Powers, eds. Journal of Northwest Anthropology, Memoir 9.

Moore, Riley D 1923 Social Life of the Eskimo of St Lawrence Island. *American Anthropologist* 25 (3): 339-375.

Muir, John 1917 The Cruise of the Corwin: Journal of the Arctic Expedition of 1881 in Search of De Long and the Jeanette. William Frederic Bade, ed. Boston & NY: Houghton Mifflin.

Murdock, George Peter 1949 *Social Structure*. NY: MacMillan.

Murie, Margaret E 1977 *Island Between*. Fairbanks: University of Alaska Press.

Nelson, Edward 1899 Eskimo about Bering Strait. DC: Bureau of American Ethnology, Annual Report #18: 3-518.

Shinen, Marilene 1963 Notes on Marriage Customs of St Lawrence Island Eskimos. *Anthropologica* 5 (2): 199-208.

Silook, Roger S 1976 *Seevookuk*: Stories the Old People Told on St Lawrence Island. Anchorage: Alaska Publishing Company.

Stephens, CA, ed 1900 At the School House Farthest West: A Tale of School-teaching in Alaska. *Youth's Companion* 74 (16): 197-198, (17): 213-214, (18): 225-226, (19): 240-241.

US Bureau of Education 1896-1905 Education in Alaska. DC: Reports of the Commission of Education.

US Federal Field Committee for Development Planning in Alaska 1968 Alaska Natives and the Land. DC.

US Bureau of Indian Affairs, Planning Support Group 1977
Savoonga: Its History, Population and Economy. Billings, MT:
BIA Planning Support Group Report #242.
1977a Gambell: Its History, Population and Economy.
Billings, MT: BIA Planning Support Group Report #243.

Young, Steven, and Edwin S Hall, jr 1969 Contributions to the
Ethnobotany of the St Lawrence Island Eskimo.
Anthropological Papers of University of Alaska 14 (2): 43-53.

INDEX

258

♀ = female, ♂ = male, c = clan, p = place, r = rite, ? = unknown

Help banish typo gnomes!

index